CONNECTED FOR LIFE

CONCORDIA PUBLISHING HOUSE · SAINT LOUIS

ESSENTIAL GUIDE TO YOUTH MINISTRY

Founded in 1869 as the publishing arm of The Lutheran
Church—Missouri Synod, Concordia Publishing House gives
all glory to God for the blessing of 150 years of opportunities
to provide resources that are faithful to the Holy Scriptures
and the Lutheran Confessions.

Published by Concordia Publishing House
3558 S. Jefferson Ave., St. Louis, MO 63118–3968
1-800-325-3040 • www.cph.org

Manufactured in the United States of America

1 2 3 4 5 6 7 8 9 10   28 27 26 25 24 23 22 21 20 19

TABLE OF CONTENTS

CONNECTED FOR LIFE

"Youth are the future of the Church." You may have heard this in your congregation. You may have thought it yourself, providing part of the reason you have an interest in youth ministry. And there's truth to that phrase. However, there is a danger if we only think about youth as the Church's future. Youth are the Church's now too. Just as every generation is welcomed and loved and important to Jesus, so also we want to make sure that every generation, including youth, feels welcomed and loved and important to our congregations.

But how do we do that? How do we make sure that we are serving our teenage neighbors well in our church home and theirs? This book begins to explore that, bringing in the voices of a great variety of those who work with youth.

CONNECTED

Picture a path of stepping stones that spans the width of a river. If the stepping stones are placed with care, you can pass from one side to the other without much difficulty. You have enough touchpoints with a secure foundation that you can move steadily without tripping. But what if some of those steps are missing? Or what if there are a few stepping stones at the beginning, but the rest of the stones are spaced out far outside of your foot's reach?

Too often, our touchpoints in the life of our members look like the last scenario. We may carefully guide children from one stage to the next, guiding them in the teachings of the faith, but we forget to make connections as our members grow older. If there's no logical next step in the life of the church, members at the high school or young adult level feel as if there is no place for them. Youth ministry, therefore, is a series of touchpoints, connecting childhood to adulthood and setting the pace so that even into old age, members have sure footing despite the rapid changes and turbulent waters that often surround them. These connections keep youth connected throughout their lives.

THEY ARE NOT ALONE

One of the most important truths that youth should internalize is that they are not alone in their church community. During adolescence, brain development often causes them to believe several different myths: everyone is staring at them, no one is paying attention to them, no one knows what it is like to be them, and tomorrow will never come. These conflicting messages further complicate the difficulties that teens face in a time of significant transition.

It is essential, therefore, that teens know that they are not alone. Those in their church love them. Those in their church need them. Most important, Jesus loves them; in Jesus, they are never alone.

You Are Not Alone

In youth ministry, you are focused on connecting youth for life. You carefully connect them from childhood to adulthood roles in the church. You connect them with one another and with those of other generations to strengthen the bonds they have with the Body of Christ. You connect their world with the Word of God so that they can navigate in their vocations through the lens of Scripture. Most important, you remind them that they are connected in Christ for life through their identity in Jesus because of Baptism and the faith they've been given by the Holy Spirit.

In all of these daunting tasks, you may feel alone. Do not neglect your own need to be connected. Read the Word of God to nourish yourself, not just to prepare for the next event. Connect with those in your congregation to remind yourself that you have roles in addition to your service to youth. Connect with others in youth ministry to share the joys, challenges, and great ideas that come with youth ministry. Connect with resources that will help you as you in turn connect with youth. That's the point of this book. In it, you will find chapters written by those who know what it is like to serve teens and their Savior. You will find help and hope and a reminder that you are not alone.

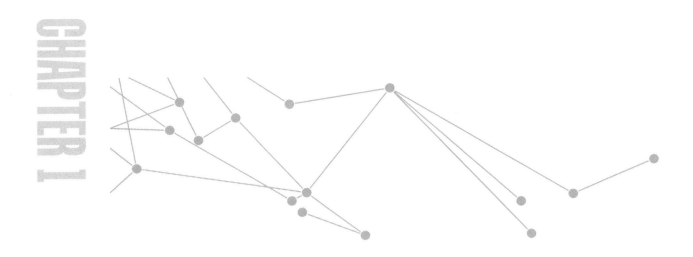

CHAPTER 1

BODY AND BLOOD YOUTH MINISTRY

BY JEFF DORIA

Can you imagine standing on the mountainside forty days after the resurrection of Jesus? Jesus stands there and tells you, just before ascending into the clouds, that all authority in heaven and earth has been given to Him. He gives His followers the command to make disciples by baptizing and teaching people of all nations (Matthew 28:18–20). As you imagine yourself standing there, you soon realize that Jesus includes you! Furthermore, all nations includes people of all ethnicities, languages, and ages as well. You come down the mountainside thinking to yourself, "I need to start a youth ministry!"

Well, okay, maybe that's not how you'd imagine yourself at Christ's ascension. Nevertheless, Christ-centered, Christ-focused ministry moved forward that day as the disciples would trust in His Word, await the gift of the Holy Spirit ten days later, and then through the power of God, begin changing the world so people experience God's love, grace, mercy, peace, and joy in this life and in the life to come.

The life of Jesus, as well as all of Scripture, reveals to us the amazing love our heavenly Father has for His creation. Genesis begins by teaching us that God made all things good, including mankind. The first man and woman were made in His image, without sin. But through the rebellion of our first parents in the Garden of Eden, we now live in a fallen, broken, sinful world as fallen, broken, sinful people. Because of mankind's sin and rebellion against God and His Word, the broken relationship remained. Thankfully, God didn't want to lose that which He loved. He promised from the very time Adam and Eve sinned to redeem the world through Eve's offspring (Genesis 3:15). Jesus, the Word made flesh, the Son of God, is the fulfillment of the Father's promise. Through His sinless life, His atoning death on a cross, and His powerful resurrection from the grave, Jesus fulfills the promise. The consequence of sin is paid for; the power of death and the devil is defeated. But it doesn't stop there. The amazing gift of God is given for all who believe in Jesus as their Savior. Eternal life is given freely to all who believe in Jesus (John 3:16).

Eternal life. Think about that for a moment. Life without end. A good life, wonderful life, joyful life, happy life, purposeful life, eternal life! Eternal life is such an amazing gift from God that we just can't completely get our heads wrapped around the idea that this gift is offered for all, young and old alike.

Yet in this world, eternal life is so often far from our minds. Consumed with the here and now, we focus on our daily struggles. World news causes concern in our hearts and minds. Family strife rips at the relationships we've sought to develop. Our own sinfulness, our willingness to put the pleasures of the here and now above God's instruction for our lives, cracks apart the very foundation of our existence. In such struggle, in such despair, God desires not to leave us alone, but to be with us, as Jesus said, "always, to the end of the age" (Matthew 28:20).

The Bible is full of this truth, reminding us time and time again of the victory we have in Jesus because of God's grace through faith in Him. This grace comes to us through the inspired words of Scripture as well as in the tangible elements of the Sacraments. These Means of Grace point us to Jesus over and over again for the forgiveness of our sins and the strength to live our lives in His love. Jesus is our focus. Jesus is our center. Jesus is the foundation on which to build lives . . . and youth ministries.

MYSTERY OF THE GIFT

Whether in person or online, many of us have seen artists paint marvelous, energetic portraits of Christ. The use of color and movement keeps us interested in what the artist will do next and what the outcome of his canvas will be. Of course, people have been painting the face of Christ for generations. Whether in modern art, Renaissance art, or art of some other time, the face of Jesus captures passion, conjures emotion, and catapults us to the cross. At the cross, we see the face of Jesus, suffering and wounded, but still a face of love, a love extending to all people. We still see this love in the face of Jesus as we encounter our Lord and Savior in Holy Communion—the sacred meal He gave us.

Can you picture the face of Jesus as He reclined at the table with His disciples? John's there. Peter's there. James, Andrew, and the others, ordinary men in the presence of the extraordinary Savior. Jesus looks at them and tells them,

> **"I have earnestly desired to eat this Passover with you before I suffer. For I tell you I will not eat it until it is fulfilled in the kingdom of God." And He took a cup, and when He had given thanks He said, "Take this, and divide it among yourselves. For I tell you that from now on I will not drink of the fruit of the vine until the kingdom of God comes." And He took bread, and when He had given thanks, He broke it and gave it to them, saying, "This is My body, which is given for you. Do this in remembrance of Me." And likewise the cup after they had eaten, saying, "This cup that is poured out for you is the new covenant in My blood." (Luke 22:15–20)**

Established at the Passover meal, Jesus connects this Jewish celebration of deliverance with His fulfillment of rescue and salvation.

The Lord's Supper is a gift of life. A gift seen in the eyes of Jesus as well as tasted in the bread and wine. A gift of forgiveness and salvation and strength for all who believe by faith that what Jesus says is true. Jesus is life (John 14:6). His desire is for His people to experience life, for He came to bring salvation and life abundantly (John 10:10). So let's take a closer look at the F.A.C.E. of Jesus (Forgiveness, Acceptance, Community, and Endurance) and see the gifts He brings through the Lord's Supper, and how that applies to youth ministry today.

FORGIVENESS: A SHOCKING WORD

Our culture has a fluid vocabulary that changes with time. Some of it can be offensive. What was fine for Mark Twain to write more than a century ago is no longer allowed on our radio or television. Yet some words that once would never have been heard on the radio or television are now used regularly in today's popular online media for teens. All the while, the culture of our world will bicker back and forth about what words are acceptable and what words are too shocking. In the Church, we use some shocking words of our own including faith, family, freedom, fulfillment, and especially in this chapter's context—forgiveness.

In the F.A.C.E. of Jesus, we see forgiveness as the most essential aspect of the Lord's Supper. Jesus tells us forgiveness is the primary purpose of this meal: "For this is My blood of the covenant, which is poured out for many for the forgiveness of sins" (Matthew 26:28). Jesus knew His disciples needed forgiveness. Jesus knows we do too. All need to know, truly know, that their sins are forgiven.

An athlete partakes in locker room pranks and smack talk; a varsity cheerleader gossips about those on the drill team; the kid in history uses his smartphone to cheat on a test; a big sister leaves the bathroom a mess in such a way that it looks like her little sister did it; a big brother gets on the computer and checks out pornographic websites. Countless scenarios of brokenness exist in the life of teens today. Whether it's sex before marriage, using drugs, disrespecting parents, and so forth, everyone has the need for forgiveness.

A beautiful illustration of forgiveness in Scripture is recorded in Luke 15—known as the parable of the lost son. In this parable, Jesus teaches about the sinfulness of the younger son and the wonderful reconciliation with his father when he repents and returns home. But it is also a great parable about the sin of the older son, who demonstrates arrogance, selfishness, and hardness of heart against his younger brother. The father's love for his sons is evident and available for both boys. Today's teenagers need to know, and be confident in, the fact that God will fully forgive them whenever they fail.

To see forgiveness in the F.A.C.E. of Jesus is crucial. It is vital for a teenager to see the importance of the Lord's Supper and the gift of forgiveness offered through this meal. Forgiveness meets a most basic need for us all, and our teenagers are in desperate need of it. If they never really experience forgiveness, they live in unnecessary guilt—or the other extreme, they live with a "who gives a flip" attitude as if nothing really matters anyway. By helping teens see the amazing forgiveness of God in the F.A.C.E. of Jesus found in Holy Communion, teens experience a crucial, foundational strength for their Christian walk. In the gift of Holy Communion, Jesus' body and blood are truly present along with the bread and wine. Body and blood youth ministry offers real presence for real forgiveness.

ACCEPTANCE: WELCOME TO THE LORD'S TABLE

Another crucial, foundational aspect of the F.A.C.E. of Jesus found in Holy Communion is acceptance. One of the primary reasons gangs are so strong in our culture is that they provide a place of acceptance. Teenagers need acceptance, and they will hang out where they experience it.

Where do they find acceptance? One difficulty in surveying teenagers is the reality that that demographic changes so quickly. Teens only remain teens for a decade—ten years of great transition and change.

Consider how quickly pop culture changes. Remember when MySpace was all the rage? Shopping malls, once the major hangout for teens, drastically reduced in popularity across the United States. Missed your favorite show on Thursday night? It doesn't matter; you can stream that program on demand whenever it fits your schedule.

Teens still find acceptance in their peer groups, whether it be in the FFA, marching band, athletics, dance, or various clubs. Many teens find acceptance in their families at home. Social media has become the place where many teens seek acceptance. But do they find it there? Well, that depends on the individual. But one thing is for sure: many teens seek acceptance from the online world. However, there is one much more powerful and important place of acceptance—the altar of the Lord.

At Holy Communion, teenagers who receive the Sacrament find themselves at a place of acceptance. The altar of God is an accepting place of love and forgiveness.

Imagine a teenager who has trouble approaching God, thinking He is a God of wrath that burns against sinners. When teens realize the powerful gift of Jesus' sacrifice, they see the altar as a place of invitation and acceptance. To kneel at the foot of the cross, at the altar of our Lord, and experience acceptance in the F.A.C.E. of Jesus is powerful for people at any age. Just as the prodigal son in Luke 15 not only experienced forgiveness, he also experienced acceptance from his father. He was accepted back into the family with all the benefits of sonship! Body and blood youth ministry offers real benefits for real acceptance.

COMMUNITY: CONNECTED TO CHRIST AND ONE ANOTHER

A third powerful benefit of the Lord's Supper for teenagers is found in the symbol central to the architecture of most churches—the cross. I've yet to find a Lutheran congregation that didn't have a cross as a focal point in its altar area. As you look at the cross, it's obvious that the two directions of the beams, vertical and horizontal, serve as a symbol of connection.

The vertical beam reminds us of God's love and connection to each of us individually. His love comes straight from heaven (top of the cross) to our lives here on earth (bottom of the cross). Holy Communion is for us personally. Remember Jesus' words when He gave the disciples the first Lord's Supper. Martin Luther emphasized the words "for you." These two important words connect sinners in community with the Savior of the world Himself.

The horizontal beam of the cross shows us another community relationship established in Holy Communion between brothers and sisters in Christ. This community is seen as people—shoulder to shoulder, kneeling at the altar rail, or lining up one after another—receive the gifts of God. In this horizontal relationship of blessing and community, we experience forgiveness and acceptance, not just for us individually, but as a community of believers called the Church.

St. Paul describes the importance of community when he writes to the Church in Corinth (1 Corinthians 11:17–34). At times, he speaks about the body of Christ, while at other times Paul writes about the Sacrament and how the bread is also the body of Christ. St. Paul also uses the term "Body of Christ" to mean the people gathered, the Church (1 Corinthians 12:12–27). In this community, in this Body, we don't just receive God's blessings on our own, but we do so as part of a larger community.

Have you ever communed at an altar in the round, where the people gather in a circle around a freestanding altar? As people stand or kneel, everyone focuses on the altar, but just past the altar, you can see the people on the other side. In that moment, God reminds us how we can see one another through the body and blood of Christ. Body and blood youth ministry offers real community for real relationships.

ENDURANCE: PROCLAIM THE LORD'S DEATH UNTIL HE RETURNS

Life in this world is tough! Tough for adults, and tough for teenagers. School pressures and temptations abound. Outside of school, the concerns take their toll as broadcast messages from across the globe include terrorism, environmental issues, protests, police shootings, government squabbles, not to mention a bleak outlook on the future status of employment for those graduating from high school and college. Jesus never tells us life this side of heaven would be easy. Instead Jesus states in very realistic terms, "I have said these things to you, that in Me you may have peace. In the world you will have tribulation. But take heart; I have overcome the world" (John 16:33).

Perhaps we don't think about endurance as a gift God gives in the Lord's Supper. Perhaps we forget about the strength the Holy Spirit works in us to face challenges of the world. Although we may yearn for that day when Jesus makes all things new (Revelation 21), we're not there yet. Instead, God gives us this gift of the Sacrament to proclaim His death until He returns.

St. Paul instructs his readers in Corinth by saying, "For as often as you eat this bread and drink the cup, you proclaim the Lord's death until He comes" (1 Corinthians 11:26).

Do you feel the sense of waiting in this verse? Do you notice how the reception of the Lord's Supper proclaims the death of Jesus until the Last Day? We need strength until that day. We need endurance to make it through until then.

One of the unfortunate states of teenage life is a sense of hopelessness. The world seems so messed up that they just lose hope in things, lose faith in God—even doubting that God exists at all. We can help teenagers realize that at the altar, strength and endurance are given so the faithful continue living for Christ even in these troubling times. Encountering the F.A.C.E. of Jesus in Holy Communion brings endurance to teens and adults alike. Body and blood youth ministry offers real strength for real endurance.

CONCLUSION

Forgiveness, Acceptance, Community, and Endurance are all parts of the wonderful gift of Holy Communion. Imagine youth being directed to Holy Communion for help in troubled times. Imagine youth leaders encouraging teens to encounter the F.A.C.E. of Jesus after they've been convicted of drug use, lost their virginity, had their reputation ruined on social media, been caught cheating on exams, been fighting with their parents, or been feeling guilty about other sin in their lives.

The F.A.C.E. of Jesus is not just for the youth today, but it will be valid for every generation still to come. Body and blood youth ministry built on the F.A.C.E. of Jesus is a great foundation on which to build youth ministry. By now, you realize that body and blood youth ministry is not a structure of leadership nor a flowchart of programming. It's a foundation of faith that as youth and adults work together developing ministry to and with teenagers, the F.A.C.E. of Jesus found in Holy Communion becomes a foundation of faith, hope, and love on which to build life today—and life everlasting.

SETTING THE FOUNDATION FOR CONGREGATIONAL YOUTH MINISTRY

Imagine a youth night. There are games and snacks and plenty of noise. But underneath it all, there is a carefully laid plan of connecting teens to one another and to the Word, which reminds them that they are connected in Jesus. The youth may not know all the work that went into this one night, but you do. You understand the days of prep work. The months of calendar planning. The years that went into your congregation's youth ministry development. The decades that the church has nurtured these brothers and sisters in Christ since their birth. A foundation has been set, building connections from past, present, and future as well as from philosophy to practice. The chapters in Section 1 help to set the foundation, reminding us all that youth ministry starts long before someone becomes a teenager.

CHAPTER 2

FAITH FORMATION

BY DAVE RUETER

In Jeremiah 18, the Lord presents the prophet with a vision of a potter working with clay to create and re-create a vessel. While the immediate context of the verse deals with the shaping God was doing with the nation of Israel, the metaphor is apt for how the Father shapes and reshapes us throughout our lives. We are clay in the Potter's hands, being shaped and reshaped according to His plan.

Building on the theological foundation laid out in Chapter 1, it becomes important to understand that faith, though given through Baptism, does not remain—certainly ought not to remain—changeless throughout the life of the believer. Faith is dynamic; it changes, and it grows. Faith is shaped by both what is taught in formal learning environments as well as life experiences. This shaping is sometimes called faith formation.

THE ROLE OF CHRISTIAN EDUCATION IN FAITH FORMATION

The primary shaper of the faith of the children and youth we work with is the Holy Spirit. The Spirit works through Word and Sacrament. The preaching and teaching of the Scriptures remain critical to the formation of faith. Some faith formation or spiritual formation theories attempt to disconnect the content of faith from the experience of faith. This is an unnatural approach to understanding how faith works in our lives.

Faith formation must begin with the simplest, most foundational content. Faith cannot be content-free. Therefore, it is critical to bring to bear quality Christian Education materials and curriculum that are solid in their content as well as the instructional methods employed.

The formation of faith takes place when the content of an individual believer's faith is lived out. Encountering people or circumstances that affirm or challenge our beliefs has a shaping or forming effect on our faith. A child who loses a parent due to divorce or death is shaped in her understanding of the world around her, as well as her understanding of

God and faith in God. A teen who regretfully loses his virginity has his faith shaped and his self-understanding altered by the guilt he now carries. Having supportive adults in the lives of children and youth can positively shape their faith as they witness a mature faith lived out in their lives. A quality philosophy of Christian Education (see chapter 3) takes into account faith formation as seeking formal and informal ways to provide positive, faith-affirming shaping. Drawing from what God promises to do in His Word and through His Sacraments, we construct an approach for Christian Education that works with God as He works in the lives of the children and youth He entrusts to our care.

UNDERSTANDING FAITH FORMATION

With a general understanding of the relationship between faith formation and Christian Education, it is now important to provide some assessment of faith formation theory. There are a number of developmental theorists whose work has at least some bearing on Christian Education. Our focus will remain strictly with two key theories of faith formation.

JAMES FOWLER

James Fowler's book *Stages of Faith: The Psychology of Human Development and the Quest for Meaning* was formative for the field of faith development and is still in common usage across theological traditions. A practical theologian with a Methodist background, Fowler attempts to describe how faith develops by drawing upon the work of developmental theories and constructing his own stage-based theory.

STAGE	AGE
0. Undifferentiated Faith	0–2 years
1. Intuitive-Projective Faith	2–7 years
2. Mythic-Literal Faith	7–12 years
3. Synthetic-Conventional Faith	12+ years
4. Individuative-Reflective Faith	21+ years
5. Conjunctive Faith	35+ years
6. Universalizing Faith	45+ years

Table 1. Based on James W. Fowler's *Stages of Faith: The Psychology of Human Development and the Quest for Meaning*

The Quest for Meaning

For children under two years of age, Fowler believed a foundational sense of security was vital. Children at this age need to experience warmth and safety in order to develop trust. This lays the foundation for the development of their faith. Neglected or abused children are less likely to develop trust, and thus, their ability to form faith may be inhibited.

Providing comfort and appropriate, loving touch during these years is vitally important. This prestage is called *undifferentiated* because the child has yet to differentiate fully between self and others.[1]

As children develop language and begin to be able to make use of symbols in play as well as in speech, they enter into Stage 1, which Fowler labels "Intuitive-Projective Faith." Children at this stage have an egocentric understanding of the world and their faith as well. With themselves as the center of their faith experience, they project their own experience onto what is taught, learning through stories, images, and the people in their lives.[2]

Stage 2, or "Mythic-Literal Faith," applies to children in the heart of the elementary school years. During this stage, children have a strong sense of justice and fairness. As children begin to grow in their understanding of how the world works and the place of others in the world, they work to apply developing concepts of right and wrong not only to themselves, but also to those around them. They are able to apply their understanding of right and wrong on behalf of themselves as well as others. They see their faith in literal terms. They struggle with understanding the symbolic language of Scripture. The content of their faith is focused on concrete objects and terms rather than abstract concepts.[3]

Fowler uses the term "Synthetic-Conventional Faith" for Stage 3. Children enter this stage during adolescence. Unlike prior stages, Fowler does not posit a concept that people will naturally progress out and onto further stages. Individuals may maintain a "Synthetic-Conventional Faith" into adulthood. This stage is marked by conformity of beliefs to authority or a religious system. Fowler holds that those who remain in this stage are marked by a fear of challenging their inherited belief systems or offering them critical examination.[4]

It is good to note at this point that Fowler's theological understanding begins to have a shaping effect on his system that may provide a tension for traditional Lutheran theology. However, there is a point to be made in support of his construct. Adolescents need to be able to examine the truth claims of their faith. In order to arrive at an adult understanding of faith, youth need to be able to ask the questions that vex them in an environment welcome to such questions. For more on this, see chapter 5 of *Teaching the Faith at Home: What Does This Mean? How Is This Done?* by David L. Rueter (St. Louis: Concordia Publishing House, 2015).

Fowler labels Stage 4 "Individuative-Reflective Faith." This stage typically begins in a young person's mid-twenties. It is a stage marked by personal ownership of one's faith. Here, the complexity of faith becomes a welcomed challenge, something to reflect more deeply upon rather than avoid. Difficult questions are embraced and more than simple answers sought. Ideas and beliefs that conflict with one's own beliefs are recognized.[5]

---

1   James W. Fowler, *Stages of Faith: The Psychology of Human Development and the Quest for Meaning* (San Francisco: HarperCollins, 1995), 119–21.
2   Fowler, *Stages of Faith*, 122–34.
3   Fowler, *Stages of Faith*, 135–50.
4   Fowler, *Stages of Faith*, 151–73.
5   Fowler, *Stages of Faith*, 174–83.

Stages 5 and 6, "Conjunctive Faith" and "Universalizing Faith," will not be addressed here as they extend well beyond the focus of this book.

THE RECIPROCATING SELF

Building on a theology of relationality, Balswick, King, and Reimer[6] offer up in *The Reciprocating Self* an intriguing framework to understand human development from a theological perspective. The reciprocating self is seen in the relational connection between self and others. They posit an understanding of reciprocation as a way to personally develop and develop one's faith through the give-and-take of human relationship.

According to this approach, the reciprocating self is best formed or nurtured (1) through covenantal rather than conditional personal relationships; (2) when failure is met with grace rather than shame; (3) when relationships are empowering; and (4) when intimacy rather than isolation is experienced.[7] Through mature relationships, they suggest that the "undifferentiated self" transforms into the "reciprocating self."

The idea of a covenantal relationship is an ancient concept. In Genesis 17, God establishes a covenant with Abraham. God would provide a family, ultimately a nation, through Abraham. In exchange, He was to be the God of Abraham and his descendants. We see this repeatedly in the Scriptures when God is referred to as "the God of Abraham, Isaac, and Jacob." While there are two sides to the covenant, it is clear that only one party is capable of keeping the conditions of the arrangement. Abraham, after all, is ninety-nine years old when this covenant is established, and for him to be "the father of a multitude of nations" (Genesis 17:5), there is little chance of this taking place without divine assistance. Further, we know from Hebrews 11:8 that Abraham was able to obey the Lord, and we know further, as noted above, from Ephesians 2:8–10 that faith itself is a gift from God. (See also 2 Peter 1:1; Philippians 1:29; and Acts 3:16.)

Parents, in like manner, are to form a covenantal bond with their children. God gifts parents with children, but also entrusts their care to parents. (See 3 John 1:4; Genesis 1:28; Proverbs 17:6; 22:6; Psalm 113:9; 127:3–5; 139:13–16.) Thus, learning from God's covenantal bond with us, parents form a similar bond with their children. This relationship is best when unconditional. Parents, on behalf of God, love and care for their children regardless of the transgressions of the covenant on the part of their children. While this may appear at times rather one-sided, it forms into a two-way bond as the child grows to return a more faithful response to this covenant of love. Only through the grace God has shown toward us are we able to have faith and grow in His love. In like manner, children grow in relationship with us and in their faith as they see the faithfulness of God mirrored in their parents.

If Lutherans are known for anything, it's grace. Grace is a natural aspect of the reciprocating self. Children and youth will make mistakes. Many times they will be entirely oblivious to those mistakes. Other times those mistakes will be willful and deliberate. Theologically, we

---

6   Kevin S. Reimer is on faculty at the University of California, Irvine and did his PhD at Fuller Theological Seminary, where Jack O. Balswick and Pamela Ebstyne King are both on the psychology faculty. Together they wrote *The Reciprocating Self*.

7   Jack O. Balswick, Pamela E. King, and Kevin S. Reimer, *The Reciprocating Self: Human Development in Theological Perspective* (Downers Grove, IL: InterVarsity Press, 2005), 51.

know some of those mistakes to be sin. Rather than making children and youth feel shamed for the mistakes, willful or not, we err on the side of grace.

While discipline in the form of natural consequences may still be necessary, this does not have to be done through shaming. The goal of discipline is restoration of relationship, not mere conformity or obedience. Grace restores the relationality between parents and children—between sinners and God. Rather than leaving children feeling that they are not good enough for our love, and by extension God's love, we need to demonstrate the inherent value in all of us that is a gift from our Creator and that cannot be removed by anything we do.

Balswick, King, and Reimer talk about power in a relationship as an ability to influence others.[8] A reciprocating relational connection entails not just the influence of a parent, youth worker, or pastor on a young person, but the influence of the young person on those adults. It brings great joy to a child or youth to be able to share what he has learned and to teach his elders something. Naturally, this is to take place in the context of a respectful relationship, but adults have greater influence on young people when the influence is mutual.

In the context of a youth Bible study, this can be fleshed out by encouraging theological reflection as a shared process rather than providing too many "answers" as the leaders. Youth who work with their leaders to understand a passage are empowered not only by the exploration but also the thought or answer not anticipated by the leader. The leader should still maintain authority and gently challenge false conclusions and beliefs, but allowing for faith to be explored and beliefs arrived at personally is not only empowering, but it is also essential for faith to flourish into adulthood.

All this leads toward an intimacy in which the teens are truly known for who they are. Many teens struggle with the belief that they are not truly known by anyone. They feel isolated from their parents and other adults who seemed closer to them when they were younger. Using the framework of the reciprocating self, parents, pastors, DCEs, and youth workers are better able to continue to nurture and foster intimate relational connections with children and youth. They not only provide for their faith development but also model healthy intimacy.

WHY YOUTH MINISTRY STARTS IN ELEMENTARY SCHOOL

This discussion of faith formation establishes a foundation for the argument that youth ministry starts in elementary school. This does not mean that you need to have youth group-type meetings or events for first graders, though you may. Some churches build toward their high school or junior high youth ministries by creating third- and fourth- or fifth- and sixth-grade youth groups. This may be a strategy for some, but not a necessity.

Keeping the elementary student in mind when structuring Christian Education in a local congregation is necessary as an intentional pathway into formal youth ministry in junior high and high school. Like with much quality work done in this world, the task must begin with the end in mind. Thus, the foundation for youth ministry is best established far sooner than the day a thirteen-year-old wanders into the youth room for the first time.

---

8   Balswick, King, and Reimer, *The Reciprocating Self,* 60.

Establishing a foundation for the place of the church in the life of a young person while parents have the greatest influence remains essential. Setting forth a pattern of church participation as a family at an earlier age lays the best foundation for maintaining the connection of youth to the church in and through high school. Worshiping together, praying together, attending potlucks and church social events together as a family lay the foundation for choices made more independently during the teen years. For more on this, see chapter 8 of *Teaching the Faith at Home: What Does This Mean? How Is This Done?*, 123–30.

At times, the conversation concerning church involvement of children and youth focuses on not forcing their participation. However, would this attitude work for school or other essential activities? Could you imagine parents arguing with a principal that they do not want to force their child to go to school because they don't want their child to grow up to hate algebra?

There is a difference between setting an expectation of church participation and forcing compliance and religious conformity. As noted above, there is true value in creating a climate in which questions can be asked freely. Yet, this does not mean that this is done without an expectation of engagement with the family practice of the faith.

Encouraging parents to see the connection between the programs and events in a church's children's and youth ministry and the formation of an adult faith is of critical importance and should be a key ingredient in the development of a philosophy of Christian Education. (See chapter 3.)

CONCLUSION

As leaders, it is critical to see the whole of faith formation and then structure age-specific programming accordingly, rather than merely addressing the immediate needs of each age group. Taking a long view in our approach to ministry takes into account how a preschooler will someday stand before the congregation for confirmation and how a confirmand will someday bring his own child for Baptism. Having a holistic vision of faith formation aids the church in addressing the needs of the individual moving through our ministries, rather than merely attempting to have a strong youth group or children's program.

RESOURCES

Balswick, Jack O., Pamela E. King, and Kevin S. Reimer. *The Reciprocating Self: Human Development in Theological Perspective.* Downers Grove, IL: InterVarsity Press, 2005.

Fowler, James W. *Stages of Faith: The Psychology of Human Development and the Quest for Meaning.* San Francisco: HarperCollins, 1995.

Rueter, David L. *Teaching the Faith at Home: What Does This Mean? How Is This Done?* St. Louis: Concordia Publishing House, 2015.

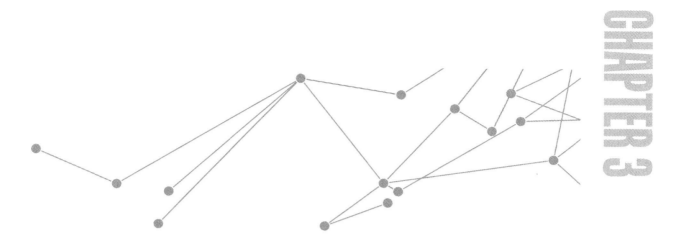

CHAPTER 3

DEVELOPING A PHILOSOPHY OF CHRISTIAN EDUCATION

BY DAVE RUETER

What is the Primary Purpose of Christian Education?

We take for granted a good many things we do in the Church. We do them year after year, often in roughly the same way. We rarely pause long enough to properly consider why we keep doing these events or activities, let alone allow enough time to put everything away before the next season of flurried activity comes upon us. I have been in many youth rooms or DCE offices following a mission trip or Vacation Bible School and have seen piles of post-event paraphernalia along with very tired church staff and volunteers who have neither the time nor the energy to deal with those piles.

Does this sound familiar? Do you find yourself running from one activity to another? Have you ever paused long enough to wonder what all this busyness is all about? I firmly believe that having a purpose for the things that we do in the Church is critically important. Further, being able to articulate that purpose in a way that helps families in your church understand the value and meaning behind the activities you offer provides a solid rationale for including those activities in their already overpacked schedules.

Whether you have a well-established ministry that is growing and thriving or you are working to reestablish or reinvigorate a ministry that has been in decline or even ceased to exist entirely, taking the time to consider the purpose for Christian Education and its relationship to youth ministry is vitally important.

What Is Christian Education?

Before attempting to articulate a philosophy of Christian Education, it would be helpful to identify what Christian Education does. The Great Commission, as recorded in Matthew 28:16–20, provides the apostles a clear direction for how to shape the ministry Christ was calling them to do in His name. They were to go and to make disciples. Their ministry was to be about baptizing and teaching.

In order to make disciples as Christ commanded, they would need to go and seek the lost. Go to where people were who could be formed into disciples through water and the Word. Therefore, the disciples went. They went far and wide. The waters of Baptism brought thousands into a right relationship with Christ. The Word of God came to many people, in a variety of contexts, who spoke many languages.

The apostles and those who followed them were to teach people "to observe all that [Christ has] commanded" (Matthew 28:20). Through the ministry of the Holy Spirit, the apostles recalled these teachings and eventually recorded them in the writings we know as the New Testament. This laid the foundation from which all Christian Education would and should properly take place.

Making disciples is not a one-time event. Disciples are not made merely through Baptism. But through Baptism *and* one's remembrance of the life change initiated in the waters of Baptism, the beginning of discipleship takes place. Discipleship enables the believers to understand and faithfully live out their vocation as a redeemed son or daughter of the King. Just as the disciples of Christ walked with Him during His public ministry, Christ's disciples today walk together under the guidance of the Scriptures and within the community of the local church.

While discipleship is primarily about learning to live out one's vocation as a believer, Christian Education provides the educational structures in which much of this learning takes place. We often see this in the programs, classes, and educational events taking place in the local church. However, much of Christian Education also occurs through the informal learning in between formal educational times.

Christian Education as an academic discipline is related to a number of larger disciplines and smaller subdisciplines. While it is beyond the scope of this book to provide a detailed accounting of these relationships, it may be helpful to understand the relational connections.

FIGURE 1

Figure 1 includes a partial list of theological disciplines. Christian Education can be seen as a subdiscipline of practical theology. The work of practical theology focuses on the application of other, more abstract theological disciplines in the lives of believers.

In addition to Christian Education, discipleship and pastoral theology are two clear sub-disciplines of practical theology.

Discipleship is a Spirit-led and Spirit-guided response to our new identity in Christ. Discipleship involves the hearing of God's Word, responding to the Law in repentance, receiving forgiveness in the Gospel, and finally faithfully following Christ. All of this is made possible not by our own strength but by the strength given to us by the Holy Spirit.

Practical theology is an academic discipline that seeks to understand how theological theory shapes theological practice. In the Church, practical theology is concerned with how pastors and other church workers put their theological training into practical action walking with people and guiding them in their relationship and life in Christ.

This means that Christian Education is a discipline in the Church grounded theologically while focused on the practical application of the theological truths of Scripture. This further means that Christian Education is always grounded to a particular theological tradition. Generic Christian Education as it applies to the ministry of the Church does not exist. This will become important further along.

How Does Christian Education Relate to Youth Ministry?

You may wonder at this point what all this has to do with a book on youth ministry. What is the relationship between Christian Education and youth ministry? Taking a look at figure 2, Christian Education can be seen, in context, related to its own subdisciplines. Within Christian Education, one can explore the teaching ministry of the Church across the lifespan, from children to adults. Each subdiscipline asks its own key questions, but must be kept in tension with the questions of other subdisciplines as well as the larger disciplines it is a part of. Thus, Christian Education must not only keep its theological foundations in mind, but also understand how it relates to youth ministry.

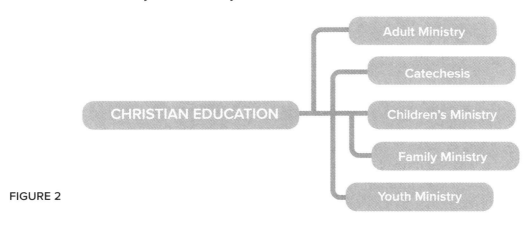

FIGURE 2

Youth ministry is a subdiscipline of Christian Education in that it picks up the work of educating youth in the Christian faith from children's ministry and catechesis/confirmation. For many churches, confirmation and a pastor's class are the only intentional programmatic approaches for catechesis. We listed catechesis in figure 2 intentionally in order to begin your thinking beyond mere confirmation toward a lifespan catechesis. For more on this concept, check out *Teaching the Faith at Home: What Does This Mean? How Is This Done?*

While there are elements of discipleship that take place in the practice of youth ministry, at its core youth ministry is an educational ministry, at least insofar as it relates to the understanding traditional to The Lutheran Church—Missouri Synod.

This understanding of youth ministry has implications for how we ought to approach our ministry to young people. Youth ministry is a theological endeavor due to its relationship to practical theology through Christian Education. Because of the connection Christian Education has with pastoral theology and discipleship, there will be an influence, though it will not be driven by these disciplines.

Understanding Christian Education in this way, we are able to see the necessity of a lifespan approach to this ministry of the Church. Each of the subdisciplines of Christian Education must relate its approach to ministry within the larger context of the whole of Christian Education. Youth ministry cannot function in a vacuum without understanding the implications of the practice of children's and family ministry. When catechesis in the local church does not take youth ministry into account, it is more likely to be ineffective. Likewise, when youth ministry is organized without taking catechesis into account, it, too, is less effective. It is only when we consider the whole of Christian Education that we are able to shape a holistic approach to ministry that cares properly for children, youth, and their families.

THEOLOGICAL FOUNDATIONS

As noted above, the theological foundations of a church's ministry have implications to how practical ministry is approached. Thus, laying out a clear and faithful understanding of the theological foundations of Christian Education in an LCMS congregation is a foundational piece that ought not to be skipped in assessing and/or developing a philosophy of Christian Education.

UNDERSTANDING SIN IN THE LIVES OF CHILDREN AND YOUTH

Lutheran theology is rightly done when it is Christ-centered. However, there are many Christian theological traditions that claim to be Christ-centered. What does it mean to be Christ-centered from a Lutheran perspective, and why is this important for the teaching of children and youth? Lutheran theology is Christ-centered in that Christ is foundational to our relationship with God the Father. Lutherans take seriously the idea of sin. While we might talk to children about sin as wrongdoing, we do not stop there. Sin, begun in the Garden of Eden, severed the relationship between God and His creation.

We are not created sinful by nature. We might talk of it as our sinful human nature, but this was not the nature God designed for us. It is, however, the result of the curse of sin. This curse was not merely something Adam and Eve had to endure throughout the remaining years of their lives, but rather a reality for all of their children. We call this original sin. The Lutheran Confessions teach that original sin has been inherited by every child since the fall of Adam and Eve. We are bent toward sin from the moment of our conception. We are in need of a Savior from the beginning.

With Christ as our center and the only hope for restoration with the Father, we recognize that we are entirely incapable of bringing anything to bear toward our salvation. The only thing we contribute to the relationship is our sin which tore it asunder in the first place. When properly applied to our understanding of children, we rightly see them as sinners in need of a Savior just as we see ourselves. They might be far more adorable than we are, but their cuteness does not negate their culpability for sin.

Lutherans are sacramental. We hold to the ancient truth that God specifically instituted particular ways and means by which His grace is available to us. Therefore, understanding the sinful nature of our children and seeking the restoration of their lives to a right relationship with God, we present them for Baptism before the assembled Body of Christ in the local church. In the waters of Baptism, Christ brings salvation and forgiveness. Baptism is entirely an act of God. Whether the baptized is an infant, teen, or adult, all that is contributed is sin. We can do nothing to restore a right relationship with God. Through the waters of Baptism, God alone acts and makes us His own.

Having been justified through the work of Christ and given faith through the waters of Baptism, both young and old begin a new life in Christ. Now empowered by the Holy Spirit, believers are able to do good works in the name of Christ, in a manner pleasing to the Father. However, as Luther rightly points out, we remain marred by sin. Luther uses the Latin phrase *simul justus et peccator,* intending to remind us that while we are made a saint through the blood of Christ, we remain sinners. We are declared just, and yet remain sinful.

From this understanding of our nature post-Baptism, Lutherans, especially since C. F. W. Walther, have emphasized the proper use of Law and Gospel. This is an exceptionally useful tool for both parents and Sunday School teachers, as well as anyone seeking to work with children and youth. Using this tool, all of Scripture is understood as containing both the Law and the Gospel. The key is to understand which you are reading in a particular passage. The Law is understood as those passages that place a demand upon humanity, whereas the Gospel is seen in those passages that explain what Christ has done in our place to fulfill the Law.

It is within this framework that Lutheran Christian Education is to approach an understanding of sin in the lives of children and youth. The implication of this framework is that a Lutheran approach to Christian Education is not merely moral training. Though many parents might find this to be a simple default setting, it is not the place of the church to train children in manners and morality for their own sake. Rather, these flow out of an understanding of our need for a Savior. Even the youngest of those we teach are in need of a Savior. Teaching children and youth that they *need* a Savior and that they *have* a Savior in Christ brings them into faith and a relationship with God. Through the work of the Holy Spirit, a desire to conform morally to the desires of God is formed. In this way, the Law serves as a guide showing us how we are to live according to God's will. A philosophy of Christian Education that does not take this into account would work counter to the expressed theology of the Lutheran Church.

MAPPING CHRISTIAN EDUCATION

Mapping Christian Education is a process by which the various programs and activities of the church are seen as a whole rather than individual silos. Too often, decisions in the church are made in isolation. Sunday School curriculum is selected without consideration of the essential educational needs to prepare children for confirmation. Confirmation programs are created without logic or structural connection to high school ministry. Pausing to consider how a child might navigate through the entirety of the educational offerings of a local congregation provides the chance to intentionally map out his or her journey of faith. Again, plan with the end in mind and with a reason to develop a comprehensive philosophy of Christian Education that provides the direction toward this common goal.

When mapping Christian Education, it may be helpful to lay out the sequence of lessons, topics, Bible passages, theological concepts, or catechetical elements to be covered, when, and in what format. Gathering this information for the first time may seem to be a rather daunting task, but the overview created will allow church leadership to identify holes in the Christian Education plan. Over- or undercoverage can be identified, prior knowledge issues identified, and sequencing of learning addressed.

BEGIN WITH PRE-BAPTISMAL COUNSELING

When laying out the map that will guide the Christian Education efforts of a local church, a great place to begin is with the counseling of parents and sponsors prior to the Baptism of their children. Keeping in mind not to overwhelm new parents, comfort and support can be brought to them in this meeting. Walk through the theology of Baptism. Invite the sponsors of the child to participate, and instruct them on both the theology and their ongoing role in the faith life of their godchild.

Then lay out how the church will walk with both parents and sponsors as they work to support the faith formation of the child. Talk about the programs, resources, and further counsel provided throughout the life of the child. Emphasize the value of family worship and Christian Education to the faith formation of the child. The goal is not only to provide information, but also to convey to parents that they are not in this alone. Help them to begin with the end in mind. Parenting often seems reactionary rather than proactive. Help enable parents to be proactive with the support of the church in both matters of the faith and general parenting support.

CONTINUE IN ELEMENTARY SCHOOL

Consider how families will be invited to participate in Christian Education efforts in elementary school. When does Sunday School begin? How are students grouped in classes? What developmentally appropriate content will be covered at each level? Make sure the content covered in elementary school is built upon prior content either covered in preschool classes or through resources provided to parents by the church.

Examine how your church can teach the whole story of salvation rather than merely a series of Bible stories. Keep the big picture in mind while teaching individual lessons. It may be tempting to simply tackle one week at a time, but try to see what is taught each week or in special events as part of a larger structure.

THE PLACE OF CONFIRMATION

Give serious consideration to how students are prepared for confirmation. Content like the Lord's Prayer, Apostles' Creed, and Ten Commandments can be memorized during the years leading up to formal catechesis. This lays a foundation for deeper reflection during confirmation. Students are better prepared to answer "What does this mean?" if they have spent more time focused on the question rather than on memorization, which is more developmentally appropriate earlier in life.

Think through the time youth will spend in confirmation holistically. What experience do you want them to have? What do you hope they will take with them following confirmation? How will relationships with ministry staff and church members be nurtured along with content learned?

If your church has a junior high youth ministry, how do confirmation and junior high ministry work with each other? How are they scheduled to support rather than compete with each other? How is content laid out to dovetail together while not proving redundant?

HANDING OFF WELL FROM CONFIRMATION TO HIGH SCHOOL

If confirmation day comes and goes and nothing intentional is done to welcome and relationally connect recently confirmed students with the high school youth ministry at your church, there is clearly work to be done. Confirmation does not have to be the end of a young person's connection to the church. Be intentional to create a bridge between confirmation and high school youth ministry.

By way of example, a church I served had a retreat designed and led by a team of high school youth who were leaders for their peers and supported the work of the volunteers and myself as the DCE. This retreat was designed as a welcome for the confirmands just a month after their confirmation. These high school youth visited the confirmation class toward the end of instruction and/or attended the confirmation banquet to extend the invitation. They called the confirmands to encourage them to attend. They planned all activities, including a time where they explained the shape of the high school ministry. Further, they held a question and answer time for the confirmands to ask questions about surviving high school. This bonded many of the youth to one another and created a relational connection to the high school ministry. How might your ministry structure such a bridge?

Up to this point, you might expect that the high school youth ministry would be seen as the culmination of the prior discussion. However, taking this as an end goal would be short-sighted. A quality philosophy of Christian Education gives consideration to how youth will be formed during high school as well as how they will be launched into their adult lives still connected to the life of the Church. Consideration should be given to how to structure a high school ministry in such a way that the connection to the larger Church is not only maintained but further supported and grown.

Just as thought should be given to when to hold other Christian Education programs so as to encourage participation in worship and the larger life of the church, the same consideration should be given to the organization of the high school ministry. What should Sunday morning programming for high school look like? Should there even be any? How can families be encouraged to worship together by the structure of the services and Christian Education programs offered?

Finally, some consideration should be given to thinking through and defining what a self-differentiated faith looks like in your context. What are the beliefs and behaviors associated with such a faith? What teachings, discussions, and experiences shape such a faith?

DIAGNOSTIC QUESTIONS FOR DEVELOPING YOUR OWN PHILOSOPHY OF CHRISTIAN EDUCATION

Sticking with the theme that developed in the preceding section, this concluding section will provide questions you can use in the formulation of a philosophy of Christian Education. Topics raised are necessary considerations to understand the unique realities of ministry in your specific context.

HISTORY OF YOUR CONGREGATION AND YOUTH MINISTRY

Every local congregation is different. Even churches in the same city are unique due to their history. This is relevant to the development of a philosophy of Christian Education in that the Christian Education practices of the past shape what is likely to work in the future. If your congregation has a long and illustrious history, more analysis might be necessary. If you are part of a new church or even a church plant, this work could be much less complicated.

Areas for consideration:

- How was the past and current support of the pastor(s) toward Christian Education?

- What were the attendance patterns over the years for major Christian Education ministries (Sunday School, VBS, midweek children's ministry, youth ministry)?

- What days and times did the various Christian Education ministries take place?

- Is there a correlation between the time an educational ministry was offered and attendance?

- What has volunteer support looked like for Christian Education in the past? Are there recent trends to keep in mind?

- Have there been any Christian Education programs that once existed but no longer exist? Under what circumstances did those programs end?

MISSION AND VISION OF THE CONGREGATION

All churches should have a well-thought-out and easy-to-understand mission and vision that guides the ministry and programming of the congregation. The mission and vision of a congregation establish the criteria to determine if a new idea for Christian Education fits with the overall purpose of the congregation. If your church has mission and vision statements, the work of Christian Education should directly support and conform to them. A philosophy of Christian Education supports and further extends the larger mission and vision of the church.

This is determined by considering the following:

- What would Christian Education need to look like in order for the vision of our church to become a reality?

- What outcomes from Christian Education programming would support members working together toward this vision?

- What place does Christian Education have in supporting the mission of our church?

- How does each age group factor into Christian Education that supports the mission of our church?

CULTURAL CONTEXT

Whether you are launching a new Christian Education ministry or attempting to give new direction to a long-standing ministry, having an accurate understanding of the cultural context of your ministry is critical. Cultural context means more than the ethnic makeup of your church. Both the culture of your church and your community need to be considered. Understanding the differences between the culture of your church and community can reveal a great deal about the approach needed to fulfill your church's mission.

Some questions for consideration:

- What is the ethnic makeup of your congregation? Is it homogeneous or diverse?

- What is the ethnic makeup of the community where your church is located? How different is this from the members of your church?

- What is the socioeconomic makeup of your congregation? Is there a wide range of financial lifestyles represented?

- How does the socioeconomic makeup of your church compare with the community at large?

- How many of your members live within two miles of your church building? Five miles? Ten miles? Further?

- What is the attendance pattern of your church members? Weekly? Twice a month? Monthly?

- What is the Sunday morning culture of your church? How has the structure of worship services and Christian Education shaped this culture?

- Are your members available for volunteer service or are they professionals who tend to be too busy? How frequently are members likely to volunteer?

AREAS OF EXISTING CHRISTIAN EDUCATION

When working on a philosophy of Christian Education, it is important to take into account the structure of the current programs offered. Being able to identify and assess what is working and what is not will help you shape a philosophy. Build upon what is working and what matches your church's mission and vision. Consider areas of weakness as places for further effort and growth.

Some questions for consideration:

- What are all the current Christian Education programs or events?

- What Christian Education programs or events from the recent past are no longer offered?

- How do these programs and events work to support one another?

- How do these programs and events support the mission and vision of the church?

- Is there a clear faith formation approach embedded across these programs and events?

- Does this faith formation approach match the theology of the church?

- Does this faith formation approach match the mission and vision of the church?

RELATIONSHIPS BETWEEN MINISTRY STAFF AND VOLUNTEERS

When laying a philosophy of Christian Education, it is helpful to clearly delineate how staff and volunteers will work with one another. The size and financial resources of your church will impact how much of the leadership of Christian Education is done by staff as opposed to volunteers. The staffing of larger churches should be shaped around how this aspect of a philosophy of Christian Education is fleshed out into an understanding of which ministry areas are prioritized as staff driven and which are best volunteer driven.

Areas for consideration:

- What kinds of decisions are to be made by staff rather than volunteers?
- What decisions and activities are best left released to volunteers? Which must remain guided by the staff?
- What training is necessary in order to best on-board volunteers?
- How large of a volunteer corps is necessary to carry out Christian Education well?
- What staffing leadership is necessary in order to support Christian Education as defined by your church?

LEARNING ENVIRONMENT

A church can have a grand vision for Christian Education, but without adequate facilities to house the programs or events, the vision has no way of becoming a reality. When developing a philosophy of Christian Education, consider the space and kinds of spaces needed to accomplish the vision of the congregation.

To assess the learning environment for Christian Education, ask the following questions:

- What formal or classroom learning environments are available?
- What informal settings can be leveraged to conduct Christian Education?
- Which Christian Education programs or events can be done well in learning environments on the church property?
- Which Christian Education programs or events would best be done in learning environments not on the church property?
- How should the use of space be prioritized?

CURRICULUM ASSESSMENT

Few things directly impact the execution of a philosophy of Christian Education more than the selection of curriculum. There is often a disconnect between the theology and philosophy of a congregation and the curriculum selected for use in Christian Education. Care should be taken to ensure that the theology of the church shapes its philosophy of Christian Education and in turn the curriculum used, rather than allowing the selected curriculum to unintentionally reshape its theology.

Questions for consideration:

- How is our church's teaching on sin reflected in the curriculum?
- How is our church's understanding of salvation reflected in the curriculum?
- What place is Christ given in the curriculum?
- Are Law and Gospel appropriately utilized?
- Is the curriculum age appropriate?

- Do the various curricula in use across the congregation work together toward the same goal?
- Do the various curricula in use across the congregation form a comprehensive whole?

GOALS FOR CHRISTIAN EDUCATION

As noted above, a philosophy of Christian Education should result in the work of a congregation orienting around a set of end goals. Keeping the end in mind when making decisions on what and how to teach the faith is the key to having an expressed philosophy that results in the fulfillment of the desired vision of the congregation.

Some questions to consider in this area:

- Based on the theology of our church, what does a mature believer look like?
- How can Christian Education in our church support the faith formation that results in this kind of mature believer?
- How can Christian Education support the realization of the mission and vision of our church?

CONCLUSION

The final question to be considered in developing a philosophy of Christian Education is how to put all the various streams of thought noted above into a coherent statement to be implemented in a local congregation. Begin by assessing the essential theological foundation of your congregation. From there, consider how you see faith formation shaping the belief systems and faith lives of your people. At this point, assess where you see various groups in your church with regard to their faith formation.

Next, lay out the current map of your Christian Education programming. Identify everything that is being taught and when. Give consideration to the connection between age groups while watching for both gaps in learning and redundancies. Finally, walk through the diagnostic question areas, gathering as much information as possible.

Based on this data, put a group together of key leaders, staff, and stakeholders, who will work together to craft a statement that takes this all into account. As a group, work toward the creation of a narrative statement that conveys your concept of Christian Education as informed by your examination of the factors above. Include a description of how this Christian Education takes place and a justification for why Christian Education is to be shaped as you believe it should be in your context. In this statement, tie together the history of your church, its theology, its approach to faith formation, cultural context, the mission of the church, and other areas from the diagnostic questions section.

Similar to a vision statement, a philosophy of Christian Education tells the story of what Christian Education looks like in your congregation. This story should connect with the larger story of the Christian Church throughout history and project the continued movement of God through His Church into the future.

Keep Christ front and center through this entire process. Seek the guidance of the Holy Spirit at every turn. When you arrive at a solid philosophy statement, prayerfully present this to the congregation for support. With their support, consider how to train both volunteers and the larger membership to understand and support this philosophy.

If your philosophy includes a change with the past, allow plenty of time for this new approach to take root. Changing the culture of a congregation takes time. A God-honoring philosophy of Christian Education should be given adequate time for people to become comfortable with and reshape the practice of their faith around. Remain in prayer as you seek to keep this philosophy in mind as you move forward in teaching the faith to all ages.

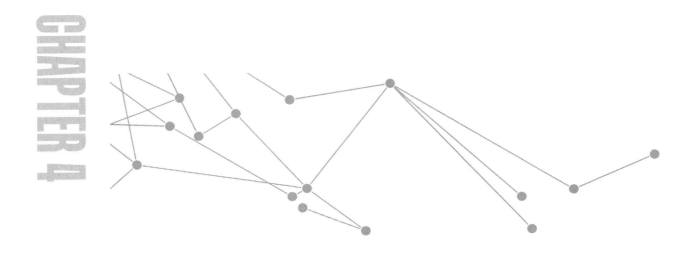

CHAPTER 4

DEVELOPING A PHILOSOPHY OF YOUTH MINISTRY

BY HEATH LEWIS

INTRODUCTION

Picture this: *You've just accepted a youth ministry position in a congregation. The congregation is a few years old, and it has recently been experiencing tremendous growth in membership. One of the pieces the congregation has yet to develop is a ministry to its young people—and this responsibility, building a youth ministry "from the ground up," will be primarily included in your position. You walk in the doors for your first day on the job. Where do you begin? What do you do first?*

Or consider another scenario: *You are a longtime member of your congregation, and you have been active for many years in various volunteer roles. Your congregation's Director of Christian Education, who maintained oversight of the youth ministry for several years, just accepted a call to another church. Because of your service as a volunteer in the congregation, you have experience serving alongside the pastor. He believes you have the gifts, abilities, and passions to help lead the youth ministry during the transition time. You agree, and begin your tenure as the volunteer youth director. What first steps do you take in this new role?*

In both of these scenarios, it would be tempting to jump in and start planning events for the coming days, weeks, and months. But before you begin with this type of work, it is critical to know where you are going—to develop a philosophy that helps guide and direct your congregation's service for and with students. Like a traveler without a GPS, map, or clear directions, planning activities without a long-term philosophy in mind can quickly lead to a greater probability of getting "lost."

Whether your congregation is establishing a youth ministry for the first time or if you have served youth in some manner for years, it is important to have a clear philosophy of ministry. A clear philosophy provides a critical component to building a healthy youth ministry, helping congregations, volunteers, and staff design and implement ministry opportunities that serve families in the present while building toward the future.

What Is a Philosophy?

At its most basic level, a philosophy involves a system of thought: the ideas, concepts, beliefs, and attitudes of an individual or group. So, when we talk about developing a philosophy of youth ministry, what we are really saying is this: this philosophy clarifies and articulates what our congregation believes about its ministry for and with young people. Your philosophy guides and directs as it defines what you are about and where you are going in your ministry to and with young people.

Why Develop a Philosophy?

The development of a philosophy is a vital first step to intentionality in youth ministry. A clear philosophy yields several benefits for you as the youth leader, as well as for the students, parents, and congregational members with whom you work. It will help you set goals. It will help you appropriately allocate resources. It will become the foundation for every decision made regarding ministry for and with students in your congregation. With this foundation in mind, there are four primary benefits of articulating a clear congregational philosophy of youth ministry.

Clarity of Purpose

If you don't understand the most basic ideas, concepts, beliefs, and attitudes regarding youth ministry in your congregation, how will you ever know what to do with your students? As described earlier, you will never know where you are headed if you don't understand your philosophy. When your purpose is clear, everyone involved—including you, as the leader—will know why you are doing what you are doing. This produces a number of advantages, including buy-in from key stakeholders in the ministry, enthusiasm from those involved, increased potential for collaboration, credibility in leadership, clear direction, measurable goals, and a focus that remains consistent over the course of time.

Consistency of Behavior

When a decision needs to be made, your philosophy helps you understand the best way for your congregation to approach it. As you articulate the things you value, as well as who you minister to and within your unique context, you establish a standard set of principles that guide the behaviors and decisions of everyone involved in your youth ministry.

Understanding of Roles

There will be no confusion about who does what when you understand your philosophy of youth ministry. The roles of parents, students, volunteers, staff members, and the congregation will be clearly articulated and defined.

Defined Goals and Objectives

The thing about congregational life is that when you bring a group of people together, everyone has their own preferences, ideas, and goals based on the things they find most important. By establishing a clear philosophy of ministry, you provide a defined set of goals and objectives for what your ministry looks to accomplish. Your philosophy will ultimately help everyone move forward together.

Whether you realize it or not, you—and your congregation—already have a philosophy of youth ministry. Think about it. Earlier, we defined a philosophy by saying it includes the ideas, concepts, beliefs, and attitudes of an individual or group. You likely already have these things when it comes to youth ministry. But since youth ministry involves a number of people, these ideas should not remain in your head! When you clearly articulate and share your philosophy of ministry, everyone involved benefits.

What Does the Bible Say about Youth Ministry?

As we begin or maintain any congregational ministry, it makes sense that we continually look to God's Word to ensure that we are in alignment with biblical principles and purposes for ministry. Youth ministry is no different. As we begin the development or evaluation of a ministry philosophy, let's dig in to see what the Bible has to say about ministry for and with young people.

Here is the bad news: the Bible doesn't give us a clear mandate about how to build a youth ministry. There is no purpose statement; no handbook that describes the scope and sequence of a well-run youth program; no planning guide for your next mission trip, movie night, or lock-in. None of it.

Here is the good news: what the Bible does provide is continual affirmation of God's care and concern for people of all ages—including youth. The following Scripture passages highlight just a few of the ways God includes young people in His kingdom work.

God is clear that the Gospel is a message for all of creation. Matthew 28:18–20 commands the Church to make disciples of "all nations," which includes youth. According to Paul, all believers—regardless of gender, race, or any other seeming difference—are a part of the Body of Christ (1 Corinthians 12:12–26). This also includes young people! Too often, congregations inadvertently fail to include their younger members in the command to reach all nations, or in their understanding of who is included in the Body. We must always remember that all means all—and in this case, that includes youth!

Throughout Scripture, God chooses and uses young people to accomplish His purposes. Biblical accounts like the calling of Samuel (1 Samuel 3), the anointing of David (1 Samuel 16:1–13), the selection of Jeremiah (Jeremiah 1:4–10), and His incarnation through young Mary (Luke 1:26–38) demonstrate God's willingness and ability to incorporate even young people in His plan of salvation.

Scripture reminds us that God uses young people to set an example for the Church. Paul reminds Timothy, "Let no one despise you for your youth, but set the believers an example in speech, in conduct, in love, in faith, in purity" (1 Timothy 4:12). In Matthew 18:1–5, Jesus uses the faith of a child as an example for adult believers, urging them to welcome the children as a part of their assembly: "Whoever receives one such child in My name receives Me." Young people are, and have been from the beginning, a vital part of the Church's existence.

Finally, in His Word, God affirms that young people need the instruction and renewal that comes from the Lord. The psalmist asserts in Psalm 71:17: "O God, from my youth You have taught me, and I still proclaim Your wondrous deeds." Psalm 119:9 states, "How can a young man keep his way pure? By guarding it according to Your word." And in Isaiah 40:30–31, we are told that "Even youths shall faint and be weary, and young men shall fall exhausted; but they who wait for the LORD shall renew their strength; they shall mount up with wings like eagles; they shall run and not be weary; they shall walk and not faint." Congregations, through Word and Sacrament, have been given a profound opportunity to instruct, renew, and bring the gifts of God into the lives of students.

In these, along with a number of other scriptural texts, God provides His Church with a mandate to serve the young people in its midst. Congregations have immense flexibility in developing ministries for and with their young people. This matters. Why? Because there has never been, and will never be, a congregation just like yours! Consider what God can do through your group, no matter if it's a handful of people in a youth group or a congregation of a thousand. A church is made up of individuals—each bringing different interests and talents.[1] Your congregation's youth ministry will serve as a reflection of your God-given concern for His young people—and as such, it should be as unique as the congregation, community, and people you serve.

CORE ELEMENTS OF A PHILOSOPHY

Whether you are just starting out or have been involved in youth ministry for years, it is vital to explore the unique nature of your congregation to develop your ministry, set goals, and plan for the future. As we have discussed, a philosophy aids in all of these components—and more! But where do you begin? What should be included in your philosophy? As you begin, or as you take a fresh look at your philosophy, here are a few questions and concepts to consider.

---

1   Will Mancini, *Church Unique: How Missional Leaders Cast Vision, Capture Culture, and Create Movement* (San Francisco: Jossey-Bass, 2008), 6.

WHY DO WE HAVE A YOUTH MINISTRY? (PURPOSE)

There are many reasons congregations engage in ministry for and with students. Before doing anything else to develop a youth ministry, you must answer this question: Why does our congregation's youth ministry exist? Is it to tell students about Jesus? to build a youth group? to provide a safe place for students? because your congregation has always had a youth ministry? to reach students who don't know Jesus? to equip students as leaders for the Church, both now and in the future? some other reason not listed here?

Whatever your reason for beginning and maintaining a youth ministry, it must be clarified and stated. This will lead to a sense of greater commitment from everyone involved—students, parents, staff, volunteers, and congregational members. Knowing why your youth ministry exists helps you determine what matters most when the time comes to make important decisions.

One key component to this idea is developing an understanding of your primary audience. Your youth ministry has the potential to reach many different students. You will encounter students who are not currently connected with a congregation—or, for that matter, maybe they are not connected at all with Christ. You will get to know students who are listed as members of your congregation but lack a deeper connection (or, perhaps, any connection!) to the Church. You will engage with students who are connected to the Body of Christ and are growing in their faith as they are involved in Word and Sacrament. You will walk with students who are discovering their gifts and finding ways to serve. Your ministry should not exist for the purpose of building up just one "type" of student, nor is the goal to pick "one or the other." The objective is to clarify why you exist and who you are trying to reach so that everyone involved is able to discover and understand his or her place in the Church.

WHAT IS IMPORTANT TO US? (VALUES)

Just like each person holds a specific set of values as important, a youth ministry also holds values. Will Mancini describes values as nonnegotiable pieces for a congregation—things pastors and leaders must never sacrifice in advancing the mission of the Church.[2] Patrick Lencioni reminds readers that values define an organization's personality, giving members of the organization clarity regarding how they behave.[3] It is important for youth ministry leaders to articulate two to three core values—pieces at the heart of the ministry's identity. These values provide a roadmap to building and developing every aspect of your youth ministry. From volunteer recruitment to activity and program selection, from communication style to room setup and more, your values influence everything that happens in a youth ministry.

HOW WILL WE ACCOMPLISH OUR PURPOSE AND LIVE OUR VALUES? (STRATEGY)

Your strategy is where the proverbial "rubber meets the road." In answering this question,

---

2   Mancini, *Church Unique*, 129.
3   Patrick Lencioni, *The Advantage: Why Organizational Health Trumps Everything Else in Business* (San Francisco: Wiley, John & Sons, 2012), 91.

you define the "how" of ministry. This is when you articulate what you will do to minister for and with students. Bible studies, mission trips, fellowship events, worship services, retreats, lock-ins, home visits, and other practices that will help you accomplish your purpose and live out your values should be articulated here. Keep in mind: your answer to this question is not meant to be an exhaustive list. Rather, it is intended to define the core practices that will support your ministry to and with young people.

WHAT DO WE PROVIDE? (DEFINITION)

Beyond the language of purpose and values, it is important to provide a clear, definitive statement of what it is your youth ministry provides for the congregation and community. It is the one- or two-sentence "elevator pitch" that shares with others exactly what it is you offer. Simply complete the sentence: "Our youth ministry provides . . ."

WHO WILL WE INVOLVE? (INVOLVEMENT)

Many youth workers try to do everything on their own in ministry. While there are a variety of reasons for this, the reality is simple: when a youth ministry is at its best, it involves more than one or two adult leaders. Let's consider a few reasons for this.

First, you don't have all the gifts (see 1 Corinthians 12 and Ephesians 4). Because you don't have all the gifts, you need help to accomplish the ministry laid before you and your congregation.

Additionally, not every student will want to connect with you personally. It doesn't matter how affable your personality, how much you care for your students, how hilarious your jokes are, or how great an event you host. There will, inevitably, be some students who don't connect with you personally. Guess what—that's okay!

Finally, you won't always be around. No matter how much you want to attend everything, it's not possible. You are not able to be everywhere at once; inevitably, scheduling conflicts *will* arise. You may move on to another position in another congregation, begin volunteering in a new role, and (someday), the Lord will call you home. What happens when you can't be at the next youth ministry function for any of these reasons when you are the only youth worker in your congregation?

One of the wonderful things about serving in the Body of Christ is that we don't have to do ministry on our own. In fact, we are blessed when we serve with others! There are likely many men and women in your congregation who are gifted in working with youth and will bless your youth ministry in so many ways. Your goal should be to connect each student with at least one adult who can share life with her and point her toward Christ.

These adult leaders can take many forms: Jesus-follower, mentor-friend, spiritual leader, cultural architect, and boundary keeper, among others.

One key person we have yet to mention is your senior pastor. No matter how much responsibility you have over your congregation's youth ministry, your pastor is still the primary undershepherd of your people, and the overseer of your flock—which includes your students. It is imperative to keep him "in the loop" regarding your ministry. Your pastor can rally members to support you, give you counsel and advice, celebrate alongside you, defend your ministry when necessary, help promote youth ministry, ensure sound doctrine, and so much more. At the very least, he will better understand how to specifically pray for you and your students. As a pastor friend recently shared with me, "I always advise my staff and key volunteers, 'Never surprise me in public.'" Even if he does not want to be directly involved in the planning and implementation of your congregation's youth ministry, always keep your pastor informed about what is happening. Your ministry will be exponentially better for it.

As a youth worker, you have an amazing privilege to equip others for service. How can you surround yourself with men and women whose gifts cover where yours are lacking? What are the gifts you need to incorporate into the life of your ministry? Consider and plan how you will incorporate other leaders into your congregation's youth ministry.

WHAT SHOULD WE SEE? (MEASURES)

One of the most important steps in developing a philosophy of ministry, yet often one of the most overlooked, is measuring the results. When students connect and engage in your youth ministry, what will you see? How will you know if you are reaching your goals? What are the things your youth ministry is measuring?

The things you choose to measure in your ministry will, ultimately, direct your activity. Think about it: if your goal is to increase attendance, you are going to do things that get students to walk through the doors. If your aim is to improve the prayer lives of your students, you spend time teaching on and practicing prayer. If you desire growing, healthy relationships between students, you spend time in activities that build community.

The most common measure articulated by youth ministries is attendance. Why? It is simple to track—a measure people understand. It is an easy "selling point" for members of the congregation to display the state of the ministry—most people would love to see more students involved in their congregation! Make no mistake; we should be tracking attendance as a part of caring for our students. Knowing who is connected, when they are connecting, and how they are connecting matters. But attendance only tells part of the story. The goal is to find other measures, in alignment with your purpose and values, to examine the growth of your students and your youth ministry. How will you evaluate other markers of growth—specifically spiritual development?

SPECIFIC CONSIDERATIONS

How you answer the questions posed throughout this chapter is dependent on your congregation's culture and context; the answers may look very different for different congregations. There are, however, a few specific ideas integral in the development of every youth ministry. Regardless of your ministry setting, all congregational youth ministries should pay careful attention to the following components.

DEVELOPMENTALLY APPROPRIATE

Spiritually, your congregation's young people need many of the same things your adult members need, such as safety, love, belonging, and more. There is, however, a difference in how preschoolers, preteens, and empty nesters experience those needs. As such, it is important that your ministry to youth addresses their needs in a developmentally appropriate manner. The generational characteristics and developmental level of your students must be considered as you develop your philosophy. This includes all aspects of their development: physical, mental, emotional, social, and of course, spiritual. To approach ministry in a manner developmentally inappropriate would be a disservice to the youth you serve.

SEPARATE, YET INCLUSIVE

There are times it is appropriate for your students to have separate events, Bible studies, and other differentiated activities separate from the rest of the congregation. That is part of operating a developmentally appropriate youth ministry! However, young people need the influence and mentoring that comes from inclusion and engagement in the larger Body of Christ. Students can learn much from the faith journeys of those who have navigated portions of the faith journey before them—and they, too, have much to share with older generations! By including both times of separation and inclusion, your youth ministry provides a developmentally appropriate space for students to grow while helping them recognize their place in the broader congregation.

SACRAMENTAL

Lutheran theology is rooted in God's work through His Word and Sacraments: Baptism and the Lord's Supper. Through these means, God offers His gifts of forgiveness, life, and salvation to His people. These gifts provide a broader connection to the larger Church—past, present, and future! As Lutheran theology is, at its core, sacramental, it is vital to point students toward these gifts in all that we do. Help your students remember their Baptism, where God drowned the old Adam and raised them to new life. Encourage them, according to your congregation's practice, to regularly partake in the Lord's Supper, where they (along with the entire communion of saints) receive Christ's body and blood for the forgiveness of sins.

ENGAGING FAMILIES

No matter how comprehensive and engaging, students will rarely spend more time in your ministry than they will with their families. According to Reggie Joiner, a typical congregation gets forty hours a year to influence the life of a student, while a parent has over three thousand hours per year with that same young person.[4] So why is it that, in many congrega-

---

4   Reggie Joiner, *Think Orange: Imagine the Impact When Church and Family Collide* . . . (Colorado Springs: David C. Cook, 2009), 87–88.

tions, we build youth ministries that focus only on activities with students? In a culture that moves more and more rapidly all the time, it is necessary for youth ministries to incorporate the family, and to equip parents for their vocation of raising sons and daughters in the faith.

A FINAL NOTE

As you walk through this process, either on your own or with your team, in the coming weeks and months, there are two key things that should happen. They comprise, perhaps, the most vital elements of the process—and they are, in many ways, the most simple. Write it down and use what you've developed! All the work you do to develop or clarify your philosophy will be wasted without doing these two things. Too often, leaders neglect the simple step of writing down what it is they believe. Make notes, write it down, and distribute it to the key stakeholders in your ministry so everyone is on the same page. Lencioni recommends developing a "playbook"—a short, simple document that provides a concise overview of your philosophy.[5] Include answers to the questions posed in this chapter. Encourage your leaders to refer to the "playbook" often as you work together to continue developing your congregation's youth ministry. As you use what you've developed, it will continue to serve as a guide to better serving students and families in the unique context and culture of your congregation.

CONCLUSION

When youth workers, parents, students, congregational members, and church staff members are able to move forward "on the same page" in a youth ministry, everyone benefits—especially students. By developing a clear, focused understanding of what you believe about your congregation's work with young people, you will enable everyone involved to take a strong collective step on the journey toward healthy youth ministry.

RESOURCES

Barna Group. "Pastors and Parents Differ on Youth Ministry Goals." *Barna*, March 22, 2017. https://www.barna.com/research/pastors-parents-differ-youth-ministry-goals/.

Clark, Chap. *Hurt 2.0: Inside the World of Today's Teenagers.* Grand Rapids: Baker Academic, 2011.

Joiner, Reggie. *Think Orange: Imagine the Impact When Church and Family Collide . . .* Colorado Springs: David C. Cook, 2009.

Krupp, Steven, and Paul J. H. Schoemaker. *Winning the Long Game: How Strategic Leaders Shape the Future.* Santa Barbara: PublicAffairs, 2014.

Lencioni, Patrick. *The Advantage: Why Organizational Health Trumps Everything Else in Business.* San Francisco: Wiley, John & Sons, 2012.

Mancini, Will. *Church Unique: How Missional Leaders Cast Vision, Capture Culture, and Create Movement.* San Francisco: Jossey-Bass, 2008.

Senter III, Mark H., Wesley Black, Chap Clark, and Malan Nel. *Four Views of Youth Ministry and the Church: Inclusive Congregational, Preparatory, Missional, Strategic.* Grand Rapids: Zondervan Youth Specialties, 2001.

---

5   Lencioni, *The Advantage*, 134–37.

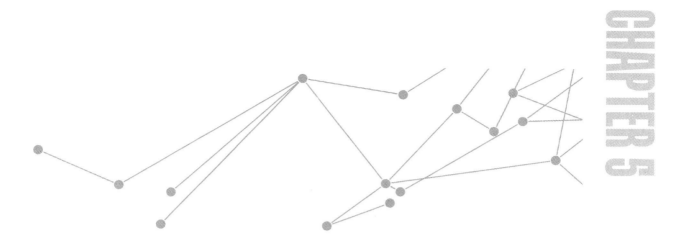

CHAPTER 5

STRATEGIC PLANNING FOR YOUTH MINISTRY

BY MARK BLANKE

Everyone plans . . . to some degree. There are those youth ministry leaders who take five minutes prior to the start of an event to plan how they *hope* the event will unfold. It may be as simple as, "I'll start with a prayer and we'll see where things go from there. . . ." While this does constitute a level—albeit a very low level—of planning, it's not necessarily advisable.

This chapter focuses on strategic planning. The dictionary defines *strategic* as "relating to the identification of long-term or overall aims and interests and the means of achieving them." Strategic planning is done in such a way that one identifies priorities for the youth ministry efforts and then directs resources (time, money, facilities) in such a way as to maximize the possibilities of achieving those priorities.

The Scriptures contain the greatest example of strategic planning. God began His plan for the reconciliation of a fallen world in Genesis. His statement to the serpent after the fall in Genesis 3:15 that Eve's offspring "shall bruise your head, and you shall bruise His heel" announced the beginning of the strategic plan. Everything that follows, the multiple covenants, the exodus, the kings, the prophets—all of it was part of the plan for Christ to come into the world to save it. God knew the direction things would take, but He allowed His plan to unfold as planned from the start of time. No wasted effort or energy. No step taken that wasn't purposeful and which didn't help the plan come to fruition. In the end, God's plan was perfectly completed through Christ's death and resurrection.

While God's plan provides us with a better understanding of the importance of strategic planning, we can't hope to come close to the effectiveness of His plan. Still, we can gain insight and clarity about our plans from making observations about *The Plan*.

DEFINING THE PURPOSE

The purpose of God's plan was to reconcile the world to Himself. What is the purpose of your youth ministry program? Think about that question . . . hard. Are you doing things just because you've always done them? Do you decide on the value of an activity based upon what you heard others say about it or how many stars it received in an online forum? Is your planning based around a large event you have done for years that seems to get the youth excited? Perhaps a conference, mission trip, ski trip, or annual talent show has become so ingrained into the culture of the group it seems to transcend all other events or purpose.

I served a congregation with such an event. When I arrived at this church, I quickly learned about the annual ski trip. This event had become one of the biggest priorities for the church, not just the youth program. Congregational leadership (not including the pastor) took special pride in mentioning how this event became so popular they rented a bus to get everyone to the ski area for the three-day event. A look at the budget showed the ski trip consumed about half of the annual youth ministry budget—most of the money paid the way for twelve or so adult chaperones.

I spent some time in my first few months trying to better understand this ski trip. I like to ski, so I had no predisposition to do away with the event. I asked about twenty youth who attended in the past what they found to be the most memorable thing, and almost universally they replied, "The cookie fight." Evidently, the retreat included another annual tradition—a large cookie fight (throwing cookies at one another) on the second night of the retreat.

While interviewing past participants, I also asked what opportunities were offered for spiritual growth; no one could think of any. While it would have been possible to modify the retreat to make it more of a growth opportunity, I spoke with the pastor and we determined that the event wasn't consistent with our purpose and we shouldn't spend half of our budget to take youth skiing and cookie fighting; so we canceled the event. This trip wasn't the best use of resources to accomplish our group's purpose.

A recent report by the Barna Group[1] found that, on the whole, there was general agreement on the main goal for a youth ministry. Seventy-one percent of senior pastors, 75 percent of "youth pastors" (including youth volunteer leaders), and 72 percent of parents identified the most important goal for a youth ministry program was discipleship.

A congregation looking to develop a purpose statement for its youth ministry should ask the key question, "What should a disciple know, feel, and do?" Once these higher-level questions have been answered, you can move on to developing the actual statement. While there are many ways to develop a purpose statement, I believe in keeping it as simple as possible.

Identify a group of mature-in-their-faith leaders who understand the dynamics of the congregation. If you have an appointed youth ministry board or committee, include committee members as part of your planning group, and plan to include other leaders as well. Ideally the planning group should have more than twelve members but less than twenty-five.

Tell potential group members that the planning meeting's goal is to develop a purpose

---

1   Barna Group, *The State of Youth Ministry: How Churches Reach Today's Teens—and What Parents Think about It* (Ventura, CA: Barna, 2016).

statement for the congregation's youth ministry. Prior to the meeting, ask group members to ponder the question: "How do we want a youth who participates in our youth ministry program to be different at the end of four years of participation than an active youth member of the congregation who doesn't participate in the youth ministry opportunities?"

Make this question the only topic for your meeting. Develop a way to encourage input from less influential or outspoken group members, who may have keen insights into the question. One method is to ask attendees to write out their answers; these are placed on newsprint around the room. Give each participant three stickers to place next to the statements they find the most helpful. Then discuss the top five statements as the group works to develop an edited version of the purpose statement.

Share this edited version of the purpose statement with your pastoral staff to make certain it remains consistent with Scripture and any existing congregational mission statement.

Finally, have the purpose statement approved by the appropriate board or committee. This very important step identifies the statement as being owned by the congregation, not just the wishes of the youth group leadership. Leaders then work toward implementing a plan to achieve the purpose.

DESIGNING THE PLAN

Thomas Edison is attributed with saying, "Vision without execution is a hallucination." A purpose statement provides a vision of a hoped-for outcome of your youth ministry efforts. If you don't build a plan of how to achieve your desired outcome, your prior planning is, in effect, a mere hallucination because it will never become reality.

STEP 1: WHERE ARE WE NOW?

At the outset, you need to see how close you are to achieving the purpose you identified. This requires evaluating. Gather individuals who have the best understanding of all aspects of the youth ministry program, including some youth who are presently involved in the program and some who participated in the past. Allow these past and present participants to review the purpose statement and give their perspective on the strengths and weaknesses of the current program relative to achieving this purpose. It is important to keep this discussion focused on the purpose statement only, since people have a tendency to share their ideas and perspectives on all things related to the youth program. There is a time for this type of feedback, but this isn't the time.

At some point, the leaders are going to have to make a subjective "ruling" on how the group is doing in achieving its purpose. After hearing feedback from those you invited to participate, determine how you would grade the success of the current program in achieving the program purpose. Give the current youth program a rating (either a letter grade [A–F] or numerical rating [1–10 or 1–100]) that allows you to quantify the current effectiveness in achieving the purpose. Once you've assigned a grade, you can use it as the youth program develops to better understand if your efforts are enhancing the program's effectiveness toward achieving its purpose.

STEP 2: DEVELOP A SCOPE AND SEQUENCE.

The term "scope and sequence" is commonly used in education. It is understood to describe how teachers logically structure the learning experiences so the correct level of complexity is presented at the correct time, and connected with the students' prior learning. Your job is to determine the most likely development process for someone who participates in your program.

Educational theorists talk about focusing on three learning domains—cognitive (knowing), affective (feeling), and psycho-motor (doing). Many churches focus energies on one area to the detriment of the other two. They may work for an emotional high (affective) found in an inspiring worship experience or the rush of feelings from the strong relational focus of a small group. Some keep their students grounded in study of doctrines and belief systems (cognitive). Some focus primarily on mission experiences and servant events (doing).

A strong youth ministry program develops efforts to move students through all three stages. Education theory supports the idea that the domains are hierarchical in nature—that is, you need to address the cognitive before focusing on the affective, and the affective should be targeted before aiming at the psycho-motor. Basically, you look to get students to know the truth, so they can feel a connectedness to that truth, and want to act on that truth.

One difficulty with developing a scope and sequence is that students arrive at different places in their development. For that reason, you want to design your program to address all three domains to some degree. An ongoing evaluation process will provide hints about which areas need more emphasis and which domains need less.

A key to your planning is designing the sequence to include leadership opportunities for each youth. It's important to see these leadership opportunities as a key step in the scope and sequence; the primary purpose is not helping the adult leaders—in fact, this part of the sequence can often be more work for the adult leaders. In reality, we learn more when we have to step into a leadership role. These opportunities allow us to apply the things we learn. When in a leadership role, we're engaged in a scrimmage where we actually get to make the call about the best way to apply what we've learned.

Consider Jesus' work with His disciples. Few would say these men were the religious elite—they served in a variety of trades and all evidence indicates they didn't fully grasp their role in ministry until Pentecost—yet Jesus sent them out, alone and in pairs (Luke 9:1–6; 10:1–17), long before Pentecost. Too often, we assume our youth will naturally find leadership opportunities as they mature. We need to intentionally design leadership opportunities in our scope and sequence.

STEP 3: CONSIDER THE CIRCUMSTANCES PRESENTLY IMPACTING YOUR MINISTRY.

Prior to setting out on implementing, you need to sit down and consider the factors that will impact your efforts, both positively and negatively.

1. **Resource options:** Resources consist of those things at your disposal for use in your ministry efforts. These include human resources, facilities, and finances. It's quite possible to put together a strong ministry with very little in the way of facility or finance resources (human resources are always a high priority), but they affect how you design your plan.

   There is no way to provide a standardized list of necessary resources; there are just too many variables, including the program purpose, youth demographics, living costs in the area, and existing congregational resources. Take the opportunity to meet with key leaders of the congregation with the single question, "What resources are available for youth ministry in the next one to three years?" Based on the answers you receive, start envisioning how you need to approach achieving your purpose.

2. **History concerns:** Every church has a history concerning how it managed youth ministry in the past. Our shared histories shape how we view something. Some of your older crowd (those over seventy) reflect on their personal history of youth ministry in what was called Walther League. For many, this approach to youth ministry has positive elements that they believe should influence youth ministry today. Perhaps surprising to some—I believe this model had a lot going for it. Most of your members are likely aware of some specifics of prior ministry efforts, youth events, youth workers, and perhaps even youth ministry failures. It helps your planning efforts to be aware of these historical influences.

   Once you are aware of these histories, decide whether you need to include them in your new plan or if they are detrimental to your plan and you need to deemphasize them in a very public way so they don't impede future efforts. One example is a youth group that had a history appealing to the wants of the youth—not necessarily their needs. The leadership decided that, in order to move to a new perspective of youth ministry, they had to bury this consumer orientation among the youth, so they held a funeral . . . for their youth program. They borrowed a casket from a local funeral home and held a service for the youth group in the church. The service included a sermon and eulogies for the prior program focus. Once they moved the casket out of the church, leaders announced a new youth ministry program with a new focus starting from that point on. I doubt there were many who missed the message. They were freed to move past an unhelpful history.

3. **Participation levels:** While true that we shouldn't focus solely on attendance, we also shouldn't ignore it either. Young people reach the age where most parents allow them to make some decisions about what they want to do with their time. If you have a low attendance percentage, you probably assume they have chosen to do something other than attend youth group.

One way to enhance participation is to tell youth why they should participate. In other words, share your purpose statement with the youth themselves. Youth are quite capable of seeing the importance of spiritual growth in their lives; in fact, some studies determined that this generation of youth prefer in-depth studies over fun-filled activities.

Get a list of all the youth in your congregation and determine how many you would consider active. Then, determine the percentage of members you would like to become active as your target. Consider also those who attend who are not members and determine a number you would like to target for nonmember attendees. This information will give you some idea of what participation levels you deem appropriate.

STEP 4: PARENTAL/GENERATIONAL INVOLVEMENT

There is a lot of research out there showing that parents are the main faith influencers for their children, and that youth benefit from opportunities to interact with older generations, especially on matters involving faith. What elements can you include in your plan to guarantee that these important faith-influencers won't be ignored?

STEP 5: EVALUATION—HOW WILL WE KNOW HOW WE'RE DOING?

Build in a regular period of evaluation. At least once every six months, plan on reviewing your purpose to see if it is still the right target. You should also assess the degree to which the activities helped you to reach that purpose. If you find an activity didn't help advance your purpose, STOP DOING IT! You have limited resources at your disposal; don't waste them on things that don't achieve your purpose.[2]

PLAN IMPLEMENTATION

Here's a question: Was God's plan for reconciling the world to Himself happening when the first covenant was made in the Garden of Eden? When Abraham received the promise? When God gave the Ten Commandments? When the Israelites were in captivity? When the prophets proclaimed God's Word? When Jesus was on earth? When the early churches were being planted? When Christians were being martyred? When Luther emphasized justifica-

---

2   For an evaluation resource, see Mark Blanke's "Program Assessment: Reinvent . . . Discard . . . Stay the Course," *YouthESource*, LCMS Youth Ministry Office, February 12, 2010, http://youthesource.com/2010/02/12/program-assessment-reinvent-discard-stay-the-course/.

tion by faith alone? When your own congregation preaches the Word and administers the Sacraments? Yes! Yes! And yes! God was and is implementing His plan through all of those things—but each piece looks unique and seems decidedly different than the others. What stays consistent is that these things are all being done at the right time and for the specific purpose of reconciliation.

Your plan for achieving your purpose may look decidedly different at different phases of development. Keep in mind that it will take four or more years of intentional efforts before your ministry program will start to resemble the purpose you developed. This isn't to say that good things won't happen during those developmental years, but things will look differently in different phases of your plan implementation.

Here's an example: Your purpose probably aims to enhance the spiritual maturity of the participants in some way. This might be stated differently, but few well-thought-out purpose statements would say that the purpose is to just have fun with youth. So, does this mean we stop doing fun activities? What about the fun games the youth enjoy so much? What about paintball, water balloon volleyball, dodgeball, blind dodgeball, one-legged dodgeball, no boundaries dodgeball, and the three hundred other dodgeball variations? Do we forego ski trips, water parks, beach trips, and scavenger hunts because they don't focus adequately on deep discipling efforts? The answer is decidedly no—and yes.

Your program may indeed infuse events and activities that would fit solely into the entertainment category—but the leadership of the ministry must constantly keep in mind that we include these events in order to achieve the ultimate purpose. Your events and activities may look different depending on the "season" your youth group is in. You may decide to rely heavily on fun, programmatic activities early in the development of your program because you need to attract youth in order to carry out the remainder of your purpose. Those activities provide a specific season for your program—these activities are developed as a step in achieving the overall purpose. The leadership of the youth ministry is responsible for making certain that resources are directed in the way that best achieves the program purpose. For a season, those efforts may be attraction events or fellowship events or mission trips, depending on what the leadership deems the most effective way to achieve the purpose.

You want youth to have some ownership of the activities of the group, but they can't be the ones directing the type of activities since they probably don't know the intricacies of the purpose statement and can't fully assess the specific group needs. Allowing input while still aiming for the events to best fulfill the purpose, you might want to employ the following technique:

> **Step 1:** Have youth generate a list of activities they would like to do. At this point, all ideas are on the table.

> **Step 2:** Your leadership team (which should include some youth) reviews the ideas, eliminating some unreasonable ones, adding some, and categorizing

activities based upon the primary focus of the activity—attraction, relationship-building, service, or focused-discipling.

Step 3: The leadership team determines the seasonal needs for the youth ministry for the next six months. If they determine that the group is weak in their relationships with one another, leaders may choose to have half the activities come from the relationship-building category and the rest of the activities be evenly distributed among the other three categories. If you have twelve activities planned in the next six-month period, for example, six would be relationship-building, two attraction, two service, and two focused-discipling activities.

Step 4: The reviewed and categorized list provides the entire youth group with the instructions they need to choose the coming activities. They select twelve choices (or however many activities you plan to have over the specific time period), but they must choose activities from the appropriate categories (in the example from Step 3, they would get to choose six from the relationship-building category, two from the attraction category, two service, and two focused-discipling).

Step 5: The leadership team takes the results and schedules the activities as chosen by the group.

Step 6 (optional): When youth complete Step 4, they are told that if they select an activity, they are expected to be willing to assist in the implementation of that activity. When an activity is chosen, refer back to the votes and contact those who selected the activity and provide them with leadership roles—even tasks as simple as bringing food for the group or calling members of the group to remind students about the activity. This involvement helps the youth understand their roles as participants and leaders.

A WORD ABOUT YOUTH AND EXPECTATIONS

I can't write about strategically planning a youth ministry program without spending some time talking about our expectations for youth. I often hear laments from church leaders about the lack of retention of youth after they graduate from high school. It seems as if our youth programs provide no staying power, no long-term church connectedness even for those who were active in their congregational youth program. While the research isn't clear on the lack of connection, it does show that there isn't as much of a connection as we'd like and expect to see. I believe the reason we see these results is because these are the results our programs are designed to achieve. Let me see if I can explain.

I have been working in the university setting for almost three decades. I work primarily with individuals who have decided to pursue a church career. I always say that Director of Christian Education students are a "youth group on steroids"—meaning they are people who were the leaders in their youth programs who all gather together for their college experience. Having the opportunity to work with these people is a great gift. I always make an effort to ask one question to these dedicated individuals: "How many of you were asked or expected to take on leadership roles in your church during your high school years?" Among the hundreds of church work students I have asked over the years, the response rate is always over 90 percent.

I believe these people seek to have a connection with the Church because they were at congregations with an expectation that youth were resources to involve in ministry, capable of making real contributions. Many youth ministries provide for the youth—making them recipients of the services the Church offers. This approach to youth ministry means you produce individuals who fit your intended design—people who look for something they want from the Church. When they graduate and the Church no longer offers targeted ministries that provide them attractive programming options, they leave.

Many churches expect high school graduates to begin entering the roles of leadership in the Church when they shoulder adult responsibilities elsewhere, but we never taught them how to do this. By the time they reach the age where we feel comfortable with these individuals in leadership positions, they have long since left the Church with little chance of returning. Mentoring youth into leadership positions should be the centerpiece of all youth ministry strategic planning.

FINAL THOUGHTS

Strategic planning doesn't come naturally for many people. Even if you have a good grasp of how planning works, it is still a difficult process because it involves other people and seeks to move a diverse group in a unified direction. We must work intentionally to make certain we are being good stewards of the resources God has given to His Church. But we don't take on this task alone. God is the only one who can plant and nurture faith in the heart of the believer. God is the one who uses the leaders, broken vessels that we are, to achieve His purpose. We must immerse our plans and efforts in prayer, trusting that God will work for us to achieve His purpose for His children.

So plan we must, just as God carried out His plan of reconciliation for a fallen world, we can be assured that He walks with us in our efforts to do His will through our plan. Seek His will through your own study of His Word and prayer. Your efforts will not be in vain.

RESOURCES

Barna Group. *The State of Youth Ministry: How Churches Reach Today's Teens—and What Parents Think about It.* Ventura, CA: Barna, 2016.

Blanke, Mark. "Program Assessment: Reinvent . . . Discard . . . Stay the Course." *YouthESource*, LCMS Youth Ministry Office, Feb. 12, 2010. http://youthesource.com/2010/02/12/program-assessment-reinvent-discard-stay-the-course/.

CHAPTER 6

DEVELOPING A SUPPORT SYSTEM

BY DEBRA ARFSTEN

Faith Lutheran Church was in a bind. Its youth ministry was declining, especially after the previous youth ministry director moved away. The right person to replace him just didn't seem to exist in their smaller congregation, but with the LCMS Youth Gathering in the near future, the congregation was desperate to find someone to lead the youth. Tara, a relatively new member of two years, was eager to take on this role; however, her controlling behavior and strong personality were not exactly what the pastor was looking for in this leadership role. However, in his desperation, the pastor asked Tara to be the leader and she eagerly accepted. The next several months were miserable. Tara's dominant personality, along with her insistence on doing everything herself, turned away volunteers who had a passion for working with youth. The ministry continued to decline since the youth didn't like Tara's over-bearing personality and didn't connect well with her. The grave was dug. It was just a matter of time before the casket would be closed.

The youth ministry at Grace Lutheran Church was thriving. Kate, the part-time youth director, was a great example of being a servant leader and truly loved those who volunteered alongside her. Kate knew she couldn't do everything on her own, so she recruited people to serve who had gifts different from the ones she possessed, and was more than happy to share the leadership responsibilities with them. Kate was a great encourager, and she always provided the resources they needed. The youth were a close-knit group who valued the different relationships they had with each of the volunteer leaders. The youth ministry was thriving and growing.

Do either of these scenarios sound familiar to you? Sadly, the first one happens way too often when youth workers attempt to be "lone rangers" in their position. Sometimes this happens because of ego and power needs, while other times it results from simply lacking an understanding of the value of a team and the positive impact it can have in ministry.

The Bible is filled with leaders, many successful but others who failed. Often those leaders who tried to lead alone, believing their way was the only way, failed. We also see many teams in Scripture, sometimes as small as teams of two while others with several members. Certainly Jesus and His disciples made up the most familiar team. Chosen by Jesus, with unique personalities and gifts, the disciples formed together to work in spreading the Gospel. The Book of Acts (chs. 13–17) provides us great examples of small teams that formed, separated, were added to, and re-formed throughout Paul's missionary journeys. Saul and Barnabas began their journey, adding John along the way for a period of time. Eventually other believers were added (Acts 15) along with Judas and Silas. Then new teams formed with Barnabas and Mark, and Paul and Silas. And then along came Timothy . . . and Priscilla and Aquila . . . and the forming and re-forming continues. This is similar to what we see in ministry. While we may initially start with our dream team, the reality is people move, or decide to leave the team, and then new ones are added, and so very often the team is back at square one figuring out how to best work together. So then isn't it just easier to go it alone? Who needs all the hassles of team dynamics and ever-present changes?

As the youth worker, you have a great responsibility and opportunity to lead a team of others to work alongside you in ministry. There is no place for ego in this kind of leadership; instead you want to create a team environment that has a heart for the Gospel, and a love for young people, in order to disciple them for their work in the Kingdom. If you want to be a lone ranger in ministry, you will most likely fail. It is not only impossible for you to do everything well, but it is not healthy or God-pleasing for you to not share this role with others. So, what are the benefits to building a team of leaders?

First of all, you have more adult leaders to help care for the youth. Whether you have a group of ten or fifty, the youth have opportunity to build relationships with other adults who benefit them in their walk with Christ. Due to numbers and personalities, it is just not feasible to connect with every youth as you might want; instead you can celebrate that youth are connected to at least one adult volunteer, whether that's you or someone else.

Second, when faithful volunteers work with you, some of your time is freed up to grow other areas of your ministry that will enhance what you are currently doing. Your energy is strengthened when you see others leading and participating, leaving you with the extra energy to do other tasks. More work gets done when more people are engaged.

Third, Ephesians 4:12 says, "Equip the saints for the work of ministry, for building up the body of Christ." By encouraging others to be part of our ministry team, we help to equip them for works of ministry that will not only bless the youth ministry, but also encourage the faith of those who serve.

DEVELOPING/CHOOSING YOUR TEAM

When you take on the role as youth worker, there may already be a team in place that you "inherit" as you begin your work. The benefit of this is that you can start strong with people who already have a handle on the congregation's youth ministry and continue to build from there. If you inherited a team, consider these things:

1. If you are new to the congregation, you won't know any of the team members. It is vital that you take the time to meet with each person individually to get to know them personally and learn the reasons they are part of the team. Do they have a love for youth? Are they actively involved in youth activities? Do they have any children who are part of the youth ministry? Or are they just on the team because nobody else would volunteer? Do they exude joy or obligation when they talk about being on the team?

2. Take time to get to know the youth. Find out their passions in ministry. Get a sense of how they feel about the adults who volunteer their time with the youth ministry.

3. Take time in your team meeting to listen to the recent history of youth ministry, listening closely for nuances that may help you identify areas of concern as well as areas of strength.

4. Even though you are the designated leader, let the team know you are there to listen and learn, welcoming their input throughout this transition process. At the same time, be confident in your own gifts of leadership, knowing some decisions or changes will be welcomed, while others resisted. All of this is part of the change process.

Sometimes, you may begin this new leadership role with no team in place, or a team in need of additional people. When it's time to choose team members, remember these things:

1. Know your own skill set. You'll want to put people around you different from yourself so your team contains a variety of gifts and talents.

2. Be picky in who you choose—not desperate. Sometimes we are tempted to choose the first people who volunteer, but they are not necessarily the right people for the team. As you think about your needs, consider the following:

   a. It is vitally important for your team to consist of people with a heart for youth and who love them just as they are. These may be parents, but don't overlook the adults of all ages in your congregation who love middle school and high school youth and would tremendously influence them.

b. Do you love details? If not, add someone to your team with strong administrative skills who manages details and deadlines well. You'll need this person to manage the budget, organize the volunteers, keep track of service hours, and keep good records of activities.

c. How about that creative soul who loves to dream and imagine all the possibilities? When you gather some creative, innovative people around the table, ideas fly and wonderful ways of doing youth ministry come to life.

d. Who doesn't love a joyful encourager in the group? Having someone who always looks at the positive side of each situation helps alleviate anxiety when things get tough, and brings joy to the group and individuals when feeling discouraged.

e. While others are dreaming of the possibilities, you also need that practical person in the group to be the realist and make sure the dreams are actually attainable and practical.

f. Do you know people who just love to *do* things but don't want to plan them? You certainly want some of those task-focused people around the table to get things done. These are often the people who do things like cook and serve the Lenten suppers, or who do the food shopping for the youth retreat.

g. While it's great to add inexperienced people to the team, it's always valuable to have some who have previous experience working with youth around the table. They bring in their experiences and ideas, and help the newer folks be more comfortable in their new role.

3. For more on recruiting and retaining volunteers, see chapter 9.

One of the most important people to include as part of your team is your pastor. While he may not have an active role on a youth board, his support, wisdom, and encouragement is key to a successful team ministry. Some things to consider:

1. Communicate with him regarding youth activities and any issues that he should be aware of. He doesn't need to know every detail of every event or concern, but it will help him to have general knowledge of what is happening.

2. Take time to build a personal relationship with him. As his teammate, it's helpful for him to know about you, your family, your work, and other areas of interest.

3. Always support your pastor in public. As a staff member or key volunteer, you may occasionally hear comments from members who are unhappy with the pastor. Refrain from those conversations and offer support of your pastor whenever possible.

4. Occasionally invite your pastor to be part of your youth ministry events. Often the youth don't have the opportunity to really talk with the pastor, so including him will allow the youth to see him in a different environment, and possibly open doors

    for more informal conversation together. You might consider using him as the devotion/Bible study leader at the youth night or retreat, a small group discussion leader, or even to lead games.

5. Pray! Pastors deal with a lot of challenging issues in ministry, so having your prayer support is vital and appreciated. Certainly pray for him on your own, but don't hesitate to pray with him as opportunity arises.

WHAT TO PROVIDE AS THE LEADER

- **Spiritual Leadership:** As a leader, you have the opportunity to provide spiritual leadership with your team. Leading devotions at the beginning of your meetings should be primarily your responsibility. You can also do a rotating schedule to allow others to take on this role as they desire. Scripture should be the foundation for your devotions, utilizing other devotional resources as needed.

- **Safe Environment:** As team leader, provide an environment that allows for open conversation without fear of judgment from others. The confidentiality of meetings and trust is critical among the group. Group members need to be confident that what they share stays within the group.

- **Clear Expectations:** Having clear expectations of job responsibilities is vital to both the team member and the team as a whole. Conflicts happen when misunderstanding about roles and responsibilities occur. Communicate your expectations clearly.

- **Organization/Agenda:** Organization is a strongly desired trait for leaders. Make sure to send an agenda for the meeting in advance. Prepare all materials for the meeting and any other activities on time.

- **Good Communication:** Key issue! Communicate verbally and in writing as often as possible. Give details, offer feedback, seek feedback, and keep your team in the loop at all times. Nothing is more frustrating than not knowing what is going on and hearing it from a secondhand source.

- **Authenticity:** Be real with your team. Let team members know when they can help with struggles. Let them be part of problem-solving. Express frustration when appropriate, but express joy and excitement as well.

- **Build Relationships:** Seek to know your team beyond your meeting time. Find out about team members' families, jobs, and hobbies. Connect with them on a personal level to let them know you care about them individually, not just in the role they serve on the team. Celebrate joys with them and be there for them in their sorrows.

- **Prayer:** Pray for and with your team members, both as a group and individually.

- **Celebrate Together:** Find opportunities to celebrate together, whether at a volunteer recognition, a birthday party, or just a gathering to have fun! This will help your team members get to know one another on a more personal level and build relationships.

- **Appreciation:** Volunteers give a lot of time and energy to ministry, so don't forget to say thanks often! Note cards, coffee gift cards, or homemade snacks are just a few ways to show your appreciation and help them feel valued. An appreciated volunteer will likely remain loyal for a long time.

DEVELOPING AN EXTERNAL NETWORK

While your primary focus for ministry is in your congregation, it is both helpful and energizing to engage with others outside of your congregation for support, encouragement, and sharing ideas and resources. Consider the following possibilities:

- **Local Youth Workers:** Seek out local youth workers in your community. It doesn't matter if they are paid or volunteer, professionally trained or not. And it doesn't matter if they are of the same denomination because you're connecting to talk about ideas and resources, not theology.

- **District/Regional DCE Meetings:** Many LCMS districts have monthly parish professional meetings that include DCEs, other church workers, and anyone else who wants to connect and be part of this community. These groups generally meet during the school year. You can find more information from the district office.

- **Area Conferences:** Check out available youth ministry conferences or seminars. You may find some offered that are fairly local so cost will not be an issue. Also see if your congregation will budget funds to attend a larger national youth ministry conference.

- **Online Support:** You can find an endless number of blogs, discussion groups, and youth ministry topics online, so search far and wide. You can connect with others across the country for ideas, ask how to deal with specific challenges in youth ministry, and just get encouragement from those who do similar ministry.

BASIC GUIDELINES IN CREATING A VOLUNTEER JOB DESCRIPTION

- **Purpose:** What is the purpose of the position? How is it tied into the purpose of the church? An usher's purpose is not "to hand out bulletins"—that's a description of what he or she does. An usher's purpose is more like "to smoothly facilitate and support worship so that our members and guests can focus on what God does in worship, and can respond to it."

- **Supervision:** Who supervises this task? This establishes accountability as well as a source of assistance.

- **Task Description:** Write task descriptions clearly so they are easily understood. Assume volunteers may have no idea what youth volunteers do. Don't expect people will understand acronyms or terminology specific to the church.

- **Time Commitment:** Include the length of time it takes to do all aspects of the job ("Sunday School teachers arrive 20 minutes before class begins at 9:30, and stay until all the children leave; plan on 1–2 hours for preparation each week; a 2-hour training meeting is held quarterly"). Also include how long a commitment lasts ("Teachers serve for 9 months, from September through June").

- **Training Provided:** Indicate what type of training will be offered and by whom. This will reassure the volunteers that they will get the information and resources they need, and not be expected to just learn it on their own.

- **Qualifications:** Include skills (computer savvy; organization/administrative skills) and qualities (ability to keep matters confidential; reliability; self-motivation). It can be helpful to distinguish between what is necessary and what may be helpful.

- **Benefits:** Be thoughtful and creative. Will the volunteer get to meet new people and make friends? build a relationship with a teenager? pray with others? share the Gospel with a person in need?

POSITION   LOCAL SUMMER SERVANT EVENT COORDINATOR

Purpose of Position

- To create opportunities for service in the local community that will provide summer servant event projects for the youth.

Supervisor

- Youth Director

Job Description

- Contact local agencies for potential servant events.
- Coordinate schedule with youth director and agency to work at events.
- Be responsible for marketing and recruitment of youth and adults to serve.
- Coordinate transportation needs and other resources needed.
- Serve as team leader on day(s) of event.
- Do a follow-up evaluation with youth/adults and agency.

Time Requirement

- 4–5 hours to make contacts
- 4–5 hours to develop materials for marketing, recruitment, and transportation coordination
- Available on day(s) of event (variable)
- 1 hour to develop evaluation tool

Length of Commitment

- One summer for service, and two months prior to summer for organization

Training Provided

- Youth director will provide support and direction as needed.

Qualifications or Special Skills

- A heart for youth
- Desire to serve in the community
- Ability to organize and implement a plan
- Ability to work on a team as a leader

Benefits to the Volunteer

- Enjoyment of serving with youth and adults
- Being part of making a difference in the community
- Grow in relationships with the youth
- Sharing your faith in action

SECTION 2

YOUTH MINISTRY COMMUNITY

In this book's introduction, we underlined the importance of making connections with one another. This section gives insights on the many connections needed for a healthy youth ministry for the benefit of both the youth and of all those who support them. In a community, youth will also realize that they, too, have an important role to support those around them.

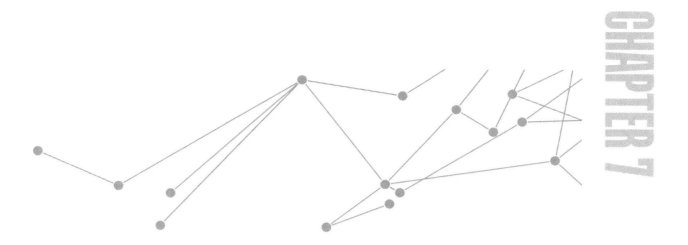

CHAPTER 7

WORKING WITH PARENTS

BY TIM RIPPSTEIN

Congregations and youth ministers must work *with* parents. The key word here is *with*. This is a respectable and versatile preposition that can have negative applications, such as, "in opposition to," "detached," or "separated." "Johnny had a fight *with* his father and therefore broke *with* his family." However, this preposition can also have a positive application: "accompanied by," "in some particular relation to," "combination," and "addition." "Emma loves to work *with* her mother. She gets along well *with* her sisters. Her love of learning along *with* her older brother's love of laughter make for an enjoyable family vacation." In our focus on working with parents, we prefer the positive approach and application.

In recent decades and over at least two generations, we have experienced some shifts in our surrounding social structures. Mark DeVries, along with many other social observers and family and youth ministers, have observed that no single factor has led to this transition. Rather, many factors have contributed.[1] DeVries goes on to quote Cornell University's Urie Bronfenbrenner's nine cultural shifts that have taken place:

Father's lengthy absence due to vocational choices.

Increase of working mothers.

A "critical" escalation in the divorce rate.

Increase in single-parent families.

Continual decline in the extended family.

Evolution of the house (family rooms, play rooms, and master bedrooms).

The replacement of adults by the peer group.

The isolation of children from the work world.

The isolation of schools from the rest of society.

---

1   Mark DeVries, *Family-Based Youth Ministry* (Downers Grove, IL: InterVarsity Press, 2004), 35, 38.

Many of us have witnessed social structures that at one time supported and combined with the parents to raise mature, well-adjusted children and teens. Neighborhoods, schools, social activities, media, and even churches now segregate our families by age or gender. The shifts in those once supportive structures have left families vulnerable to pressure, and they are buckling. One remaining support is the Church, still openly supportive of the home and intergenerational faith family. Yet this institution is under fire and struggling.

Another significant impact, which cannot be overestimated, is the development of technology. Certainly technology and the digital age is a positive force *with* parents as well as all of society. It is also creating dissension *with* families, separating them from one another. It is not possible to justly explore the changing and exponentially advancing impact on our topic. So, we will simply raise some concerns and guidelines.

PARENTS, TEENS, AND SOCIAL MEDIA

Fact: teenagers are the largest portion of our culture to be online. Fact: teenagers are one of the largest portions of our society to own smartphones. Amanda Lenhart and Pew Research in a 2015 study reported that about 25 percent of teens go online almost constantly and about 75 percent have smartphones or have access to one.[2] What are teens using smartphones for? Social media. Facebook continues to be the largest social media platform (71 percent of teens 13–17); next is Instagram (52 percent), Snapchat (41 percent), Twitter (33 percent), Google+, Vine, Tumblr, and so forth.[3]

Such a rapid rise and such prevalent access to digital social connections has afforded us many opportunities. Who among us has not reconnected with old high school friends or stayed in touch with family members over great distances? Yet digital opportunities have also led to such new phenomena as cyberbullying, Facebook depressions, online stalking, and the new behavioral disorder known as "Problematic Internet Use," resulting in tragedies among teens. What's a parent to do? Some ideas or guidelines have surfaced.

Parents need to have multiple conversations with their kids about what they encounter online. Parents should share their own media use. Remind kids often that the internet is not private. Marketers as well as potentially harmful people are tracking their viewing habits.

Parents should install, with their kids' knowledge, blocking or monitoring software. Turn on parental controls. This is not to shame kids, but it is being responsible parents. Family psychologist Dr. John Rosemond reminds us how to parent with a child and a cell phone. The parent has the right, maybe even duty, to monitor. As the adult in the equation, it is the parent's role to support the child, but in the end, the phone is the parent's, not the child's. The parent is loaning it to the child, and the child needs to know that.[4]

---

2   Amanda Lenhart, "Teens, Social Media & Technology Overview 2015," *Pew Research Center*, Internet & Technology, April 9, 2015, accessed March 29, 2017, http://www.pewinternet.org/2015/04/09/teens-social-media-technology-2015/.

3   Lenhart, "Teens, Social Media & Technology."

4   John K. Rosemond, "Smart Phone, or No Smart Phone?" *ArcaMax*, June 23, 2016, accessed June 25, 2017, https://www.arcamax.com/homeandleisure/parents/johnrosemond/s-1844399.

There is much to learn about the impact of gaming on children and teens. Their brains are malleable and social skills are in development. We are already seeing ratings being applied that recognize the content suitability for different ages, related to violence, fantasy, sexual content, language, even gambling. Parents can pay attention to these ratings.[5] A rule of thumb to keep in mind: the smaller your kid's screen, the more you lose control.

John Rosemond points out that there is evidence gathering that points to a likelihood of brain development delays in preteens and teenage years as smartphones are addictive.[6]

BUSYNESS, FOMO, AND IDOLS, OH MY!

Three more specific social shifts in recent decades have significantly impacted parents, families, and churches: busyness, FOMO, and idolizing youth. It was Eugene Peterson who first flagged and labeled the phenomenon of busyness for me. This retired pastor (and who is more busy than a pastor?) identified two reasons people are busy today. Some are busy because they are vain. (Ouch! That will be a bruise on my ego.) Overpacking my days and weeks become proof to myself and others that I am important. The second reason is people become busy because they are lazy. Now that sure seems like an irony. I let others decide what I will do instead of resolutely deciding myself. Busyness is in epidemic proportions; a single person cannot fight it. It is too contagious. It takes a whole community to identify this infection, to consistently support one another in order to eventually develop immunities. Does your church support you against busyness or is it one of its carriers?

FOMO, or "fear of missing out," has been identified as a recent generational phenomenon. Here we see people who want to do everything, parents who enroll, sign up, register their kids in every opportunity so they don't miss out and grow up deficient somehow. These kids learn to go, go, go, to band practice before school, eating meals in the family van while on the way from school to soccer to confirmation before hitting homework at 8:30 p.m. and to bed in time to do it all again. This pace of busyness and FOMO has given rise to a small but growing reactive culture, which may be exemplified by Mark Yaconelli's book *Downtime: Helping Teenagers Pray*. Here he draws attention to the negative spiritual impact of such a lifestyle and attempts to offer classic, tried-and-true Christian spiritual practices to a healthier, faithful lifestyle.

A third observable shift is the idolizing of youth and youthfulness. In previous generations young people desired to grow up and mature. Older people expected them to become contributing, responsible adult members of society. However, a glance at commercials and media ads gives clues to this regressive change. Adults now try to hold on to adolescent activity and youthful irresponsibility; refusing to become responsible adults seems to be the new goal. From avoiding superficial wrinkles, gray hair, and sagging body parts to the deeper

---

5   "Entertainment Software Rating Board (ESRB) Ratings Guide," accessed March 10, 2017, https://www.esrb.org/ratings/ratings_guide.aspx.
6   John Rosemond, "Remove the Smartphone, Regain the Child," *Herald & Review*, February 10, 2017, accessed March 29, 2017, http://herald-review.com/news/opinion/editorial/columnists/rosemond/john-rosemond-remove-the-smartphone-regain-the-child/article_699a-92ca-77f3-5d9f-a5a5-9f72ab35bb4c.html?utm_medium=social&utm_source=email&utm_campaign=user-share.

recesses of self-centered immaturity and irresponsibility, teenagers are the new heroes to whom many adults aspire. Princeton University ethicist Paul Ramsey has observed that in no other time in human history have the "elders" of a community asked its younger members to define rules and standards.[7] To whom is the teen going to look in order to see what a mature Christian adult is like? Is there even any hope for a meaningful life after adolescence? One might conclude not if the teen years are the best years. How can churches and parents team up to offer mature Christian adult role models and instill hope that a full and satisfying life in Christ is still ahead? Doug Fields, who has over thirty years of youth ministry experience and is senior director of the HomeWord Center for Youth and Family at Azusa Pacific University, starkly says that a youth ministry that fails to minister to entire families is about as effective as a Band-Aid on a major wound.[8]

A partnership is needed. In fact, a whole community is needed for parents to raise healthy, well-adjusted Christian teens into adulthood. To coin a new twist from an old tribal adage, "It takes a community of believers to raise a Christian teenager."

THE SCARY STAGE OF DEVELOPMENT

Here is where working *with* parents is vital. Ours is an age of collaboration, task forces, teams, and partnerships. The "task" of raising a teen to become a mature Christian adult is in need of such collaboration. The teen years are relationally developing years. Many who work with adolescents are familiar with Dr. Erik Erikson's seminal work on the stages of psychosocial development. He identified eight stages of social maturity. Stage 5 hits in the adolescent years (11–25), and can be called The Scary Stage, but Erickson titled it the "Identity vs. Identity Confusion" stage. This is when a teen begins to challenge that which she has been taught in order to see if it will hold up. It is a painful process, but necessary to adopt parental beliefs and values. Relationships outside and beyond the parents develop and grow. It is scary to parents because while their teen more openly begins to challenge parental values, beliefs, and practices, she also embraces an ever-increasing circle of friends and outside influences. This is a necessary but potentially challenging phase. But it is also an opportunity for the community of believers to support parents and to become more relationally engaged with the teens. It is also an opportunity for the perceptive pastor, youth minister, or DCE to connect teens with other mature adults in addition to her parents.

The days of separating the teens from the rest of the community and giving them a hip, young, attractive youth leader must go. This has not been successful nor has it been the practice for the first nineteen centuries of church-parent team practices. Here a review of Deuteronomy 6:4–9 is insightful:

> Hear, O Israel: The LORD our God, the LORD is one. You shall love the LORD your
> God with all your heart and with all your soul and with all your might. And these

---

7 DeVries, *Family-Based Youth Ministry,* 34.
8 Doug Fields, *Purpose Driven Youth Ministry: 9 Essential Foundations for Healthy Growth* (Grand Rapids: Zondervan, 1998), 251.

words that I command you today shall be on your heart. You shall teach them diligently to your children, and shall talk of them when you sit in your house, and when you walk by the way, and when you lie down, and when you rise. You shall bind them as a sign on your hand, and they shall be as frontlets between your eyes. You shall write them on the doorposts of your house and on your gates.

This identifies a style of ministry with children and teens that has served God's people from the beginning. In fact, Mark DeVries rightly calls segregation a crisis.[9] Reggie Joiner points to many churches that claim to partner with the family but still separate parents and kids into separate programs.[10] This separation of teens from the adult world has led many to agree with Tom Gillespie (quoted by DeVries), who asserts that the decline in church membership is directly related to our inability to translate faith to the next generation.[11] At a developmental stage when adolescents are becoming more and more relational and pushing against the values and beliefs of their parents, they need to be immersed in a multigenerational community of mature adults. What is traditionally more intergenerational than a worship service? What can the community of faith provide that puts teens with those younger and older to help them accept responsibility, model maturity, and see what it looks like to be a mature Christian adult?

This community and these relationships also support and guide the teenager as he embraces and walks through life's crucibles. We are a church born and formed through the cross, we have a scripturally faithful doctrine of this theology of the cross, and our Lord has even promised such challenging crucibles in this life. "And He said to all, 'If anyone would come after Me, let him deny himself and take up his cross daily and follow Me. For whoever would save his life will lose it, but whoever loses his life for My sake will save it'" (Luke 9:23–24).

We can give intellectual assent to the belief that we grow through struggles. This larger community of believers can also help our young to grow *through* life's struggles, rather than buying into the current belief that our highest value is to avoid pain and struggle. We do our children and teens a long-term service by showing them that struggles are part of the Christian life, not the punishment of an angry God. We help teens by showing how to faithfully work through struggles, whether they be school related, church related, gender or identity related, emotionally or socially related, even physically related. We must model faithfulness and support for these teens and their parents.

The geometry of adolescent faith formation is stark. The traditional youth ministry has been labeled as a "one-eared Mickey Mouse."[12] Imagine a circle of about five inches in diameter. This represents the church programming, also Mickey Mouse's face. Now imagine a two-inch circle sitting atop and to the right of that face, Mickey's ear. This represents youth

---

9   DeVries, *Family-Based Youth Ministry*, 21–22.

10   Reggie Joiner, *Think Orange: Imagine the Impact When Church and Family Collide. . . .* (Cumming, GA: The reThink Group, 2016), 165.

11   DeVries, *Family-Based Youth Ministry*, 25.

12   DeVries, *Family-Based Youth Ministry*, 42.

programming. It is separate and isolated from the rest of the church. Give the youth their own youth minister, a youth room filled with old couches, toys such as a Ping-Pong table or foosball table, a TV and internet access, and keep them out of trouble and away from the rest of the church. This has become the *de facto* idea of youth ministry. Instead, what has been the Church's practice for nineteen centuries and what is needed today is teens integrated into the life of the Church. The Church needs to shift its focus away from separating teens and toward giving teenagers opportunities to be in conversation and relationship with Christian adults. Mark DeVries says this is the most important priority a church can have.[13] Churches, in their supporting role with parents, can encourage, equip, and empower parents as they raise teenagers.

WHAT CAN A PARENT DO?

By way of encouraging parents, we must believe that most parents, regardless of marital status or family type, truly want to do a good job as parents.[14] It is a parental insider's truth that most parents are feeling guilty and can easily be shamed. The law of perfect parenting constantly weighs heavy, and parents live under a significant burden. The Church, the Body of Christ, can help ease the burden with words and actions of grace, yoking with parents as the Lord has expressed in Matthew 11:28–30: "Come to Me, all who labor and are heavy laden, and I will give you rest. Take My yoke upon you, and learn from Me, for I am gentle and lowly in heart, and you will find rest for your souls. For My yoke is easy, and My burden is light." Remember, what used to be performed by neighborhoods, schools, churches, and families is now done largely by parents alone. They are struggling and need encouragement.

Churches and ministers can help by equipping parents. Specific ideas are limitless, and some will be suggested below, but let it suffice here to say that anything the Church and its ministers can do to equip parents *in the home* impacts teen development much more than anything they can do at church or in the youth room. Rick Lawrence, longtime educator and youth minister, has observed that the impact parents have on their teenagers far exceeds even the greatest youth leader.[15]

If I were to pose just one idea for both parents and youth ministry, it would be to commit to eating together. Powerful formation happens when we eat together regularly. Isn't it exciting that the Lord also blesses us when we eat or commune together around His Table! A study by the National Merit Scholars organization, seeking to identify factors that influence high achievement among their teens, indicated that one common factor in the lives of these teens is that they regularly eat dinner with their families.[16] For it is around the dinner table that each person talks about things going on, values, faith, deep issues and humdrum tasks, what brings joy and toil. This simple commitment to eating together regularly is powerful.

The church and its ministers can empower parents in their roles. The church can assist

13 DeVries, *Family-Based Youth Ministry*, 56.
14 Joiner, *Think Orange*, 160.
15 DeVries, *Family-Based Youth Ministry*, 58.
16 DeVries, *Family-Based Youth Ministry*, 63.

parents in developing a plan. Through blogs, parenting classes, online/paper/audio resources, and so on, the church can help develop a big picture or end goal of the mature Christian young adult prepared to assume an adult role. Then provide and direct people to resources at each developmental stage to work toward that goal.

Lastly, the congregation can show parents how the strategy works. A strategy could be to adjust home rhythms to include eating together. Such supports might include no meetings, no phone, no TV, and so on at dinnertime. What is helpful here are words of encouragement to stay the course when challenges to a new rhythm come.

Use a small-step approach. When my son was a young boy, he was told, numerous times, to clean his room. He tried but quickly gave up. My perceptive wife then stepped in and told him to pick up all his cars and put them in the box. Then take clothes on his bed and put them in the drawers. Next pick up books and put them on the shelf. Voila! Success. What he needed was a small-step approach since "cleaning the room" was overwhelming. (I've noticed her applying this strategy on me from time to time too.)

The power of the family to influence cannot be overstated. A study by Search Institute looked at the children of parents who considered religion important, were service-oriented, were concerned about their child's morals, allowed them to question rules, and prayed. What they found in these young adolescents was their preferences about with whom they would prefer discussing particular problems. When teens needed to talk about school, feelings, drugs and alcohol, sex, guilt, and life decisions, they were mostly influenced by a parent or guardian. As teens got older, a parent's influence did diminish, but the study showed that the influence of friends never equaled or exceeded that of parents.[17] Parents simply must be a priority in this partnership.

The primacy of priorities is illustrated by your stove. You have front burners and back burners. The front burners are the position of priority. Here is where the eggs are cooked, the bacon sizzles in the pan, that which gets immediate and regular attention. The back burners are further away; they are where the oatmeal is moved to keep warm, where the bacon goes once it is crispy. They require neither immediate nor constant attention. It is a matter of priorities. Parenting must be on the front burners. Dr. Christian Smith, University of Notre Dame sociologist, led the mammoth National Study of Youth and Religion and concluded that the greatest influence to the spiritual development of teens is their parents.[18] And if we were to put an even finer point on it, fathers have the greatest impact.[19] By so many measures, it is concluded that the community of believers must encourage, equip, and empower parents.

WHAT CAN CONGREGATIONS DO?

There really is no limit to ways the congregation can partner with parents, and we have

---

17 Merton P. Strommen and Richard A. Hardel, *Passing on the Faith: A Radical Model for Youth and Family Ministry* (Winona, MN: Saint Mary's Press, 2008), 52–54.

18 Kara Powell, Brad M. Griffin, and Cheryl A. Crawford, *Sticky Faith: Youth Worker Edition: Practical Ideas to Nurture Long-Term Faith in Teenagers* (Grand Rapids: Zondervan, 2011), 117.

19 Strommen and Hardel, *Passing on the Faith*, 47.

the gift of imagination and blessing of the Holy Spirit to develop strategies. We'll take a look at some ideas from both sides of this partnership.

- **Congregations can guard and protect intergenerational worship.** This is one of the last remaining bastions in society where all ages can and should remain together. Children can learn to be quiet and respectful. Members can be patient and supportive of noise blessings among the younger members of the family of faith. Research shows that teens and young adults participating in intergenerational worship show more maturity in their faith.[20]

- **Congregations can make an effort to follow the 5:1 rule.** Facilitate ministries and articulate congregation-wide expectations that there are at least five adults investing in each teen. Hebrews 12:1 states, "Therefore, since we are surrounded by so great a cloud of witnesses, let us also lay aside every weight, and sin which clings so closely, and let us run with endurance the race that is set before us." These five or more adults become part of this cloud of witnesses, the cheerleaders cheering teens on to adulthood.[21] Ideas: traditional potlucks, intergenerational usher teams, extended family scavenger hunts, family road rallies, "speed friending" using all ages, and discussion guides.

- **Congregations can provide resources to get them talking, such as devotional discussions from Bible class lessons and sermons.** Provide family devotional resources, prayer suggestions, and family Bible reading plans. Provide resources online to support parents, question and answer sites, blogs, parental support groups, and adolescent parenting chat rooms. Here are some ideas to get parents talking: Parents share their favorite part of the worship service, sermon, or Bible class in the car ride home. They could share highs and lows each day and add, "How did you see God at work today?" Parents can ask kids, "How can I be praying for you?" Help parents learn to ask questions and listen. Use this to replace parental lecturing by following the rule of thumb, "Never explain something if you can ask a question instead."

- **Congregations can offer parent training.** Include role playing on tough issues, share horror stories of conversations gone bad, and celebrate what went well. Give parents regular updates on youth culture and tips on discussing issues with their kids.

- **Congregations can help parents develop faith rituals.** These rituals need to fit into each unique family system; therefore, they should be creative and organic. An example could be a regular movie night and discussion. My own daughter's favorite question on the way home from the theater is, "What was your favorite part?" She enjoys telling us what captured her imagination and how it fit into the plot.

- **Congregations can provide community rituals that teach, develop identity, and**

---

20   Powell, Griffin, and Crawford, *Sticky Faith,* 75.
21   DeVries, *Family-Based Youth Ministry,* 84–85.

celebrate progress. We are familiar with the Rite of Confirmation, teaching the doctrines of the faith, developing Christian identity, and celebrating a more mature confession of the faith given at Baptism. What other milestones or rites of passage can be celebrated through ritual? Receiving the first Bible, reading the New Testament, Old Testament, getting a driver's license, entering middle school, graduating high school? Celebrating through rituals in worship, among the family of faith, is most appropriate and significant in teaming with parents.

- **Congregations can provide examples and demonstrate countercultural living to help parents battle busyness, FOMO, and idolizing youth.** These can be addressed in sermons and discussed in Bible class and around the dinner table at home. Brief articles and websites can be sent out supporting this countercultural posture.

Start Small, Start Now

Finally, we want to consider what can be facilitated in the home and the parents' side of this partnership. The key is to start now. The earlier in children's lives the better, but start now. Consider what you want to do; discuss it with older, mature Christian parents, your pastor, DCE, or youth director; and write it out as a goal. Do it! Here are some ideas. Schedule what you want to do into your family schedule, get it on the calendar, fit it into the rhythm of your lives together. Make regular meals together a front-burner priority, and talk. Add family devotions and prayers together. For many, this works nicely after family dinner and discussion. It is likely that prayer topics will surface in these dinner discussions. Design family time so it is tech-free. One family I know rotates among members to choose what to do together as a family with appropriate parameters—visit the zoo, go on a bike ride, watch a movie, play a board game, and so on. Another family plans a meal out each week, rotating who picks the restaurant, within set limits such as cost, guests, and day. Use downtime such as car rides, bedtimes, TV viewing, and walks for intentional discussions. Here parents can even combine the biblical concept of Sabbath with family. Set aside time to cease from regular demands and remember the Lord together. This can be a relaxed time of being together. Another idea can be to have accountability families. As families support one another in your new goals, give permission to check up on one another. Share ideas and especially pray for one another.

Working with parents is a must in this fast-paced, familial-fractured, and challenging time. It takes a family and a family of faith to raise a mature, healthy Christian teen into adulthood, ready to take responsibility as a man or woman of God.

Working with Parents Discussion Questions

Rather than try to address every question listed, it is better to pick and choose the ones that challenge parents and make congregations think deeply and act to make a difference in working *with* parents.

Working with Parents

- How does the congregation work with parents in a negative way? in a positive way?
- A number of social shifts are mentioned that have put a greater burden on families in the twenty-first century. Which ones have you personally observed? Would you add another one not mentioned?

Parents, Teens, and Social Media

- Does this section seem to bemoan or take a negative view of technology? What makes you think so?
- According to this section, how can parents be more supportive and vigilant in their teens' use of social media? Would you add any other suggestions?
- If you have tried to be vigilant, what has worked better? What has not worked out so well?
- What more support would you like the congregation to do to help you in this area?

Busyness, FOMO, and Idols, Oh My!

- Are you busy? Why?
- Where do you observe FOMO around you? Do you experience this cultural tendency in yourself?
- What will it take to help wean you and your family from this FOMO phenomenon?
- Over the next week, keep an eye out for social clues of youth idolization. Write down what you observe. Draw attention to these in your group.
- Where can you find modeling of healthy Christian adulthood in your surroundings? List these. How can you maximize these opportunities?

The Scary Stage of Development

- Why might this developmental stage be called the Scary Stage?
- Do you remember this stage of development in your own adolescence?
- How might a pastor, DCE, or youth worker help teens and parents in this stage?
- Drawing upon Deuteronomy 6:4–9, what was the setting for the children and teens for Israel? Is this prescribed or simply described? What other biblical text might guide you in intentionally ministering with parents in raising mature Christian teenagers into adulthood?
- Notice what Jesus says about this to an inquiring scribe in Mark 12:28–34. How does Jesus view this text, which likely was taught to Him by His own parents?
- What might be "the most important of all" for parents to pass on to their children and

teens? How is the congregation helping them to do this? In what ways might the congregation be unintentionally hindering this?

- What might be "crucibles" in teens' lives today? How can the congregation support parents of these teenagers as they experience these crosses trusting that Christ is with them? When and where do the kids and teens experience and understand our theology of the cross?

- How is the cross countercultural? What "culture" does your congregation offer for the parents of these teens? Where might this community of faith culture more effectively support parents to walk with their teenagers through the crucibles?

- Does your congregation lean toward the de facto, one-eared Mickey Mouse image of youth ministry? If so, in what ways? What suggestions are offered in this chapter? How might this be addressed? Where do you anticipate resistance?

- Brainstorm areas where the teens might get involved in the life of the church. To prime the pump, consider teen usher teams, teen greeters, teen technology assistants, family service projects, family of faith mission events, and so forth.

What Can a Parent Do?

- How does your congregation encourage parents of teens? What might it do more effectively? Remember to consider the nontraditional family (e.g., single parent, blended family, working parents, absent parents).

- What does the congregation currently do to equip parents for the spiritual support of teens in the home? What do parents think about these? What do parents suggest to enhance what is already being done?

- What will it take parents to make eating together at least five times a week a priority? What priorities must be shifted by teens, parents, and congregations?

What Can Congregations Do?

- Pick one of the suggestions to support or to refute.

- What additional suggestions have surfaced by the group?

- Has your congregation ever held the discussion regarding taking kids out of adult worship for one of their own? What might this chapter suggest in this discussion?

- Who specifically are in your teen's "cloud of witnesses"? Does he or she have a 5:1 ratio of mature Christians who know and engage him or her?

- What resources from your congregation are helpful for deeper discussions at home?

- When was the last time your congregation provided you with resources or encouraged you to participate in parent training? When is the next time?

Start Small, Start Now

- As leaders in the congregation, set up and work toward S.M.A.R.T. goals—goals that are specific, measurable, achievable, relevant, and time-bound. These are first-priority goals. Communicate these goals with parents, boards, and other leaders to get their input. Use these goals for evaluation at meetings and in discussions. Then, once these are pretty well in place, pick a couple more with which to build upon the first-priority goals.

- As parents, pick a couple of goals that can be implemented at home. Set up S.M.A.R.T. goals, share these with a trusted, mature Christian friend, and ask that friend to check up on you and pray for you. Consider meeting regularly with other parents or families to support one another (this can be fun around a meal, activity, or movie night). This can also help to serve as a countercultural community. Then work on these ideas. It may take some effort to get into a habit. Be kind to yourself, but stay the course. Keep your goals nearby to review and remind yourself. It is okay to revise these goals based upon experiences.

RESOURCES

DeVries, Mark, *Family-Based Youth Ministry*. Downers Grove, IL: InterVarsity Press, 2004.

"Entertainment Software Rating Board (ESRB) Ratings Guide." Accessed March 10, 2017. https://www.esrb.org/ratings/ratings_guide.aspx.

Field, Genevieve. "Parenting against the Internet: What Are Our Kids Doing Online, and How Can We Protect Them from Danger?" *RealSimple*. September 2016. http://www.realsimple.com/work-life/technology/safety-family/internet-safety.

Fields, Doug. *Purpose Driven Youth Ministry: 9 Essential Foundations for Healthy Growth*. Grand Rapids: Zondervan, 1998.

Greenwood, Shannon, Andrew Perrin, and Maeve Duggan. "Social Media Update 2016." Pew Research Center, Internet & Technology. November 11, 2016. http://www.pewinternet.org/2016/11/11/social-media-update-2016/.

Joiner, Reggie. *Think Orange: Imagine the Impact When Church and Family Collide . . .* Cumming, GA: The reThink Group, 2016.

Lenhart, Amanda, "Teens, Social Media & Technology Overview 2015." *Pew Research Center*, Internet & Technology. April 9, 2015. Accessed March 29, 2017. http://www.pewinternet.org/2015/04/09/teens-social-media-technology-2015/.

LifeLong Faith Journals, http://www.lifelongfaith.com/journal.html

Powell, Kara E., Brad M. Griffin, and Cheryl A. Crawford. *Sticky Faith: Youth Worker Edition: Practical Ideas to Nurture Long-Term Faith in Teenagers*. Grand Rapids: Zondervan, 2011.

Rosemond, John. "Remove the Smartphone, Regain the Child." Herald & Review, February 10, 2017. Accessed March 29, 2017. http://herald-review.com/news/opinion/editorial/columnists/rosemond/john-rosemond-remove-the-smartphone-regain-the-child/article_699a92ca-77f3-5d9f-a5a5-9f72ab35bb4c.html?utm_medium=social&utm_source=email&utm_campaign=user-share.

Rosemond, John K. "Smart Phone, or No Smart Phone?" ArcaMax, June 23, 2016. Accessed June 25, 2017. https://www.arcamax.com/homeandleisure/parents/johnrosemond/s-1844399.

"Social Media and Mobile Internet Use among Teens and Young Adults." *Lifelong Faith* 4, no. 1 (Spring 2010): 52–53, http://www.lifelongfaith.com/uploads/5/1/6/4/5164069/lifelong_faith_journal_4.1.pdf.

Strommen, Merton P. and Richard A. Hardel, *Passing on the Faith: A Radical Model for Youth and Family Ministry*. Winona, MN: Saint Mary's Press, 2008.

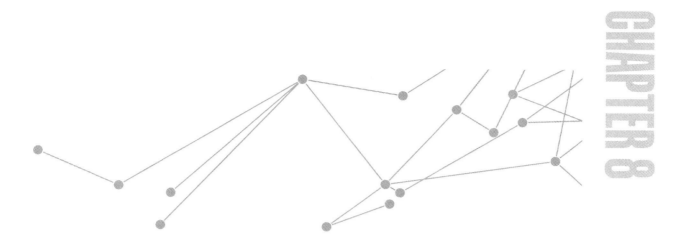

CHAPTER 8

FIVE ROLES OF THE YOUTH LEADER

BY A. J. MASTIC

When I showed up for my first youth ministry position in 2007, I was fired up and ready to get started! I had just graduated with a Director of Christian Education (DCE) degree and I was excited about using my skills to make a difference in the lives of young people. When I was younger, the youth ministry at my church made such a profound impact on me that I found myself drawn to becoming a youth worker. I wanted to help young people trust in Jesus and give them a sense of community, like the one I had growing up.

Your story might be similar, or maybe serving in youth ministry is a new journey for you. Perhaps you trained for this—or maybe you're a new volunteer and you're wondering what you've gotten yourself into! No matter how you got to this point, what's important is that as you take your first steps in youth ministry, you do so with an awareness of not only your *skills,* but your *roles.* Am I a teacher? chaperone? dodgeball referee? friend? mentor? A good understanding of your roles will help define your work and the nature of your relationships with the youth.

Role 1: Follower of Jesus

In Acts 8:26–40, we read the powerful story of how God used Philip, a deacon in the Early Church, to bring the Gospel to an Ethiopian official. Read what happens:

> Now an angel of the Lord said to Philip, "Rise and go toward the south to the road that goes down from Jerusalem to Gaza." This is a desert place. And he rose and went. And there was an Ethiopian, a eunuch, a court official of Candace, queen of the Ethiopians, who was in charge of all her treasure. He had come to Jerusalem to worship and was returning, seated in his chariot, and he was reading the prophet Isaiah. And the Spirit said to Philip, "Go over and

join this chariot." So Philip ran to him and heard him reading Isaiah the prophet and asked, "Do you understand what you are reading?" And he said, "How can I, unless someone guides me?" And he invited Philip to come up and sit with him. Now the passage of the Scripture that he was reading was this: "Like a sheep He was led to the slaughter and like a lamb before its shearer is silent, so He opens not His mouth. In His humiliation justice was denied Him. Who can describe His generation? For His life is taken away from the earth." And the eunuch said to Philip, "About whom, I ask you, does the prophet say this, about himself or about someone else?" Then Philip opened his mouth, and beginning with this Scripture he told him the good news about Jesus. And as they were going along the road they came to some water, and the eunuch said, "See, here is water! What prevents me from being baptized?"

Do you see what happened? God tells Philip to travel along a dusty wilderness road—*and doesn't seem to tell him why*—but Philip goes faithfully. When Philip arrives, God only tells him to go over to the chariot—no more. With essentially zero instructions, Philip reads the situation, figures out what the Ethiopian needs help with, and determines that God has placed him there to share the Gospel. It's amazing! God *doesn't need* to give Philip detailed instructions, because God knows that He's sending Philip. He doesn't need to lay out a detailed plan, because Philip is who he is. He's a follower of Jesus. He's firmly rooted in who God is and who God has made him to be. He's very familiar with Isaiah because he's a student of God's Word. The things Philip is able to do as he ministers to the Ethiopian official are the direct result of his "being." Philip leads by being who God has made him and being present in the moment that God placed him into. So do we.

I cannot stress this enough: as youth workers, we draw from the well of our identity in Jesus when we lead. That's why our first role is to be a faithful follower of Jesus. Obviously, as Christians, that's our first role no matter what vocation we have. God's powerful Word works in the lives of the youth we lead, even when we're not at our best. We will be more effective as youth workers when we immerse ourselves in God's Word daily, as lifelong students of Scripture. It shapes our hearts, molds our thoughts, and causes us to be more attuned to what our youth need to hear. Studying the Scriptures causes us to be people of prayer, kindness, and so forth—the sort of people who are "the real deal." That's how we inspire young people. The book *Sticky Faith: Everyday Ideas to Build Lasting Faith in Your Kids* by Dr. Kara E. Powell and Dr. Chap Clark says the biggest reason young people leave the faith is because they don't see faith prioritized or modeled in the lives of Christian adults they know. Young people sense hypocrisy a mile away—but they absolutely listen to and learn from those who are genuinely devoted followers of Jesus.

Role 2: Mentor-Friend

The role of mentor-friend is an important one, and more than any other, it's also a role that when misunderstood, carries a huge possibility for disaster. Here's what I mean. As youth workers, we should have good relationships with the youth we lead. We should relate to them, speak their language, and have fun together. As we guide young people along the journey toward a life of faith, there needs to be a friendly bond. Yet, we are not peers. We are mentor-friends. We are friends in much the same way parents befriend their children. There is a line of clear authority, expectations, and boundaries. Consider Jesus' relationship with His disciples. In John 15:12–15, Jesus spoke with His disciples saying:

> **This is My commandment, that you love one another as I have loved you. Greater love has no one than this, that someone lay down his life for his friends. You are My friends if you do what I command you. No longer do I call you servants, for the servant does not know what his master is doing; but I have called you friends, for all that I have heard from My Father I have made known to you.**

Notice how Jesus is clearly a friend to His disciples. He's able to relate with them. He spends a lot of time with them. He cares for them on a personal level. Yet, He is not *just* a friend. There's no question that He is the rabbi and they are His disciples. Likewise, youth workers should be trusted mentors who can also have fun and empathize with young people. There is a big danger that can arise when youth workers let their mentoring role slip. The risk for this is particularly high if you're entering youth ministry leadership as a college student or a young graduate, as I did. You're closer in age; therefore, the opportunity to relate is higher—but so is the risk of slipping into a poor mentor-friend role balance. Here are a few questions that can help you evaluate your balance:

- Do I just hang out with the youth, or am I also looking for ways to mentor through teachable moments?
- Has my desire to be seen as cool caused me to sacrifice my mentoring role in any way?
- Do I need emotional validation from the youth or am I comfortable with the appropriate relational distance that results from me being a mentor?
- Has the youth group become my peer group?

The mentor-friend role requires a balance you need to be intentional about setting, from day one. The first thirty days are essential to establishing that you are both relatable and a genuine follower of Jesus who has something to share. I highly encourage you to take a trip with your youth group during that first month. Trips and other shared experiences provide great opportunities to get to know your students, demonstrate your authenticity, create teachable moments, and generate excitement for your group. DCE students are assigned to a church to complete a one-year internship following their coursework, and I was blessed that my internship church brought the whole youth group on a road trip to Austin to meet me after our internship locations were announced. That trip helped me jump-start my relationships with the youth. *If your church will be getting a new youth worker soon, I encourage you to work in advance to plan a group trip about two weeks after your new youth worker starts—you'll be doing him or her (and your youth ministry) a huge favor.* Another way many youth workers increase face time with their youth is by occasionally eating lunch with them at their schools. Most important, remember every interaction with your youth is a gift from God, which we honor by intentionally seeking to be a mentor-friend.

ROLE 3: SPIRITUAL LEADER

A youth worker's distinctive role is that of spiritual leader. If we don't assume this role, our churches and youth ministries will likely be spiritually malnourished; they won't take on the distinctive qualities of a Christian community. While we can't personally cause young people to grow in faith, it is our role to "lead them to water," so to speak.

Pastors are *called* to be the chief spiritual leaders in our churches. However, the task of leading God's people is so great that pastors cannot do it alone—nor should they, if they are concerned about raising up the Body of Christ (Ephesians 4:11–12). Youth workers, whether commissioned church workers or volunteers, are a part of the church leadership team, led by the pastor(s). When I started out in youth ministry, I was blessed to work with an amazing pastor who mentored me *and* served me; I pray that for you as well. You might not be best friends with your pastor(s) and your relationship with them will require some work, but it will be a blessing if you can respect and support one another. A wise youth ministry veteran taught me early on that we should always speak well of our pastor(s) and put the best construction on everything as you work together to engage people of all ages in the life of the church.

So what exactly does it mean to be a spiritual leader for the youth? It means teaching God's Word (through lessons, discussions, mentoring, and teachable moments), modeling a life of faith, and leading the youth ministry team.

In many cases, teaching God's Word means first deciding what to teach—which requires asking yourself, "What do the youth need to hear?" Regardless of what passage you choose to teach, I encourage you to prepare and teach it passionately. Don't just go through some Bible study sheet you haven't even reviewed ahead of time! Create or find great content and then refine it. Determine which questions won't work well for your group and which ones will. Think of additional questions you can ask or stories you can share. Think about how the Scripture passage applies to youth in their everyday life and then be *passionate* about teaching it. If you're having trouble getting excited about the passage, it's likely you need to take a step back and first apply it to your own life. Take some time and let it soak in; perhaps read a commentary. You need to know why the passages make a difference in your life if you're going to teach the youth why it makes a difference in theirs. Another way you can help your youth apply the passage to their lives is by doing an initial teaching time with the whole youth group, and then splitting up into smaller discussion groups led by volunteers. This can really help the youth internalize what they learn from the teaching time.

As we teach, we must realize that it's impossible to teach our youth the right answer to every question, or the right way to act in every situation. However, in addition to teaching our youth to memorize important truths, we can and should teach them theological and practical thinking skills. This skill set will equip them to process through each situation in light of their Christian faith and navigate the world as a follower of Jesus. For example, instead of beginning the lesson by saying, "Don't smoke marijuana," you might lead a discussion in which you ask youth to evaluate marijuana by asking, "What does God's Word say? Is it legal? Is it beneficial?" That's just one example. The point is, we must teach what God's Word says and how it informs our decision-making when the issue is not plainly laid out in Scripture. This requires that you yourself know God's Word, which is one reason why the first role (being a Jesus follower) is going to be the foundation of your ministry. It also requires learning the art of asking open-ended questions and waiting long enough for students to process your question and respond. I can't tell you how many discussions I led my youth through. These discussions stretched me as a leader and helped the students own their faith. The first few discussions will definitely be a bit shaky. You'll have to teach the youth how to dialogue respectfully. This includes teaching listening skills, reeling in the tangents, dealing with conversation dominators as gently as possible, and of course correcting with God's Word as needed. These discussions go a long way toward raising up young people who are bold and confident enough to dialogue about their faith. Your youth will grow to counter the stereotype that Christians lack substance and ignore science. They'll also be much better prepared for the onslaught of faith-challenging issues that often arise in college.

Another way youth will learn how to put their faith into action is by seeing it modeled by how you live out your own faith. For example, they'll be watching to see if you stop to pray, if you give of yourself to serve others, or if you're involved in a small group. They'll want to hear how you've processed through difficult issues of faith and life. My encouragement is to be appropriately open about your struggles, understanding of how others have dealt with their challenges, and courageous to share how your faith has led you to live differently. This will go a long way toward establishing yourself as a trustworthy spiritual leader.

As we seek to raise up youth who are faithful and knowledgeable about their faith, it's also important that we not view ourselves as soloists. Do you ever wonder why many youth groups peak at twenty to thirty youth, regardless of church size? It's because that's about the number of youth one youth worker can relate to on his or her own! Perhaps you've heard the Lego example—we only have so many pegs! We must view ourselves as team leaders who work in concert with parents and raise up volunteers. Training volunteers is an important way that we live out our calling to make disciples. Volunteers not only help you with your responsibilities, but they also serve as additional role models and spiritual leaders with whom the youth can connect and learn from. In time, your volunteers can even replicate themselves, creating even more spiritual leaders.

ROLE 4: CULTURAL ARCHITECT

Youth workers set the tone and culture of a church's youth ministry through their language, actions, and decision-making. They are cultural architects, sitting at the drafting table, sketching out a group identity. All youth workers have this influence, but only the best know it and use it intentionally.

Setting the culture of the group is a delicate balance of vision-casting while also allowing for parent/volunteer/youth input. It's important to think about how you're going to build in opportunities for input to be shared. I highly encourage you to consider creating a youth leadership team, which provides opportunities for your youth to develop a team mentality, give input, and participate in the planning of youth group or other events. They know their peers best, and if you want youth to invite their friends to youth group, let them have ownership! You'll be amazed at the creative ideas they have and how much more comfortable they'll be inviting other youth to their church. I'm very proud of the youth I've led over the years; they have been so creative! They helped transform a boring youth room into a functioning coffee bar. They came up with a thrilling tag-based game called "Zombies," got high school bands to play concerts in our youth room, created a day-long Hunger Games event played with nerf blasters, and helped hundreds of their peers encounter the Gospel. They knew best how to engage their community and create opportunities for others to encounter the love of Jesus—they just needed someone to believe in them and offer a little guidance. Dreaming big can result in some messiness, but holes in the wall can be fixed. You can even learn to appreciate them when they're the result of community being created and the Gospel being shared.

When it comes to being a cultural architect, one thing I've learned from my mentors is that it helps to take time to identify and speak about your cultural distinctiveness. This means highlighting the language and actions in line with your group's identity. It often means stopping to thank an individual for something he did and explaining how it was an example of living out your group's mission. If you want your parents, youth, and volunteers to replicate certain language or actions, say so! Claim them. Things left uncommunicated don't get acknowledged or repeated; things communicated clearly become a part of the group's DNA.

Being a cultural architect means acting with intentionality. For example, it's important to give some careful thought as to the "flow" of youth group, whether you've only got one hour on a Sunday or two hours on a weeknight. When youth are arriving, I encourage you to make sure they're not just sitting on couches looking at their phones; create a fun space so they can hang out and enjoy their time together! Put on some music, have some snacks, get a Ping-Pong table—whatever you need to do to help students get excited about being there. It's also important for you to use your time intentionally. Don't just sit in one spot; make your way around the room, interact with every youth, and connect isolated youth with others (you can teach your youth leadership team and volunteers to do the same). Also, how you order your time together matters. It can be a good idea to do a group game first in order to get their energy out before you sit down for the lesson and/or small group discussion time. Ask your volunteers not to look at their phones, but to be fully engaged in games, the lesson, and small group time. When you're done, plan on hanging out for a bit longer. It's a great time to be available for follow-up conversations. These are just a few examples of being an intentional cultural architect, in order to create a group culture that helps young people connect with Jesus.

ROLE 5: BOUNDARY KEEPER

Nobody wants to be the boundary keeper, yet it's an important part of a youth worker's responsibilities. Setting appropriate boundaries honors everyone, keeps the focus on Jesus, and ensures that your ministry isn't derailed. Youth workers set and properly communicate boundaries in three important areas:

RELATIONSHIPS

It's important to have appropriate personal boundaries for yourself and volunteers. You might observe practices such as these:

- Don't initiate or force physical touch; let others initiate appropriate touch if they want to.
- Opt for side-hugs instead of full hugs.
- Stay away from jokes about sexuality, relationships, or gender.
- Don't be alone with minors or members of the opposite sex, even in the car.
- Ask parents if it's okay to accept friend requests from their child on social media (one youth worker I know tells parents that at any time, they can look at his social media account communications with their children).
- Background check your volunteers.

SAFE SPACE

Youth workers communicate what is acceptable behavior when participating in youth group activities. This means rules such as no drugs, weapons, physical violence, bullying, PDA, or swearing at youth group. Youth workers should not take delight in being an authoritarian, but rather utilize appropriate authority as necessary to ensure that safe space is respected. This means that trained school teachers will likely need to use less authority than they are used to and that all youth workers should avoid being overzealous about what they say no to. However, it also means intervening as necessary. For example, I once caught a youth sharing cigarettes with three other youth (all minors). This behavior doesn't honor their bodies nor their parents' wishes and it was important for me to intervene in that moment.

OFF-CAMPUS EVENTS

Youth workers work in conjunction with parents to set appropriate policies regarding activities that take place off of the church property. For example, off-campus events usually require permission slips and authorized drivers. Overnight trips require separate sleeping arrangements for men and women. International trips might require supplemental insurance.

CLOSING THOUGHTS

Whether this chapter has been one big review for you or you had several "light bulb" moments as you encountered new ideas, I hope that it causes you to reflect on the complex roles that you play as a youth worker. What you do is so important! Thanks for giving of your-self so others might know Jesus. I hope this chapter has given you a foundation to keep your ministry thriving for many years to come.

PRAYER

Father, thank You for leading me into youth ministry. I'm grateful for the opportunity to use my gifts to make a difference in the lives of young people in the name of Your Son, Je-sus. I pray that You would continually renew me in Your forgiveness, solidify the roles that You would have me play, and give me wisdom as I work with parents and other volunteers. May Your Spirit be with me and guide me to be a lifelong student of Your Word. Fill me with Your passion as I model what it means to follow Jesus and encourage the youth in their faith journey. Amen.

QUESTIONS FOR DISCUSSION

- In 1 Corinthians 11:1, Paul urges new Christians in Corinth to "be imitators of me, as I am of Christ." As a Jesus follower, which parts of your faith walk are currently exam-ple-worthy and which ones need a little work?
- Ask yourself the questions on page 73. Would you say that you currently have an appropriate mentor-friend balance with the youth? Why?
- What steps can you take to improve your relationship with your pastor?
- If you got a coach to observe you teaching your youth group, what improvements do you think he or she would suggest?
- Make a "DNA" list of items that are currently important to the culture of your youth ministry. Do you think all of those items are being adequately communicated?
- Are there good opportunities for parent/volunteer/youth input in your youth ministry?

- Out of the example boundaries on pages 77–78, are there any you're not sure are necessary? Are there any you would add?

- What other roles might be important for youth workers?

RESOURCES

Crabtree, Jack. *Better Safe Than Sued: Keeping Your Students and Ministry Alive.* Grand Rapids: Zondervan, 2008.

Fields, Doug. *Your First Two Years in Youth Ministry: A Personal and Practical Guide to Starting Right.* Grand Rapids: Zondervan, 2002.

"Kretzmann's Popular Commentary," http://www.KretzmannProject.org.

Powell, Kara E., and Chap Clark. *Sticky Faith: Everyday Ideas to Build Lasting Faith in Your Kids.* Grand Rapids: Zondervan, 2011.

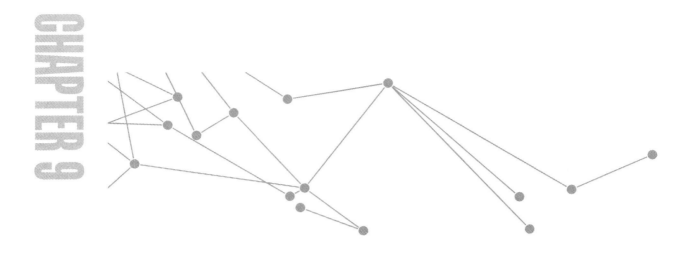

CHAPTER 9

VOLUNTEERS

BY BO CHAPMAN

THE POWER OF VOLUNTEERS

BY THE NUMBERS

The national numbers are amazing when it comes to the number of people engaged in some type of volunteering within nonprofit organizations and the number of hours those volunteers put in. The Nonprofit Academic Centers Council noted that the nonprofit sector accounts for more than one hundred million volunteers.[1] Within those one hundred million volunteers, it is estimated close to five million individuals work as full-time equivalents (FTEs) in these organizations. This figure is staggering in terms of the hours, cost savings, and work these nonprofit organizations accomplish because of the involvement of so many volunteers. Without volunteers, many of these organizations wouldn't exist.

The reality is individuals serve nonprofit organizations in large numbers, and they do so without compensation. If these individuals out in the world give of themselves for various organizations, then you can rest assured they exist in your congregation as well. You just have to find out who they are, what motivates them to give of their time and talents to make a difference, and how you can connect them with the larger mission of the church. Once you have a fuller understanding of the depth of talent around you; you can tap into that talent by connecting it with the deeper purpose that drives volunteers. I believe you will see some undeniably exciting ministry opportunities take place right in your congregation.

REALIZATIONS

Numerous gifted and talented individuals fill your congregation. In your pews sit individu-

---

1   Nonprofit Academic Centers Council, "The Role of Nonprofit Organizations and Academic Centers," 2015, http://www.nonprofit-academic-centers-council.org/.

als smarter than you, more creative than you, better speakers than you, and so forth. I'm not saying this to bum you out, but instead to open your eyes to the reality and boundless possibilities right in front of you. When we take the time to realize our shortcomings and place them in the context of the vast array of gifts and talents in our midst, we begin to honestly structure a successful volunteer program that brings forth the best of everyone.

When we begin effectively utilizing volunteers, the opportunity to touch more lives relationally, emotionally, and spiritually in a positive, deeper way becomes a greater possibility. You don't have to do it all (because you can't), and you shouldn't try to do it all (because you won't). Instead, set the foundation of the ministry and then surround yourself with these untapped resources to build on that foundation and watch the wonderful things that take place.

Engagement in the Larger Mission of the Church

Having individuals assist you in various areas of ministry is not just about that particular aspect of ministry. Yes, you want to see your particular area of ministry growing and thriving. But remember, you and the volunteers who serve alongside you are involved in something so much larger than children's ministry, student ministry, Sunday School, and so forth. When we engage people to serve as volunteers and then place them in an area of ministry where they can use their gifts and talents, they impact the lives of others both consciously and inadvertently. The lives they impact will, in turn, have the opportunity to move out and touch the lives of others.

You and your volunteers have the opportunity to be part of something bigger than your ministry, something bigger than yourselves. You have the opportunity to be the hands and feet of Jesus in your congregation, community, and the world at large. When we are faithful with what God has given us, we get the chance to see some wonderful things happen in the kingdom, and it serves as a blessing for our ministry, for our church, and for so many people around us. Never lose sight of the reason for what you do and why you do it.

Getting Volunteers Involved

The potential is right there in your church—gifted people who could bring a lot to your ministry—if you could just get them to say yes. What does it take to move people from their pew to the point where they willingly commit their time and talents to assist you with the area of ministry God has placed you in? Three factors are very important:

1. Set forth a vision that gives people a clearer idea of what you are about and how that ties in with their specific gifts and passions. When people see the bigger picture and their role in it, it tends to motivate them to get involved.

2. Establish different levels of commitment because people are going to enter the ministry in various capacities.

3. Make the formal "ask." Too many people wrestle with this step for whatever reason—usually out of fear of rejection. If you want someone to say yes, you have to ask the question first.

SETTING FORTH YOUR VISION

If you could succinctly share your vision for your particular ministry with those in your congregation, what would you say? What would you tell people to let them know this is who we are, what we are about, and where we are going? What would you say that would get others excited about being part of something bigger than themselves? How would you help people visualize the "what could be"? Vision is important because it not only gives direction to your ministry, but it also develops a visual and tangible purpose for volunteers to rally behind.

Begin personally praying for God to make it very evident for you what He wants for your ministry. Ask God the hard questions. Take time to dig into Scripture. A good place to start might be the Great Commission (Matthew 28:19–20) and the Greatest Commandment (Mark 12:29–31).

As you discern God's desires for the ministry, start processing how you are going to accomplish it. Where do you begin and where do you want to go? Don't be too ambiguous. Write it down. Having a visual outline helps you know what pieces need to be in place and when to start setting various items in motion. What quantifiable and qualitative elements let you know you are moving in the right direction?

Begin to communicate the vision. Start with those close to you to get valuable feedback for possible refinements and then get the word out. This is who we are, what we are about, and where we are going. Let people hear it and hear it often.

ESTABLISHING DIFFERENT LEVELS OF COMMITMENT

As you set forth the plan to achieve the vision for your particular ministry, realize that people will want to help but they will also have reservations. Leaders can assist volunteers by giving them specific information with regard to what you are asking of them. Concerns include the timeframe needed, what they will be doing, and who they can go to for help. Potential volunteers need you to answer these critical questions. Having good information upfront helps allay some of the reservations potential volunteers have with regard to being involved in the ministry.

In addition, be cognizant of the value of establishing different levels of commitment and involvement for volunteers. Some individuals have limited availability. Others may want to explore the ministry before making any form of extended commitment. Still others may have very specific gifts or skills so certain areas of ministry might resonate better with them.

With this in mind, work to provide varied opportunities for volunteers to engage within the ministry. These opportunities include a very low commitment, such as driving students to and from an event or helping to serve at the Easter breakfast; to a mid-level commitment, such as serving as a chaperone on a weekend retreat; all the way to a very high-level commitment, such as leading a small group every Wednesday night or being a part of the board of student ministry.

No matter the commitment level, each individual is important in the life of your particular ministry area especially as you begin to grow and get more and more people involved. By setting forth these various levels of commitment, people have the opportunity to engage at their comfort level and within a structure that works for them. It also makes it easier to have them become a more active part of the ministry. When events are done well, you establish trust, and volunteers begin to capture more of the vision.

MAKING THE "ASK"

You've laid out your vision. You have a plan in place. You know *who* and *what* you need to set things into motion. Now comes the most difficult part for many people: asking others to commit as volunteers for a specific role within the ministry.

Why is this so difficult? Are we afraid of rejection? Are we scared that maybe we're asking the wrong person to do the job? The list can go on, but stop for a moment before going down that list and start scanning another list.

- Have you prayed about this person and this particular position?
- Do you feel that the direction you want to move the ministry is the direction God wants it to go?
- Have you done your due diligence in planning what you need and making those needs public?

As you start answering yes to those answers, then you know you are on the right track. So, make *the "ask."*

Let individuals know exactly what you would like them to do. Give them pertinent information. Share why this is valuable. Then let them make the decision. Some will say yes, others no, still others will say, "Let me think about it." In the end, you asked and it will become easier the more often you ask. Even if someone says no to your first appeal, look for other ways you might engage them in the ministry.

The primary goal is to consistently engage people as part of the bigger picture. When people say yes and have a positive, purposeful experience, you can be guaranteed that the power of word of mouth will take place. Excitement builds because God is at work and people get to be part of the growth in your program. It all starts with prayer and stepping out of your comfort zone to ask.

Developing and Retaining Volunteers

Volunteers, like all people, have all types of gifts, talents, and skills that combined with their particular passions allow for some very purposeful and powerful ministry to take place. These individuals are in your midst—once you have them involved in the ministry, how do you do more than just keep them involved? How do you help them flourish?

Give Clear Direction

The first key component is for volunteers to get continued clear direction from you. They need to know what you want them to do, when you want it done, and any specifics regarding how you want it done if the task requires a level of precision. There is a balance between dictating everything for volunteers, and thereby stifling their gifts, to being very laissez faire in your directions, thereby allowing people to potentially wander from the direction you are trying to go.

All people are different, and time and experience will help you determine how much direction you need to give to various individuals. But if ever in doubt, always lean to more direction because this helps to alleviate the frustration that comes with not knowing if you are doing something correctly. Volunteers want to do well with the responsibility you have given them, and a clear direction helps them to thrive.

Provide Adequate Resources

Resources can mean anything from actual supplies needed to complete a project to training opportunities for continued growth and improvement. Resources are critical for volunteers to accomplish the role you have given them. Make sure they have the items they need when they need them. Set them up to succeed by taking potential frustrations away and establishing greater opportunities for them to shine and, in turn, impact the ministry in a positive manner.

Consistent Encouragement/Support

Volunteers need to hear it, see it, smell it, taste it, and touch it when it comes to encouragement. From a handshake to a card to a gift card for the local coffee shop, take the time over and over again to say "thank you" and to mean it. Your encouragement of your volunteers lets them know that their time and energy is important, and that means a lot.

In addition, make sure you support your volunteers. They need to know that you have their back. When it comes to an upset parent, an unintentional mistake, and so on, volunteers appreciate the fact that you, their leader, support them and will diligently gather the needed information and then take action when needed. Be proactive in letting your volunteers know that if issues do arise, to please keep you informed and you will handle them from that point on.

PROVIDE AVENUES OF COMMUNICATION AND FEEDBACK

Volunteers in the trenches see things you miss. Their insights can lead to doing things better or differently. Give these individuals the freedom and the avenue to share their ideas and be heard. It is important that you take the feedback as constructive criticism and really hear what they are saying to you. The back-and-forth dialogue that happens within a successful communication and feedback structure gives the ministry a stronger foundation to grow from because ideas are well thought out and people bring their differing gifts to the table.

Some questions to consider:

- Is there a process for both formal (written) and informal (verbal) feedback?

- Do you want the feedback to be anonymous?

- Have you established guidelines for feedback? Guidelines might include making constructive not destructive comments, differentiating between feedback and new ideas, and understanding that receiving feedback doesn't necessarily mean you agree with it.

- Do your volunteers feel heard? Ask them.

SAFETY FIRST

ESTABLISH GUIDELINES AND POLICIES TO PROTECT STUDENTS AND ADULTS

In this day and age, congregations must have a well-thought-out child and youth safety policy manual in place for your ministry. For volunteers, this manual systematically lays out the steps used before approving volunteers to work with children and students. These steps should include getting a national background check, having a waiting period before recruiting volunteers (child predators attempt to get involved immediately upon joining a congregation), obtaining references when possible, and participating in training.

In addition, you need to set guidelines for all volunteers with regard to adult/student ratios, meeting places, gender interaction, and so forth to alleviate scenarios detrimental to either the child or the volunteer. You must also draw up formal guidelines for reporting claims of any type of abuse.

Though these types of items tend to add an extra step for getting people to volunteer, it is important that we remain vigilant in protecting those entrusted to us. This applies to both the children and the volunteers who serve in various capacities of ministry. When guidelines remain above reproach, it limits the possibility of improper conduct and/or accusations of inappropriate conduct.

Most district offices provide a substantial framework of material for you to utilize in establishing your child and youth safety manual. In addition, feel free to contact local law enforcement to determine what your particular state's requirements are for reporting abuse. Lastly, organizations such as Protect My Ministry can walk you through different areas including background checks, training videos, and so forth. Though these services come with a cost, it is worth the investment in additional safety for your youth and volunteers.

RESOURCES

Kahnweiler, William M. "Non-Profit Organizations: A Primer for OD Researchers and Practitioners." *Organization Development Journal* 29, no. 4 (Winter 2011): 81–89.

Nonprofit Academic Centers Council. "The Role of Nonprofit Organizations and Academic Centers." 2015. http://www.nonprofit-academic-centers-council.org/.

Pynes, Joan E. *Human Resources Management for Public and Nonprofit Organizations*. 3rd ed. San Francisco: Jossey-Bass, 2009.

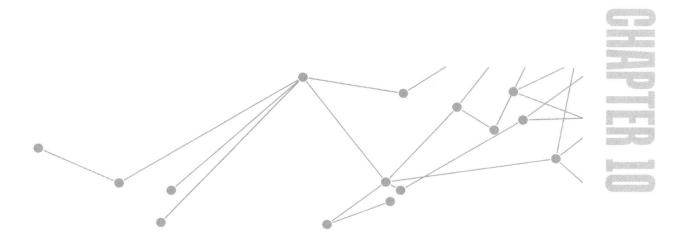

CHAPTER 10

THE FAMILY OF FAITH

BY LEAH ABEL

I grew up in a small church in rural Iowa. We had sixty to eighty people in worship on a good Sunday. Over my first eighteen years of life, I remember at least five pastors who came and went. My church wasn't cool. It wasn't hip or happening. It wasn't intentionally youth-friendly or youth-focused. We didn't have a youth worker or a DCE. We didn't have a youth room with old couches. We didn't have activities or events that I invited my nonmember friends to. Our confirmation program had lots of memorizing and homework without a lot of practical application. Our church basement contained an out-of-tune piano and the ugliest yellow-green carpet you have ever seen.

My church was a place where I learned to know Jesus.

The church where I grew up was far from perfect, but my church understood what it meant to be a family of faith. They surrounded me and my fellow youth, however few of us there were in a given year, as a community of faith. In my church, I knew I wasn't an afterthought or a problem to be solved, but part of a family.

After college, my first call as a DCE was to a large congregation in Florida with Sunday morning Bible studies bigger than my home congregation. We had lots of teenagers, a hip young youth worker (me), a freshly painted youth room with couches, a gym for games, and weekly youth events designed with food, fun, games, and Bible study. This church was not a perfect place either. We had successes and failures in ministry to teenagers. Guess what still mattered most to the students? Being family. On our best days, our students understood that they were not an afterthought or a problem to be solved, but a part of a family.

Spending time comparing your youth group and program to other churches may seem easy. They have more youth. They have more money. They have a youth director on staff. They are cooler than we are. In the end, every congregation has the same job—becoming a family of faith with and for their teenagers.

This chapter could cover hundreds of pages as we consider how to best live as a family of faith and parent our teenagers in the faith. Practically speaking, there are three key roles of a congregation in the life of youth ministry:

- Support ministry by and for teenagers financially.
- Support those who serve teenagers.
- Engage teenagers as members of the church family.

We will quickly cover the first two roles and spend the majority of this chapter considering how and why to engage teenagers as members of the church family.

BUY THE DONUTS

Paying for youth ministry is not only the responsibility of the parents of youth but the entire congregation since the members serve as parents in the faith to students. As in any family, the priority given to most things can be determined by considering where money is spent. Financially supporting ministry by teenagers and for teenagers is an important responsibility for any congregation. Make sure the church budget reflects the importance of youth ministry.

There are many ways to consider this number. Ministry Architects, a youth ministry consulting firm, suggests an investment of $1,000 per youth per year.[1] (This includes staff and other resources.) Others suggest making youth ministry a percentage of the overall church budget rather than simply setting an arbitrary number. This approach helps congregations think in terms of investing in youth rather than just taking care of a few expenses.

Supporting youth also means attending and participating in their fundraisers—buy the donuts. Buying the donuts has a dual purpose in that a member's financial contribution provides the ability for youth to go on a mission trip, attend a youth gathering, or go to camp while also showing tangibly a desire to support teenagers. Imagine if the average member put in an extra $5 for their donut and said, "I'm praying for you," instead of, "How much?"

My small Iowa congregation wasn't able to set aside large amounts of money for youth ministry, but one commitment it kept every year was to budget money to a scholarship designed to help students attend a Lutheran summer camp. My decision to enroll in a Lutheran college and become a church worker is directly linked to my camp experience, made possible by my church's annual budget.

SUPPORT THOSE WHO SERVE YOUTH

The second key responsibility of the family of faith in youth ministry is supporting those who serve teenagers. This group includes youth volunteers, church staff, and parents. Youth ministry can be challenging, time consuming, and at times downright demoralizing. Support those who serve youth with prayer, encouragement, and resources.

---

1   Ministry Architects, "FAQ," https://ministryarchitects.com/frequently-asked-questions/#Q9.

- **Pray** for and with those who serve teenagers in your congregation. Include them in petitions of the church regularly as well as in your personal prayers.

- **Encourage** parents, volunteers, and staff. All members of the family of faith play a role in this as fellow believers. Stop a parent on a Sunday morning and tell him about something you've seen his child do right recently. An empty nester can ask a parent how it's going and take time to listen. Provide opportunities for parents to gather together and share their successes, failures, and questions. Encourage youth volunteers with an occasional note telling them why what they are doing is important. Share Scripture with them and let them know when you see big and small victories in youth ministry. Be sure staff who work with youth hear about what they and the youth they serve are doing right.

- **Resource** those who serve youth. Send staff or volunteers to a youth ministry conference. Provide a budget for books and materials to equip volunteers who teach and serve students. Bring in guest speakers to talk about social issues teenagers face. Offer video-based parenting classes geared toward middle and high school parents. There are countless resources available to support those who serve teenagers. Be intentional about providing these resources on an ongoing basis.

ENGAGE TEENAGERS AS MEMBERS OF THE FAMILY

In one model of youth ministry, youth are given their own space, their own programs, and their own leaders so they can focus completely on issues that matter to them. This method for youth ministry allows students to do their own thing without being bothered by adults. It allows adults to concentrate on their relationships with people their own age and properly enjoy their coffee on a Sunday morning. It allows youth and adults to each stay in their comfort zones. In their book *The Godbearing Life*,[2] Dean and Foster refer to this as the "One-Eared Mickey Mouse Model of Youth Ministry."

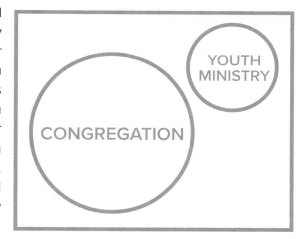

There are benefits to this model, since we are able to address the specific needs of adolescence. This method for youth ministry is easier and more efficient. It also has the potential to rob the whole church of the benefits that come from being connected as the Body of Christ. Certainly teenagers enjoy being with others their own age, and we should work to provide opportunities for students to be together and address the specific needs of this pivotal developmental stage. We should not, however, disconnect students from the

2   Kenda Creasy Dean and Ron Foster, *The Godbearing Life: The Art of Soul Tending for Youth Ministry* (Nashville: Upper Room Books, 1998), 31.

larger family of faith. Within the family of faith, students have opportunities to serve and lead alongside the rest of God's people.

What if your congregation viewed youth ministry as a part of the whole congregation rather than a separate entity? Effective ministry to students means inviting students to be a part of the family.

Recent research from the Fuller Youth Institute set out to discover what churches in America that teenagers really love are doing right. Their research found six practices of churches that effectively nurture faith in teenagers. These practices engaged youth effectively and include, among others, a focus on being more warm and inviting than cool; inviting youth into service and leadership; and taking the message of Jesus seriously.[3]

CHURCH AS HOME

Growing up, I knew for sure that my church wasn't cool. But I also knew, beyond a doubt, that my church was *home*. I knew the church loved me. I knew that because Mr. Hillers, who I think was perpetually eighty years old, would always smile and take the time to ask me how I was with his deep gruff voice. Then he would genuinely listen to my response and tell me if he saw me in the paper or had run into my grandparents. I knew my church was home because Mr. Bradley answered the barrage of questions that my fellow fifth and sixth graders and I threw at him during Sunday School. I knew it was home because Greta would sometimes help us talk my mom into going to the nearby truck stop after church to talk and eat deep-fried cheese curds. I knew it because Carol, whose kids had long since graduated from high school, continued to show up every week and teach high school Sunday School in the church kitchen. I knew my church loved me because of Janet Fisher, who loaded up her big brown cargo van with a bunch of teenagers and one other adult and drove us to San Antonio, Texas, for a National Youth Gathering.

When it comes to entertainment, we can't outdo the culture in which we live. Students are not easily impressed by technology, music, amazing games, or even a young, hip youth worker with a millennial haircut and skinny jeans. Students are, however, stopped in their tracks by a community of people that wants to know them. It seems my church may have lived instinctively what the Fuller Youth Institute's research discovered—that being warm is cool.[4]

Research by Fuller Youth Institute and others seems to indicate that young people are

---

3   Kara Powell, Jake Mulder, and Brad Griffin, *Growing Young: Six Essential Strategies to Help Young People Discover and Love Your Church* (Grand Rapids: Baker Books, 2016), 42–43.

4   Powell, Mulder, and Griffin, *Growing Young*, 167–69.

less concerned with the cool factor in their church and more likely to invite others, connect, and stay connected because of the warmth, welcoming, accepting, belonging, caring, and authenticity of their church. Genuine and deep relationships keep young people connected to the church as they explore the faith.[5]

Warmth is difficult to pin down in terms of how our churches function week-to-week, but we know it when we see it. And we cannot fake it. Consider ways to help students and their families feel at home, listened to, and valued through one-on-one conversation. Developing a culture where every member sees themselves as responsible for the care of others is a tall order. Inviting older members of the congregation to see themselves as spiritual parents and grandparents to the young people in the congregation is a beautiful way to cast the vision.

INVITE TEENAGERS TO LEAD AND SERVE

At the church where I served as DCE several years ago, we had a weekly Wednesday night dinner. It was a big church and it could be easy for individuals to get lost if adults didn't keep their eyes open. We had a chef who helped us cater the meal each week. Chef Scott was a master at involving young people in the kitchen. He would take the quiet youth, give them a big knife, and spend ten minutes teaching them the proper way to cut up a pineapple. The next week, that same student would be back in the kitchen cutting up a pineapple while Chef Scott was busy doing other things. Chef Scott learned names, exuded warmth, and knew how to find a job for everybody. They had a job that needed to be done. They were invited personally to do it, and they were cared for by an adult while they served.

The Fuller Youth Institute's Growing Young Research cited "keychain leadership" as a vital strategy in churches effectively engaging teenagers and young adults. They define this as leadership that shares and gives away authority in a way that connects young people to the life of the congregation in a meaningful way.[6]

The church is being family when we include students as young leaders within the church rather than a separate entity of the church. When student service is always separate from adult service, we may give the impression that our mission is somehow different. When students are not given age-appropriate responsibilities, we may give the impression that students will be able to really serve Jesus and witness to their community only when they grow up, but not now. Inviting students to lead in ways that are both meaningful and connected to the mission of the larger congregation has great benefits. Consider these possibilities:

- What if students knew where the dishes went in the church kitchen because they were invited to serve alongside other adults during Lenten dinners?

- What if students were asked personally to serve by a member of the church who is not the youth worker, rather than asking the youth worker to get the youth to do it?

---

5   Powell, Mulder, and Griffin, *Growing Young*, 170–71.
6   Powell, Mulder, and Griffin, *Growing Young*, 67.

- What if instead of sending students to their (youth) room while adults do the real work, we give students a voice in decisions that impact them?

- What if students were paired up with adults on church work days?

- What if some teenagers were given not just instructions to lead a game during VBS, but time to prepare ahead to lead a time of games and devotion with younger students?

- What if the pastor invited one or two students to lead the adult Bible study for a week? Adults and students may both learn valuable lessons.

Sometimes adults become controlling because we are afraid students will mess up a task. Oftentimes this fear is based on real life experience. It can be difficult to hand youth the keys and let them lead, and yet, seeking out appropriate ways for students to lead is important to the faith development of students.

ENGAGE TEENAGERS BY TAKING THE GOSPEL SERIOUSLY

Engaging teenagers means much more than planning events that students will want to attend, giving them a budget, and being kind to them. Engaging teenagers in the family of faith means engaging them with God's Word. It means taking the message of Jesus seriously. These churches are effectively reaching young people.[7]

OPENING THE WORD

The family of faith has been entrusted with God's Word and the duty to "teach [God's Word] to your children, talking of [it] when you are sitting in your house, and when you are walking by the way, and when you lie down, and when you rise" (Deuteronomy 11:19). We no longer live in a society where basic biblical literacy is the norm. Our biblically based worldview is not necessarily being taught in schools and is certainly not being celebrated by the media our students constantly consume. If we don't tell them who Jesus really is and teach them what God's Word really says, who will? They will be left with some watered-down version of the Bible.

Fuller Institute's research marked three shifts in churches whose students articulate a clear understanding of the Gospel. Here are some of those shifts:

1. Less talk about abstract beliefs and more about Jesus

2. Less tied to formulas and more focused on the story of redemption

3. Less about heaven later and more about life here and now[8]

As the faith family lives out this responsibility of teaching God's Word, we must be mindful

---

7   Powell, Mulder, and Griffin, *Growing Young*, 126–60.
8   Powell, Mulder, and Griffin, *Growing Young*, 136.

of *what* we communicate as the most important things. Students may get the message that we are more concerned about being good or being a nice person than the Good News of Jesus if lessons focus primarily on dos and don'ts of the Bible, Bible trivia, and the Bible as a handbook for living. The Bible is primarily the story of God's incredible plan of salvation through Jesus Christ. It is an epic story of love in the face of ungrateful, undeserving, sinful people. It is the story of true healing. It is, at its heart, the story of Jesus. When we teach lessons zeroed in on various aspects of God's Law, Bible characters, and the Bible's teachings, we put these things in the context of the larger story of salvation.

Intentional work by youth staff, youth volunteers, or a youth board to plan what will be taught in a given year is important. Taking a year-by-year look at the content taught to teenagers helps ensure that students get the big picture of God's Word and are regularly reminded of the most important doctrines we hold as Lutheran Christians. It is easy to get trapped in Bible trivia or jumping from hot topic to hot topic. Certainly these issues have merit, but keeping Jesus at the center means always ensuring that lessons point us to Jesus' work in our lives now rather than pointing students to their own willpower or choices.

A GOSPEL COMMUNITY IS DIFFERENT

On a weekly basis, students are involved in lots of communities—everything from their fourth-period history class to their basketball team to the group of friends they sit with at lunch to their co-workers at their part-time job. When we take the Gospel seriously, the Church has the opportunity to feel very, very different from each of these other communities.

Fewer and fewer youth experience church life as part of their regular family routine. According to the Hartford Institute for Religious Research, only 40 percent of Americans claim to attend church regularly, and as few as 20 percent actually attend on a weekly basis.[9] When students and families do walk through your congregation's door, they should be overwhelmed by how different it feels from all of the other communities they experience. As students experience hope, healing, love, and purpose that only Jesus can provide, it can change their lives forever. Because of Jesus, Christians have an ability to "love one another with brotherly affection" and "outdo one another in showing honor" (Romans 12:10) in a way that is decidedly different from what the world offers.

As we outdo one another, we bring a warmth and compassion that shows what we already know to be true: Jesus makes all the difference.

For the sake of the youth and the spreading of the Gospel, exhort church leaders to fight fair, forgive easily, and love one another for real. When conflict big or small exists between students, encourage them to do the same. These practices set the Church apart and are only possible because we know our own sin and Christ has paid it all.

---

9   "Fast Facts about American Religion," Hartford Institute for Religion Research, accessed May 1, 2017, http://www.hartfordinstitute.org/research/fastfacts/fast_facts.html#attend.

My Church, My Family

What makes a warm, welcoming, authentic, Gospel-centered church? What makes church home for a teenager? It's a place where people of all ages smile at them, ask them how they are, and maybe even know their name. It's a place where they know where the candy is hidden and they are welcome beyond Sunday mornings. It's a place where they hear about Jesus and see faith in Him lived out in the lives of others. It's a place where they know they belong and are invited to live out their purpose. It's a place where they are invited not just to attend a church, but to participate in the church as fellow servants and leaders.

I know and follow Jesus today because of the family of faith that surrounded me back at my tiny church with no youth room and ugly carpet. There were hundreds of seemingly insignificant conversations over my eighteen years there that encouraged me in my faith. There were adults who surrounded me and others who made the Gospel tangible. I was given opportunities to lead and serve. That congregation invested in me and in my developing faith. They showed me the love and acceptance of Jesus. That church lived out love for one another, not perfectly because no family is, but beautifully for my sake and the sake of others. Your church isn't perfect, but it is a place where teenagers can be at home as they are loved by the faith family that surrounds them.

Practical Help for the Family of Faith

Questions to Consider about How Your Church Does Family

How warm and "homey" is your church? Consider the following:

- What words or phrases are youth most likely to use to describe your church? (Ask some teenagers rather than assume their answers.)
- What words or phrases are youth most likely to use to describe the people in your church?
- What words or phrases do you hope youth use to describe your church?
- What do the youth in your congregation love about their church?
- How likely are the average members of your congregation to talk to a teenager they are not related to?
- When was the last time you introduced yourself to a teenager in the congregation whom you didn't know?
- How often do adults in your congregation stop a teenager just to ask him how he's doing? How did they respond?
- What parts of the church building are teenagers discouraged from visiting? (Do youth seem to feel as if the church building is more like home or more like a china shop where they should look and not touch?)

How well does your church share leadership with teenagers? Consider the following:

- Make a list of ways that teenagers are encouraged to volunteer at your church.
- Make a list of all the other volunteer opportunities available in your church or participated in by your church out in the community.
- How many of these positions could be held by a teenager?
- Are there any teenagers who come to mind who would be particularly gifted in any of these roles?
- Are there any projects within your church initiated by teenagers rather than adults?
- How can you show teenagers that they are important members of the church today?

How are you doing at taking the Gospel seriously? Consider these questions:

- Ask students to explain Christianity to you in their own words. Listen closely to their answers and don't be quick to correct. Listen to understand their understanding before responding.
- Ask students during Sunday School—what would you say are the main teachings of Christianity?
- Look back at the lessons taught to youth over the last year. What are the topics covered? What does this list of classes indicate is being communicated as the most important thing? Discuss this with a team of valued adults and students.

Gather the youth ministry board or a group of youth volunteers and parents and plan out a year of topics and lessons for youth group or Sunday School. Ensure that your plan includes study of a book or books of the Bible, study about relationships with others, study about our relationship with God, and study about witnessing and sharing faith with those who do not know Jesus.

A Few Practical Ideas with Church Size in Mind

There are some tremendous advantages to being a big church . . . and a small church . . . and a church somewhere in between. Below are a few ideas on how you might best play to your strengths when it comes to church as family.

Small Church

Your struggles: You struggle with having critical mass so an event feels vibrant, fun, and full of energy. You don't have enough students for a dodgeball game.

Your strengths: You can know every youth in your church. Your ministry can exude warmth and authenticity because it is personal. Also, you can fit your whole youth group in a minivan.

What you can do:

- Know your students' names and talk to them. In a small church, it is both easy and possible to know the names of all the teenagers. Show genuine care and interest in their lives outside of Sunday morning.

- Make sure all adults in the congregation (everyone 25–75) understand that knowing the names of youth and making a point to talk with them is a job for every member.

- Only two young people show up for youth Bible study? Bring them to the adult class. Ask them questions. Ask them for their insights. Treat them as real members of the class.

- After Bible study, take the students to the truck stop for cheese curds or breakfast (or the equivalent in your community).

- Send them to camp to meet other Lutheran Christian young people.

- Team up with other youth groups in your area for occasional events.

- Pair students with a great Sunday School teacher who can mentor them and let them teach. Caution: While it is a fantastic idea to ask youth to help teach Sunday School, it is also a bad and dangerous idea to ignore the ongoing discipleship of the youth themselves. Be careful to have them teach for seasons of time but not all the time. They need to be aware that Sunday School isn't just for little kids. When we end education ministries for young people at elementary or middle school, we may inadvertently send that message.

- Attend their sporting or arts events. It speaks volumes when young people see that you care about them outside the four walls of your church building.

- Host events for youth and their entire families (backyard BBQs and kickball work well).

- Don't pretend to be big. Love who you are as a small church family and don't give youth the impression it would be better if you were bigger.

Big Church

Your struggles: There are too many young people to get to know well. They attend multiple high schools, and it is hard to feel connected to them.

Your strengths: Your size allows for a larger pool of volunteers with a variety of gifts. You likely have a larger budget. When you can get all your students together, you can do big things.

What you can do:

- To manage your size, you need to get smaller to grow bigger. On Sunday mornings and on retreats, put students in small groups with adult leaders they can grow to trust. The family group model is key for a large group.

- Recruit key leaders. Capitalize on the gift of a larger pool of volunteers by designating key leadership.

- Focus resources on the training and deployment of a team of mentors.

- Intentionally team your youth ministry leadership with other ministry boards or groups in the congregation. Look for ways other ministries can invite students into ministry instead of asking the youth worker to do the inviting for them.

- Celebrate youth events and achievements in worship, such as a brief commissioning for servant events, mission trips, and youth conferences.

- Large churches can be easier places for students to bring friends. Encourage students to do this and introduce others to their family.

- Pray specifically for the challenges and struggles of teenagers in worship. Prayers in our churches often focus on the sick and dying, which in most cases is a small percentage of children or teenagers.

- Provide regular fellowship and support opportunities for parents. Connecting parents to other parents is key to the development of faith-building households.

RESOURCES

Dean, Kenda Creasy, and Ron Foster. *The Godbearing Life: The Art of Soul Tending for Youth Ministry.* Nashville: Upper Room Books, 1998.

Hartford Institute for Religion Research. "Fast Facts about American Religion." Accessed May 1, 2017. http://www.hartfordinstitute.org/research/fastfacts/fast_facts.html#attend.

Ministry Architects. "FAQ." https://ministryarchitects.com/frequently-asked-questions/#Q9.

Powell, Kara, Jake Mulder, and Brad Griffin. *Growing Young: Six Essential Strategies to Help Young People Discover and Love Your Church.* Grand Rapids: Baker Books, 2016.

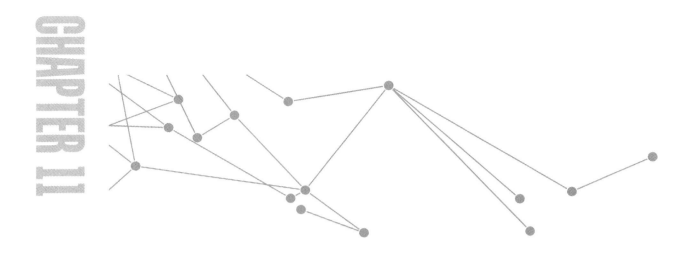

CHAPTER 11

ENCOURAGEMENT FOR THE YOUTH WORKER

BY JACOB YOUMANS

Thank you. When spoken genuinely and with sincerity, these are two of the most powerful words in the English language. I do not know how often you hear these words from youth, parents, volunteers, church members, elders, pastors, and so forth; but I do know that no matter how many times you hear it, it's not enough! Thank you for loving youth!

In the classic movie *Wayne's World,* one of the characters constantly tells everyone he loves them. He says it again and again until the recipient of the love says, "Thank you!" Then he or she is given a great big hug! Thank you for loving youth!

As you know from reading the New Testament, St. Paul liked to write letters. In the Letter to the Romans, in 1:8, he thanks God for the believers in Rome. In 1 Corinthians 1:4, Paul says the same thing about the believers in Corinth. In Ephesians 1:16, he gives the same sentiment. Again in Philippians 1:3; Colossians 1:3; 1 Thessalonians 1:2; 2 Thessalonians 1:3; 2 Timothy 1:3; and Philemon 1:4. Catch a pattern here yet? Paul is thankful for his co-workers in the Kingdom. He never wants them to forget how much he appreciates them, and he thanks God for the gift they are not only to him but to the Kingdom at large! So from one youth worker to another, thank you for loving youth!

In the 1990s I got to meet one of my heroes, Christian music recording artist Michael W. Smith. I stood in line for an hour to take a picture and get an autograph that is hanging in my office to this day. When I told him that I worked with youth for a living, he said, "Thanks for loving kids!" Those simple words of encouragement have stuck with me over the years! So I tell you, thanks for loving kids!

I know it doesn't often feel like it, but you are making a difference. I know that no one may ever really tell you this (especially not the youth or parents you serve), but you are making a difference. I know you have sacrificed time and money to do this job—but know you are making a difference.

You may not get to see the full fruit of God's work through you. You might be the instrument God uses to plant seeds. You might be the watering mechanism that God uses to grow those seeds. You might be the one God uses to prune and show tough love in difficult circumstances. But great will the day be when we're all in heaven and former youth are there because God used you to love them! Thank you for loving youth!

Youth Ministry: One of the Hardest Jobs in the World—but One of the Best Jobs in the World

I was speaking at a high school youth gathering recently, and after my session four students wanted to talk privately with me. The first one told me about how her mother died a year ago due to a lifetime struggle with drug abuse. The second told me how he was wrestling with his calling, and he felt God might be calling him into ministry but his parents were not supportive. The third told me she was mad and frustrated because she wanted to get into an elite leadership team at the university she was going to next year and was denied acceptance. The final student told me how she was the product of rape. Her biological father raped her mother—she was born nine months later. My heart broke in different ways for each one of them. Youth ministry is the toughest job in the world! Our students are dealing with so much more than we will ever know!

God also blessed me with the opportunity to speak the Gospel into each one of their lives! I got to witness the drying of their tears. Nothing necessarily changed about their different and unique situations at that moment, yet they encountered Jesus in personal ways. Jesus worked His healing and grace, and I got to humbly be a part of it. Youth ministry is the best job in the world!

I have been blessed to serve with an Apache tribe in Arizona for about fifteen years. During one of our visits, we got time with the principal at the high school. He told us the basic statistics of his tribe: a 40 percent pregnancy rate among teenage girls in the tribe, a 50 percent attempted suicide rate, and a twenty-eight-year life expectancy for Apache males. When I asked the principal what was their greatest need, he said without skipping a beat, "Jesus!" I don't know the statistics of where you are called to do ministry, but the greatest need is the same—Jesus.

All of these situations typically come back to the same issues: feelings of rejection, loneliness, and isolation. My favorite account of a lonely outcast in Scripture is Zacchaeus. Zacchaeus's life story is only recorded in Luke 19:1–10. Interestingly, in Hebrew, Zacchaeus's name means "pure and righteous one." But he was anything but righteous. Zacchaeus was a traitor to the Jewish people. He worked for the hated Romans. Many of you probably know Zacchaeus was a tax collector—but it's actually much worse than that. He was the chief tax collector! In ancient times, the people hated the tax collectors. The hatred must have been one hundred times greater for the chief tax collector. He was at the top of a pyramid scheme that terrorized the people and made him very, very wealthy.

Zacchaeus is one of the ultimate outcasts in Scripture, essentially kicked out of the Jewish race and no longer part of the family. Yet, somehow he had heard about Jesus. He probably heard that Jesus ate and interacted with outcasts and sinners. He needed to see this Jesus for himself.

This brings us to the point where Zacchaeus climbed the tree. But why did he really climb that tree? Yes, he was a short person, but my guess is he was not the only short person assembled to watch the Jesus parade. He didn't climb the tree because he was short; he climbed the tree because he didn't have any friends who would help him see Jesus. If he wasn't the outcast of society, the people probably would have made way for him to get to the front of the line to see Jesus and they would just look over him. Zacchaeus climbed the tree because he was an outcast. Zacchaeus climbed the tree because he didn't have any friends. Our calling in working with youth is to help them see Jesus.

Jesus loves the outcast. Jesus stresses urgency when he says to Zacchaeus, "Hurry and come down, for I must stay at your house today" (Luke 19:5), so Zacchaeus does. During their time together, Jesus proclaims this in Luke 19:9, "Today salvation has come to this house, since he also is a son of Abraham." Did you see what Jesus did? He not only brought salvation and forgiveness of sins, but He welcomed the outcast back into the family. Zacchaeus is a part of Abraham's tribe. Our calling in working with youth is to help them experience what it means to be a part of Jesus' family. Our call is not to replace the parents, but to work alongside and by God's grace create an inclusive family for all people. This is really hard—but it's also the best job in the world!

YOU CAN DO THIS!

If you cannot sing like angels, if you cannot preach like Paul—good! God wants you to be you. You have been given all you need to be the best youth worker you can be! Instead of focusing on what you can't do, I encourage you to focus on what you can do. In the book *Growing Young: Six Essential Strategies to Help Young People Discover and Love Your Church*, Dr. Kara Powell suggests that *warm* is the new *cool*.[1] We do not have to try and impress young people with how cool we are—or used to be. (It's dangerous to tell about all the hell you raised in high school, college, before you knew Jesus, and so on.) By being warm, loving, caring, compassionate, and sincere, youth will want to connect with us.

When I used to teach "Youth Ministry 101," I spent most of the time going over wacky youth group games, silly songs to sing, creative ways to teach the Bible, and the like. While there is certainly a time and a place for those things, I would much rather have you focus on your unique context and how to connect with the youth God has blessed you with and with the youth in your community. I want to go over four simple yet profound things everyone can do to serve in youth ministry. These are not easy by any stretch of the imagination, but

---

[1]   Kara Powell, Jake Mulder, and Brad Griffin, *Growing Young: Six Essential Strategies to Help Young People Discover and Love Your Church* (Grand Rapids: Baker Books, 2016), 26.

anyone can do them. I believe that if you do them, by God's grace, you will be able to do the best youth ministry you can do!

LOVE

You can love every youth who walks through the door. You can love every youth you come into contact with in the community. Most important, you can show them and teach them about Jesus' unconditional and everlasting love for them.

When it comes to the concept of unconditional love, we have to understand that many youth know only conditional love. They have been told (usually unintentionally) that they are loved if they win, if they succeed, or if they make the significant adults in their life look good.

A sixteen-year-old girl once told me that she had lost her virginity to her boyfriend. She was grief stricken, weeping uncontrollably thinking she disappointed me. I told her that Jesus forgave her and still loves her. I also encouraged her to tell her parents, so they could also remind her how much she was loved and forgiven. She finally built up the courage to sit down with her mom and dad. After she poured out her heart to her parents and confessed her sin, her father's first response was, "Give me back your purity ring." I recognize that he was in shock and didn't know what to say—a prime example of conditional love.

As youth workers, we have the incredible opportunity to love youth with an unconditional love, not because of anything they have done or not done, but because of who they are in Jesus. The amazing thing about modeling unconditional love is that it becomes contagious! Soon the youth desire others to know this unconditional love too. They'll start telling their friends about Jesus and His unconditional love lived out in their lives.

Think about how you can give students opportunities to practice unconditional love. Take them to the homeless shelter. Take them to the senior citizen center. Take them to the soup kitchen. Give them the opportunity to be the hands and feet of Jesus, and the message of Jesus becomes even more real.

LISTEN

Listen to your youth. Ask them questions. Listen to their stories. And while you listen, pay attention and remember! Take notes immediately after the conversation if you have to, but remembering the details of their lives will allow you to go deeper with them. Many youth are not used to being listened to; change that for them.

The Columbine school shooting in 1999 was not the first school shooting, but from my perspective it changed high school culture and youth ministry forever. It was orchestrated by a pair of outsiders seeking revenge.

In the 2002 documentary *Bowling for Columbine*, we see an interview with Marilyn Manson. Manson's music was believed to be an inspiration for the school shooting, and he was actually blamed by many people for the massacre. In the interview, they asked Manson what he would say to the shooters from Columbine, and he said, "I wouldn't say anything; I would listen."[2] Wow! What if someone did take the time to sit and listen to them? What would it mean for any youth if they believed that someone actually cared enough to listen to them?

LANGUAGE

Of all the great things the reformer Martin Luther did, perhaps one of the most important was translating the Bible into the vernacular language of the people. We often take this for granted. I do not know how many copies of the Bible I currently own. There is great power when people hear the Word of God in their native language.

When I travel abroad, I love collecting Bibles in different languages. It's a beautiful reminder that God is so much bigger than me and my people and my language. I developed an interesting problem with these Bibles. God forces me to give them away to people whose native language is the language of that Bible! This has happened with my Thai Bible and with my Chinese Bible. Both were given away to spiritually curious people who could not find a copy of the Scriptures in their native language, and they were both led to Baptism through the powerful Word of God! Language is powerful!

What is the language of your youth? How do they think and connect? In a book I wrote, *Talking Pictures: How to Turn a Trip to the Movies into a Mission Trip*, I argued that in the context in which I served, popular culture, specifically movies, were the vernacular of teenagers. I could communicate the Gospel to a fuller extent using movies as a means and metaphor. How can you speak the language of your youth? Maybe it's sports? Maybe it's school? Maybe it's 4-H? There is great power when we can speak the Gospel in their vernacular.

LEAD

Youth crave significant adult relationships. They want you to relate to them, not be them. Be their friend and not their buddy. Meaning, be the one they call at 2:00 a.m. because they're drunk and need a ride home from a party—but don't be at the party with them! You have the opportunity to be a real, genuine, loving role model and adult in their lives. You are not trying to replace anyone, but simply be a friend for them.

As you think about leading youth, think about which of the following metaphors you connect with. When you are in your twenties, you are more of the big brother/sister figure in their life. When you are in your thirties, you are more of the uncle/aunt figure. The forties bring more of a mother/father-type relationship. In your fifties, you become more of the great aunt/uncle figure, and then in your sixties and beyond, you become more of the grandfather/grandmother figure. You are never too old to do youth ministry! Now you might get too old to do an overnight lock-in—but that's a different story altogether! The problem becomes when you're in your forties and act like you're in your twenties. That's not real and genuine. Fit into the metaphor God blesses you with, and youth will connect with you!

2   Michael Moore, Kathleen R. Glynn, Jim Czarnecki, Charles Bishop, Michael Donovan, Charlton Heston, Brian Danitz, Michael McDonough, Kurt Engfehr, and Jeff Gibbs, *Bowling for Columbine* (United States: MGM Home Entertainment, 2002).

As you lead youth, there are two more important things to understand. Lead them into God's presence, and lead them into a real community. In everything we do, how can we keep the great commandment in the forefront? How can we show them how to love the Lord and love their neighbor?

By the way, all of the events and programmatic pieces of ministry will fall into place as we love, listen, speak their language, and lead. When we get this foundation, we will know what retreats, mission trips, Bible studies, games, and so forth will truly connect with our youth. Thanks for loving youth!

So That's Why I Keep Doing This! Stories in Youth Ministry

Brian was a sophomore in high school, a natural leader who loved to be goofy. One of those too-smart-for-his-own-good kind of kids. During a youth gathering, in front of a hundred other youth, he thought it would be funny to poop on the beach, set it on fire, and then dance around it. I did not witness this, but as you can imagine, I heard about it. When I confronted him, he acknowledged it, and instead of sending him home, I decided that he would not leave my side for the rest of the weekend.

When we got back to church, I called a family intervention with his parents. I tried to communicate grace, love, leadership potential, and forgiveness, and I failed miserably. What Brian heard was judgment. I didn't see him for the next year.

Thank God that He was still at work in Brian. During his junior year, he started getting involved in our mission work to the Apache. He kept going and going and you could see God transforming his thoughts, words, and deeds. Brian was growing up and leading!

A few months before graduation, I had to call another major family intervention with Brian and his parents. This time was because Brian wanted to move to Africa to be a missionary, and his parents didn't want him to leave the States. After an hour or so of tears and frustration, I called time-out. I reminded them that we should look back on how far we'd come in two years. Brian—the guy who once pooped on the beach—now wants to serve Jesus as a missionary. Let's stop for a moment and rejoice in the transformation Jesus brings!

So they compromised. Brian went to Cyprus, an island in the Mediterranean, for a year. He had an incredible experience and then went back to school and now is a middle school youth minister. (Because when you poop on the beach, that is what you become.) You never know how God is going to work in the lives of His youth!

The next story started on a mission trip to Inglewood, California (think next to Compton). Our youth group spent three days living like the homeless and served a local church with upkeep of their facilities. There were no showers and we got very dirty and sweaty, so as you can imagine the room in which we stayed smelled absolutely aromatic.

During the last few hours of the weekend trip, a teenager named John and I were jumping up and down in a dumpster manually compacting the trash so we could get even more garbage in there. With dirt all over his face, sweat flowing down his cheeks, and a big smile across his face, John looks at me and says, "Don't you get the feeling that if we quit everything else and did only this that we could change the world?"

I love it! God has big dreams for our youth! God is going to use them to change the world! What an honor to be a part of their journey for a season.

When my oldest daughter Maile was seven, her Sunday School teacher taught on original sin. The teacher kept saying to the students over and over again, "You're not perfect." After half a dozen times of hearing this, Maile raised her hand. Somewhat surprised that anyone would have a question or comment at this point of the lesson, the teacher called on her and Maile said, "I'm not perfect, but I'm awesome!"

I love this! Now I fully recognize that it's not doctrinally correct. I wish she would have said, "I'm not perfect—but thanks to Jesus, I'm awesome!" But she was seven. She'll learn.

Youth ministry allows us to see Law and Gospel on a daily basis. Middle and high schoolers are going to make mistakes. In fact, they will make lots and lots of mistakes. I did, too, and I'm guessing so did you! But by God's grace, we get to teach them that even though they are not perfect, God still loves them and sent Jesus to not only forgive all of our sins by His life, death, and resurrection, but also to give us the promise of everlasting life. That's pretty awesome! And that makes them awesome! And that makes you awesome! Thanks for loving youth!

QUESTIONS AND PROCESSING

- Why do you keep doing this?
- What are you going to do this year to grow in your ministry skills?
- Research local youth worker groups in your community. Who in your community can you look to for support in working with youth?
- Who else can you involve in the ministry? How? Why?
- How can you show love to the youth in your congregation/community?
- How can you listen to the youth in your congregation/community?
- How can you learn the language of youth in your congregation/community?
- How can you lead the youth in your congregation/community?
- Youth ministry is not just working with youth—it's also being their advocate for the Church at large. How can you be an advocate for youth in your church? community?
- Thank you for doing what you do. Whom do you need to thank?

RESOURCES

Moore, Michael, Kathleen R. Glynn, Jim Czarnecki, Charles Bishop, Michael Donovan, Charlton Heston, Brian Danitz, Michael McDonough, Kurt Engfehr, and Jeff Gibbs. *Bowling for Columbine*. United States: MGM Home Entertainment, 2002.

Powell, Kara, Jake Mulder, and Brad Griffin, *Growing Young: Six Essential Strategies to Help Young People Discover and Love Your Church*. Grand Rapids: Baker Books, 2016.

Youmans, Jacob. *Missional Too: The Trip of a Lifetime*. Anaheim Hills: Tri-Pillar Publishing, 2013.

Youmans, Jacob. *Talking Pictures: How to Turn a Trip to the Movies into a Mission Trip*. Anaheim Hills: Tri-Pillar Publishing, 2010.

Youmans, Jacob. *Youth Ministry 101*. Anaheim Hills: Tri-Pillar Publishing, 2017.

YOUTH MINISTRY 101

It's not always easy to connect the objective you have for learning and growth with the educational tools that will get you there. It can be tough to even know where and how to get started! Now that you have a solid foundation and a network of support, it's time to engage with some basic youth ministry practices to move forward with your youth ministry. From selecting curriculum to equipping adolescent witnesses in the world, this section prepares you for some essential learning for all who work with youth.

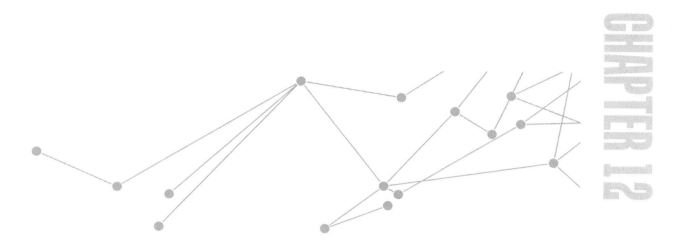

CHAPTER 12

TEACHING THE FAITH TO YOUNG PEOPLE

BY BRANDON METCALF

PART 1: WHY DO WE TEACH?

If you were to go to a typical youth group and ask each young person why they are a part of the group, you'd likely get a variety of answers depending on how the youth ministry is structured. When a youth says, "I love the music there," hopefully it's because he's connecting with the theology of the songs and not just the tunes or melodies. For a youth who answers, "I just want to hang out with my friends," it could mean that she's developed strong Christian friendships as a part of the group, or it could be your group is simply a social gathering and nothing more. If a young person answers, "I love that I can be accepted for who I am," either you're doing a great job of building an environment of support and encouragement, or as Christian comedian Tim Hawkins would say, "You're at a bar!"

While hopefully you're not doing youth ministry at a bar, sometimes young people do want to find a place "where everybody knows their name." There is absolutely something to be said about building an environment where young people can feel safe, build strong friendships, be challenged and encouraged, and enjoy fellowship. But my prayer for you is that ultimately your youth ministry will be defined by something greater. Young people are drawn to a church ministry by different factors: friends, food, silly games (typically involving food), interaction with caring adults, competitive sports games, music, or being locked in a church overnight. (I will never understand why youth who won't normally step foot in a church show up when you tell them they will be locked in all night, but God works in mysterious ways.) All of these are reasons to attract youth to a group and are great ways to connect with nonbelievers, but ultimately none of them will keep them there. These factors could perhaps keep young people connected until they graduate but will definitely not keep them in church as young adults because "regular church" often looks so different from what they grew used to.

Many churches focus mainly on having a fun place for young people to hang out, but they miss out on giving these teens something more than that. Youth can always find somewhere to hang out, so what makes us different? Gordon MacDonald summarizes this idea nicely when he tells us that just about anyone can build houses, feed the hungry, or treat the sick. But unlike the world, the Church can offer grace.[1] At what point in your ministry do you get to the core of the Church, which is grace? Certainly we can share grace with one another in the midst of our ongoing relationships. In fact, Luther called this the mutual conversation and consolation of the saints[2] and identifies it as a Means of Grace. But the primary way in which grace is heard, read, and applied is in the teaching of the faith to young people.

So why do we teach? The simplest answer to this question is that teaching is what we do as Christ's Church. We are commanded by Christ to do so:

> **And Jesus came and said to them, "All authority in heaven and on earth has been given to Me. Go therefore and make disciples of all nations, baptizing them in the name of the Father and of the Son and of the Holy Spirit, teaching them to observe all that I have commanded you. And behold, I am with you always, to the end of the age." (Matthew 28:18–20)**

To put it plainly, we make disciples by baptizing and teaching; therefore, teaching is one of the primary jobs of the Church, and by extension, the youth ministry. Disciples of Christ is the "who we are" of youth ministry, which means that teaching the faith is the "what we do" aspect. Teaching the faith is the primary thing that separates us from all the other choices that youth have with which to fill their time.

PART 2: WHAT DO WE TEACH?

Knowing that we have to teach the faith is fairly obvious and hopefully self-evident. Knowing *what* to teach is a somewhat different story. Most churches have a plan or idea of what to teach children (i.e., whatever is outlined in the Sunday School curriculum they use), but the planning oftentimes stops there. Very few churches have an intentional plan for education from youth all the way up through adults. We typically offer a variety of Bible studies, and some people show up to them, so we assume we're doing our job. Technically, yes, we are doing our job and bravo to these churches for doing something! But we could be doing our job so much better! I firmly believe that having a plan for what you teach is one of the easiest and most beneficial tasks that you can do in youth ministry, or any congregational educational ministry, for that matter.

As we look at Scripture, God's instructions to the young nation of Israel in Deuteronomy give us a great model of the foundations of Christian Education:

---

1   Philip Yancey, *What's So Amazing about Grace?* (Grand Rapids: Zondervan, 1997), 15.
2   Robert Kolb and Timothy J. Wengert, *The Book of Concord* (Minneapolis: Fortress Press, 2000), 319.

Hear, O Israel: The LORD our God, the LORD is one. You shall love the LORD your God with all your heart and with all your soul and with all your might. And these words that I command you today shall be on your heart. You shall teach them diligently to your children, and shall talk of them when you sit in your house, and when you walk by the way, and when you lie down, and when you rise. You shall bind them as a sign on your hand, and they shall be as frontlets between your eyes. You shall write them on the doorposts of your house and on your gates. (Deuteronomy 6:4–9)

From this passage, we get two key ideas as to what we are to teach: who God is (v. 4) and what He wants for us (vv. 5–9). We also see that parents are given a primary responsibility in the teaching of the faith (v. 7), as well as the fact that teaching is an ongoing "on the go" concept and not just for designated Bible study sessions (vv. 7–9). The more the Church can help parents, the better. We as the Church can provide ways for families to have faith conversations "near, far, wherever you are" (what I call "the Titanic rule," which we'll talk more about later in this chapter) so they're not dependent on their children getting spiritual content only while they're physically at church.

In terms of content, the main three categories and questions I see in Scripture are these: Who is God? Who am I? And how is God calling me to live? Not only can any Bible study topic or idea go into these categories, but any Bible passage can be discussed using these three areas. Take any given passage and, after reading it, ask these three questions:

1. What does this passage say about who God is?

2. What does it say about who I am?

3. What does it say about how I am to live as a result of who God is and who I am?

That is an instant Bible study right there and is a great introductory way to teach youth how to read and study the Word on their own.

The other reason that I highlight these categories—which are certainly not the only way to discern the message of Scripture; we'll talk about another way (Law/Gospel) later on—is to highlight the concept of balance in planning a curriculum. If you're working on a twelve-month curriculum and you're studying how we respond to various current issues for nine of those months, you could be out of balance.

If all we talk about is life application without learning the reason for the changed life—who God is and what He has done for us in Jesus Christ—then we're just teaching behavior modification, which is not the same as sanctification. On the other hand, if we only talk about the character of God and never get to how we live as a response, we miss out on the Ten Commandments and how God wants us to live, which is so important to Him. The key is to not only find balance overall in a curriculum plan, but also in each individual lesson or unit.

THE GUIDING QUESTION FOR TEACHING CONTENT

To get at the heart of this issue, I want to share a question that changed my way of viewing youth ministry: *How is a senior different from a seventh grader and what are we going to do to get them there?* I want our youth to grow and change over their years in our youth ministry, not just show up and over the years get taller, have more hair, and be able to drive themselves places (one of the reasons why I recommend parking far away from the main church entrance). If your ministry team can answer this question and then develop a plan based on that answer, you will take a huge step toward building an intentional lifelong disciple-making machine of a youth ministry instead of just being a "hangout" spot for a few years before they potentially leave the faith in college—which is the unfortunate state of so many well-meaning groups.

To give you an example of what this can look like, I'll share the journey that this question has taken me on. As I wrestled with the idea of what I want to see different in a senior, it led me to try to better define the areas of living life as a disciple of Christ. In an effort to avoid getting too lost in the details, I summarized the life of a disciple in seven key areas (personal spiritual growth, congregational life, Christ-centered relationships, prayer, studying the Word, worship life, and service). For each of these areas, the next step was to set a couple of specific goals for each group. The hardest part for me is that most of the goals I had been setting were attendance or outcome-based goals like "have ten kids in the program" or "get confirmed," which do not help measure where a youth is at in his discipleship walk. The new aim was to set "discipleship-based goals" like "take personal ownership of your faith" that go back to either learning more about what it means to be a disciple of Christ or finding ways to live that life out in service to the Church and world. Once I had the goals set, the last step was to address the ways that we seek to meet those goals as a church and through which programs, resources, or opportunities. I filled in any blanks with additional ways that our congregation could meet these goals in the future.

Asking the question, "How is a senior different from a seventh grader and what are we going to do to get them there?" not only helps us focus the educational aspect of our youth ministry, but helps us to make sure every program we offer has a purpose and fits into our goal of making disciples. The end result even morphed into a cradle-to-grave discipleship guide for our whole congregational programming. The reason I mention that is to remind you that in some form or another, you have to make sure you look at how the youth ministry fits into the larger picture of the congregation too. Here is a sample of two categories—personal spiritual growth and service—for our youth ministry:

MIDDLE SCHOOL (6TH–8TH GRADE)

Personal Spiritual Growth

- Take public ownership of their faith
- Confirmation
- Be able to better articulate what they believe
- Youth group, Sunday Bible class

Service

- Find an area of regular service inside the congregation
- Acolyte, usher, VBS, and the like
- Participate in church-sponsored service events
- Youth group or confirmation servant projects

FRESHMAN/SOPHOMORE

Personal Spiritual Growth

- Build a foundation on their identity in Christ
- Youth group
- Have faith-reinforcing "mountain-top" experiences
- National Youth Gathering, mission trips, youth retreats

Service

- Actively serve with fellow church members
- Church service events, various on-going service opportunities
- Find opportunities to serve outside of church-sponsored events

- Various school, community, and neighborhood opportunities
- Engage in service outside of our own community
- Mission trips/servant events

JUNIOR/SENIOR

Personal Spiritual Growth

- Be able to articulate "the Lutheran difference"
- Youth group
- Have biblical opinions on important social issues
- Youth leadership team
- Prepared to enter "Grade Thirteen"

Service

- Gain experience organizing service projects
- Deeper involvement on youth leadership team
- Transition toward more relational service opportunities
- Youth servant events

I hope the above example helps you think about the overall design and flow in your youth ministry. Having a guide like this not only helps you be intentional about your ministry, but it also helps you evaluate how you're doing along the way. You can certainly make it more or less detailed than you see it here, but it comes back to the key question, *How is a senior different from a seventh grader and what are we going to do to get them there?* As you go through this process, also keep one more question in the back of your mind: "What about the thirteenth grade?" The focus of this question is when they leave our youth ministry. What have we prepared them for? Are they ready to live out their faith in college or in the workplace? Do they want to be an active member of a congregation on their own, outside of the youth ministry? Having a discipleship focus enables you to build a ministry that prepares youth for life after high school.

As you plan topics or key ideas to cover over the course of a year or a student's time in your youth ministry, remember that we learn through repetition and themes. Don't be afraid to repeat a topic from year to year, though I would recommend changing the lesson a bit each time you use it. Our youth group, for example, hits the topic of dating and relationships for six to eight weeks each year. Each year the theme is different but a lot of the content is similar. One of the positive effects of this pattern is that by a student's senior year—the fourth time around with these same scriptural themes—some of the content finally starts to set in. Perhaps a familiar illustration hits students in a new way because of the new situations they've experienced. I had one of my seniors stop a group discussion recently and tell the younger members of the group to pay special attention to what we were talking about, because she wished she would have done so when she was their age. I'd rather a student learn and internalize six concepts over the course of their years in our youth ministry than learn facts about twenty different things but internalize very little.

Another way to connect across the span of your curriculum or different topics is to have a theme that runs through everything you do. Some youth groups have a yearly theme that they focus on, and each topic studied during the year goes back to that theme somehow. Others have a group name referenced frequently. (I've seen lots of names involving fire like Ablaze, Hearts on Fire, or Fan the Flame because we apparently either really like Pentecost or are pyromaniacs at heart.) For our group, I connect each series or topic to an overall theme, which is "Identity in Christ," and a phrase repeated regularly, "You are worth dying for." For example, we approach the topic of dating by talking about how your identity in Christ informs who you should be looking for, and the phrase "you're worth dying for" is at the core of talking about your infinite value and how you should be treated in a relationship. At the end of the day, these are the key understandings I want our youth to have as a part of their DNA when they graduate and are no longer a youth group participant. I encourage you to think about the burden on your heart that you want your youth to remember above all else and focus what you do around that core idea.

There is so much more that can be said about this topic that can't be covered in this brief chapter. I would encourage you to continue these conversations in your congregation and to seek out a DCE (Director of Christian Education) in your area if you don't have one at your church, because this will be one of their areas of expertise.

HOW TO CHOOSE AND EVALUATE CURRICULUM

Some youth workers (including myself) choose to write and create curriculum themselves the majority of the time so that it fits their teaching style and learning environment. Many others rely on getting curriculum from another source and adapting it to fit their circumstances, saving time on the lesson preparation that can be used in the numerous other jobs a volunteer or youth worker has (like finding their desks among mounds of paper, unread books, bulletins, and glitter that has been stuck there for the last eight years). Finally, there are a select few who don't use any sort of curriculum and decide to "see what happens" when they get there. Those people likely aren't reading this or any book (chances are it's buried among all the stuff on their desk), but if you are . . . please change categories! Have some kind of a plan!

Regardless of which camp you fall into, consider the following questions to help you evaluate any resource or curriculum, whether you're teaching from it or using it as a take-home or family resource. Use these to evaluate and improve your own curriculum or to help you determine whether a particular resource is worth using.

QUESTIONS TO ASK ABOUT ANY RESOURCE:

- **Does it focus on Jesus?** If the focus of the curriculum is all on me and how I can improve myself in my own power, take a look at where you are. You may have wandered into the self-help section (or the questionable parts of the "Christian Inspiration" section) and will need to redirect yourself back to a more sound location or a different website (for those of you who haven't been in a bookstore in ten years or more).

- **Does it challenge me? Does it make me too comfortable?** A good resource shouldn't just pat you on the back for being exactly where you're supposed to be. God's Law should mess with your pride and convict you of your sin while also encouraging you to live more like Christ. It's so easy to be basic and generic with youth out of fear of overwhelming them, but they grow so much more when they are challenged. Find or create resources that make them think and wrestle with God's truth. A book that has a slightly different worldview may actually help some of your older youth learn more because your discussion could focus on why you believe what you believe instead of just taking everything in the book as truth. The only infallible book is the Bible. Don't be afraid to wrestle with other belief systems as a tool to reinforce your teaching of the true faith as revealed in Scripture.

- **Where does this resource tell me my confidence should be?** Again, if the resource points your trust, hope, and confidence to anything other than the God revealed in Scripture, you may need to check the title. If it's called *Idiot's Guide to Creating Your Own God*, then it's actually pretty accurate, but still should be avoided as well as anything with this same theme under a different, more sensible title. We're good enough at making our own gods already; we don't need a book to encourage us toward sin.

- **Could I replace the word "Jesus" with something else and have it still make sense?** This is especially helpful with music. If a "Christian" song can change out "Christ" for "Sharon, James, or tacos" and still mostly make sense, you may need to find something that conveys deeper Christian truths.

- **Which version(s) of the Bible is being used?** The big concern here is that if a book uses twelve different versions of the Bible, then the author is probably proof-texting frequently and trying to find the wording that fits the point he or she is trying to make rather than letting Scripture speak for itself. As a rule of thumb, if a curriculum references the book of Second Opinions, it's probably using a translation of the Bible that's not credible.

- **Will it hold the hearer's attention? Is it understandable?** If something is doctrinally vapid or incorrect, then we don't really need to get to this point, but once I know something is credible, I need to ask if it is beneficial. Will anyone be awake to learn from it? Is the material engaging? Is the vocabulary too advanced for use in a junior high class but might work great for a senior high small group? Can I give this to an adult leader and expect him to figure it out or do you have to be trained at the seminary to know what's going on?

- **Are the issues too big to ignore, or can I still get some benefit out of this?** Ultimately, this is what all the other questions lead to. Can I adapt this and still get good use out of it or are there too many problems that I can't work around? Do I need to just use part of this and combine it with something else, or will it take so much time to make it work for our group that it's better left alone?

PART 3: HOW DO WE TEACH?

Now that we've dealt with the ideas of why we teach and what we teach, we can get into the practical specifics of how to teach the faith to young people. We'll start with some overall ideas focused on Law and Gospel and then hit on a couple specific topics such as teaching methods, classroom management, and getting feedback. By the way, what I just did was provide a road map for the upcoming information, which is a great tool to use when teaching the faith. Share at the beginning what's going to be learned, how things will wrap up, and where any transitions are (we're going to ask a few questions, then watch a video, and close with an activity involving duct tape, a rubber chicken, and Ping-Pong balls).

LAW AND GOSPEL

One of the first concepts we have to at least introduce when discussing how to teach the faith is the Law and Gospel throughout Scripture. This is one of the best ways to view, teach, and discuss the Word and one of the hallmarks of Lutheranism. In basic terms, the Law is what we do (and fail to do) and the Gospel is what God does for us. The Law shows us our sin, the Gospel shows us our Savior. The Law functions as a curb (keeps us on the right path), mirror (reveals our sins), and guide (shows us how God wants us to live). The key in teaching the faith is to not only teach how to identify Law and Gospel in the Scriptures, but to balance our lessons and teaching in light of it.

The Book of Ephesians serves as a guide for us in this area. Paul starts out the letter and hammers home all that God has done for us (chs. 1–3) and in the midst of that he lays out that we are sinners in need of God's grace (2:1–3, 12) and then finishes out the letter (chs. 4–6) talking about what it looks like to be God's people and live in light of what He has done for us.

Just like Paul's letter, our lessons should consist of the Law (wrestling with our sin and how we fall short of God's standards), the Gospel (what God has done to reconnect us to Himself), and back to the Law (how we should live in response to God's grace). We can't skip straight to the application, but we don't want to neglect that either. The more we can show how Scripture, both Law and Gospel, is relevant to their lives, the more youth will grow in their love for the Word and for the Lord.

TEACHING METHODS

So you have a group of youth in front of you, now what? Thankfully, you have a couple different options! We'll go through each of them briefly and give a few tips along the way, including some ideas on how to help youth stay engaged in the learning.

Lecture

The classic, for sure—also the source of so many naps. Lecture gets a pretty bad reputation, but this style has stuck around for so long because on some level, it does work. When done well, lecture can even be inspiring. But it does take focus to stay engaged as a learner, especially if the speaker is not very skilled. That is why I think it's better to have a ten- to fifteen-minute, focused talk versus a thirty-minute lesson that hits on a bunch of different topics. Pick one key idea and use that in the lecture format, using a key story to bring it to life, while saving the other points for a group discussion afterward. If you can't summarize your talk in one sentence, chances are you're trying to do too many things at once. The more focused you are, the better youth are going to learn. A format that works for me is starting with a story or illustration, connecting that to a problem we all face, going to God's Word to find how He is uniquely the solution to the problem, and then explaining what it looks like for us to live that out with a few application points.

Standing up and talking in front of a group of people is not a skill set a lot of people have right off the bat, even those who work in a church, so make sure if you're going to do this regularly that you work at it. Work on crafting your message not only so it remains focused, but so you have it practically or altogether memorized. This enables you to maintain eye contact with your youth (just don't stare down any one person unnecessarily, that's weird) and enhances the whole experience. Also, keep an eye (yes, that was an intentional segue) on how your tone and your message connect. For example, if you are sharing good news in your content, your tone should be excited. I often see this mishandled when we announce the forgiveness of sins, but out of reverence perhaps, we share it quietly and monotonously. I want to shout out, "You're sharing the greatest news this world has ever heard, that God forgave all of your sins, and you're making it sound as exciting as the stock market changes! Come on!!!" If our tone matches our content, it enhances the message. When a speaker passionately and emphatically shares the Good News of Christ with an audience, even if people don't remember everything that was said, they'll likely say, "Wow, that person really was on fire for the Good News!" Isn't that what you want your youth saying about you? Can I get an amen? (Bonus points if you read that "amen" with more than two syllables.)

One of the best ways to check in on all of this is to get feedback. Utilize technology and either video or audio record yourself so you can gain valuable feedback and work to improve continually. By doing that, you can spot a lot of poor habits that you've developed like filler words, distracting hand motions, awkward transitions, out-of-place pacing (don't use your message time to get your step count up for the day), or speaking either too slowly or quickly. You may be able to pick up on a lot of that on your own, but I'd highly recommend having another adult that is well-versed in public speaking help you too. When I was in high school, I participated in our school's Mock Trial team. After giving what I thought was a dynamite closing argument, my coach got up and said, "Brandon, you're a rock star!" I was like, "Yeah, I know," with some of that teenage arrogance that we all know and love, when my coach cut me off and said, "No, I mean you rocked back and forth the whole time you were giving the closing argument. It was distracting. Stop it." I was rocking without even realizing it, and I never would have noticed if she hadn't pointed it out to me. The same is true with speaking in church. Don't be afraid to have someone critically watch you either in person or on video to help you improve.

Helping Youth Stay Engaged during Lectures

- **Use stories and humor that enhance your message.** Sharing a story is one of the best ways to keep someone engaged during a lecture, as long as the story isn't too long and it fits with the point of the message. Don't share stories for the sake of telling a great story, but use stories to teach about who we are, who God is, or what it looks like to live that out. In that same vein, humor is a great tool for keeping youth listening, but make sure that it is related to whatever you're currently saying and not just a funny one-liner that comes out of the blue.

- **Use illustrations that your youth can relate to.** If you're talking to a bunch of middle schoolers, examples of losing a job or the stresses of college are not going to hit home with them nearly as much as those would with a group of upperclassmen. Similarly, make sure any cultural references that you make are actually known by your audience. Not long ago, I made a reference to Mr. Rogers to make a point about loving your neighbor, and only one of the youth had any clue who he was. Let's just say it was not a beautiful day in the neighborhood for that example, because I had no clue I would be showing some age with that one. The point is that the more you can connect the Word to what they experience in their lives and see in the world around them, the more they're going to perk up and listen to what you have to say.

- **Your setting makes a huge difference.** This is a lesson I learned in the past year, and it has helped me out tremendously. For a few years, I had done the lecture-style message for our youth group in our youth room at the end of our discussion time. The problem was, this room is not conducive for sitting and listening for a long period of time, so it was harder to keep the youth engaged. When I switched that worship time to the sanctuary, there was a dramatic change in how many youth I could see were actively listening and involved. The acoustics in the sanctuary worked better, there was a change in location from the discussion so they were ready for a new style of learning, and sitting in a pew versus a couch really helps lessen the side conversations. Find a space that matches the style of your learning at the time.

- **Give each youth an outline or a place for notes.** Printing a handout that goes through the Bible study or message is such an easy avenue toward increasing engagement. Not only does it give youth a place to visually follow along, it also opens up the door to taking notes (gasp!). For some youth, even just having something to doodle on helps them pay attention. Educationally, if you can hear information, see it, and then tactilely write it down, you're going to remember it better than just listening to it. Plus, then there's the possibility of students taking it home and reading it again that night, or many years down the road when they're going through old papers. God can work through that too.

Large Group Discussion

This is where you gather the whole group in a big circle (which coincidentally is the hardest shape for any group of young people to make) and you go through either a list of questions about the topic or you start with a topic and ask the next questions based on where the discussion is going (the "tangent" method isn't as bad as it sounds, really, which reminds me . . . did you hear about the time that . . . okay wait, maybe you need some control in order to succeed this way). A key advantage to this way of teaching is that now you have the opportunity for some interaction with the youth. They can offer answers and ask questions, which helps them learn better than them hearing you tell them all the answers. This implies that you're not just asking questions and then answering them yourself after no one answers two seconds later. On that note, shoot for ten seconds of wait time after you ask a question before you rephrase it (note, I said "rephrase" not "answer yourself and comment on how quiet they are being today"). If you pull out a timer on your phone and time how long ten seconds actually is versus what you think it is in the moment, you'll be shocked at how quickly you normally jump in that silence. Give your youth time to think, which especially gives your introverts time to formulate their answer and then build up the courage to speak. Speaking as a proud internal processor, it's much appreciated.

I've found that having the discussion time after the message, lecture, or video is the best place to put it. It gives everyone a chance to process out loud about the video or teaching and share what stood out to them and what they learned. If you're the one who spoke in the message or video, this is a golden opportunity for feedback without coming out and asking for feedback. If you ask what they learned and the youth say "nothing," the discussion is your chance to redeem this learning experience and maybe explain in a different way what you apparently didn't get across earlier. This is also the prime time for specific application to each youth's life. The discussion is their opportunity to see how God's Word directly impacts their life, so push for specific versus generic application. You also have the ability to have a more interactive learning experience, so explore object lessons, come up with skits acting out biblical accounts, discuss case studies, and ask for real-life examples from your youth.

Helping Youth Stay Engaged in Large Group Discussion

- **Don't lecture in a group discussion.** Especially if you cut some talking points out of your message and saved them for the discussion, it's so easy to go off on long stories or tangents in a group discussion. Nothing kills the discussion more than listening to one person (normally the leader) go on for five minutes or more and then close it with "Does anyone have any questions?" Actually, yes, their question is, "Are you done yet?" I may or may not be speaking from previous experience here. Keep any points you make short and to the point, remembering that in a discussion, a youth is far more likely to remember a good idea that he offered to the group (and got praised for) than a great idea that you told him yourself. When in doubt, ask questions way more than you offer answers.

- **Avoid sharing the "I feels" in a Bible study.** This is one of the downfalls of many Bible studies. It happens when the group reads a Bible passage and the follow-up question is "What do you feel like this verse is saying?" Someone inevitably responds with, "I feel the passage is saying . . ." and oftentimes continues on with some form of hideous heresy or rambling nonsense. Here's the proper response to the "I feels" about Scripture: "Someone's feelings are about to get hurt, because I feel you're twisting God's Word and that makes me feel angry! You wouldn't like me when I'm angry." Hulk references and pseudo-threatening language aside, teach your group how to actually read Scripture in context rather than just sharing uneducated guesses about various topics. The honest truth is that I don't care what you *feel* Scripture is saying. What I care about is what it actually *says*.

- **Summarize the message using social media.** Have group members come up with a caption or tweet that summarizes either the message or Bible study for the night. This is a great way to not only grow the community platform of your youth ministry, but to help solidify the key learnings of the teaching. If youth know going into the lesson that at the end of the discussion, they're supposed to have a key point to post on social media, they're more likely to be looking for those points during the lesson, and thus are more engaged in the discussion. If you're going to allow technology to be a part of the group dynamics, then find ways to help it enhance the learning experience rather than detract from it.

- **Have a handout!** Just like during a lecture, having a handout for a discussion can be very handy (pun intended). The printout gives a direction for the discussion, provides a place to take notes, and allows another leader to take the lead on the discussion. And yes, you can ask a question even if it's not on the handout, but it's like reading words not on the teleprompter, so don't get too crazy. It also helps avoid some of the one million "what verse are we on" questions you'll get each year. Notice I said some, not all, because even if the verses and questions are printed very clearly on the handout, you'll still have people who are clueless. Jesus died for them too.

Small Groups

A great chance to get more people involved in a discussion is to split into smaller groups. There are a number of different ways to format these groups, like breaking your group in half at youth group, having everyone assigned to a small group with designated leaders, having these groups meet outside of your Bible study, having youth or adult group leaders, and the options go on and on. Regardless of how you structure them, small group discussions allow the opportunity for greater involvement across the group and provide an environment where shy youth can put forward their thoughts and ideas more easily. It also is a chance to train youth workers or adult volunteers to help out with the group. Some powerful relationships can be born from these interactions.

Helping Youth Stay Engaged in Small Groups

- **Have leaders exercise the "one-third rule."** The one-third rule states that a small group leader should aim to talk less than one-third of the time in the small group. Note, the one-third rule is that the amount of time a leader is talking should be about one-third, not one out of every three comments. Otherwise, two youth make a short contribution and the leader talks for five minutes. That squelches the conversation, and we want the opposite effect. Effective small group leaders invite group members into the conversation, ask questions, and offer a listening ear.

- **Utilize case studies.** Whether via video, testimony, or a printed story, case studies are great for small groups to apply biblical truths to their lives. Have each small group member think of what they would do in a certain scenario, how they could share God's love with a specific person, or what they could say in a tough moment. Group members will learn from one another concerning how they can live out their faith and maybe even develop action plans for how to impact their school or community together.

- **What about having a handout?** What a great idea! Wait a second, I think I've heard this before. Is there a theme going on here? Yes! Theme repetition is the mother of all learning—having a Bible study printout is a great idea! In the small group setting, this helps ensure that each group is talking about the same topic and questions, at least in theory.

- **Experiential learning:** You can create experiential learning experiences in any of the above formats, and I hope you take the opportunity to do so. Getting youth to *do* rather than just listen is important. This type of learning lends itself very well to off-site events such as servant projects, retreats, leadership training, and mission trips. These events can be "mountaintop" experiences resulting in lifelong memories tied to Scripture lessons and enhancing everything else you're doing in youth ministry. You could take a devotion given in your normal youth setting and replicate it word for word, same speaker and everything, except read it outside around a campfire, and it will be more memorable almost every time. This same idea is why youth seem to learn more on a mission trip or youth gathering, because it's an overall experience, not just a lesson. Find ways to enhance your program not only with small experiential learning opportunities in your youth gatherings, but also have those other events to help reinforce and internalize what you've been teaching.

A Note on Classroom Management

There are volumes of literature devoted to classroom management techniques like maintaining eye contact and close proximity with those causing the disruption, having frank and honest conversations with youth afterward regarding behavior issues, and having multiple leaders there to help youth stay engaged. I would encourage you to read more from those sources and continue to grow in this area, but I will share the one technique that has helped me with managing behavior in a youth ministry setting.

Our group had been having some issues with a number of younger members causing a distraction for the rest of the group. I tried various methods and was seeing little long-term impact other than increasing frustration from other youth and even parents. What I decided to do was create a written set of expectations for the group, but instead of making it into a list of rules or calling it a contract, the document was our "identity statement" as a youth ministry. The statement focused on who we are as a youth group, what we're all about, and as a result, here's what we do and how we act. Not only did this spell out the behaviors we wanted, but it was laid out in such a way that it created a sense of group ownership; this is who we are!

If youth were not ready for a faith-driven experience like this, I was happy to direct them to another area of ministry more suited to their level in the hopes that given some greater maturity over time, they would be ready to handle the youth group again later. Most of our major behavior issues stopped in the subsequent weeks because the group was refocused around the ideas of "this is who we are and what we do." I would strongly encourage anyone working with youth to do this way sooner than I did and reference it often as a group. Have the youth be a part of the creation of the identity statement; with strong ownership of the group comes a decrease in behavioral issues overall. The thinking changes from "I'm just here to hang out with my friend and I don't really have to pay attention" to "I don't want to ruin the learning and growth experience of the rest of the group, because this is my group and that's what we're about."

Connecting with Youth When They Aren't There

How can I teach the faith to a young person when they're not at church? This is a tough question, but one with an increasing number of decent answers. If you follow what I call "the Titanic rule," then you will have a way to reach your youth with your teaching even when they're not at a particular event or program, as well as give those who were there additional ways to engage with the information. The Titanic rule is derived from the famous Celine Dion song from that movie, specifically the line "near, far, wherever you are." (One bonus point if you sang along to that last sentence, five points if you sang it out loud, and ten points if "near" and "far" got you thinking of the classic lesson Grover taught about those words on Sesame Street.) The point of the rule is that each of our lessons should engage youth near, far, and wherever they are. Here's what that looks like:

- **Near:** This is the part of the lesson that takes place at the actual church event or small group, which we have spent the majority of this chapter discussing. Remember, we learn differently, so differentiating your instruction between large group and small group, involving various senses, and engaging the three domains of learning (cognitive, affective, and psycho-motor) are so important in helping all members of the group learn. Give each individual, regardless of their learning style, multiple chances to wrestle with the material.

- **Far:** Here is where we focus on the lesson interacting with youth when they are at home, whether they attended the gathering or not. Technology is a huge benefit in this area. Posting recap pictures or status updates on social media (or having the youth do so on their personal profiles), putting a video of the teaching message onto Facebook, creating an audio podcast of the information, and putting your youth handouts on your church website are all ways to help get the information from the learning experience into the home. The next step is to create ways to engage further with the teaching, like having follow-up discussion questions for use in the home, facilitating a Bible class for parents that teaches ways to create disciples in their own home, or having a prayer prompt or journal idea for youth to try out that week. The more you can get families talking about their faith in their home, the better!

- **Wherever You Are:** This is the application in the everyday life of your youth. This is where your application points in the discussion or message are reiterated and ultimately lived out. Maybe a few days later you send out a reminder via social media or text message to reinforce that week's main theme. Take time to invest in building skills in your youth (like how to read the Bible, pray, and grow in various spiritual disciplines) so they can continue to grow throughout the week. Have youth share stories each week about how they were reminded of the lesson over the past few days or how they were able to apply it to their life. Send out a memory verse to your group each week and have a prize for those who have it memorized by the next gathering.

- One idea we used this past year was to take our theme for the year, which was "worth dying for," print it on various colors of silicone bracelets, and then give each youth a few of them to wear themselves or pass out to their friends. These bracelets serve as a constant reminder to them wherever they go of who they are and whose they are. That's what we want to foster in a youth ministry—they live out who they are as believers wherever they go. The more we can encourage and reinforce that, the better!

Getting Feedback (aka How Am I Doing?)

One of my favorite comedy routines is when Tim Hawkins talks about school bumper stickers. He says they need one for people like him: "My kids are homeschooled. We have no idea how they're doing!" I think that's how we oftentimes feel in youth ministry in regard to teaching the faith. I'm telling students something, but I have no idea how I am doing. While there are various ways of getting feedback, I think the easiest way is to have a short evaluation handed out at the end of each youth series or topic (about every four to six weeks). This gives your youth a chance to make their voices heard and offers you a way to see if the main points of what they're learning are what you're hoping they're going to learn, which teaching methods or illustrations resonate best with them, what they're looking for additionally out of the group, and so much more. I recommend handing these out toward the end of a gathering but giving students time to fill them out before they leave, otherwise you won't get them back. Here are a few sample questions or prompts I've used at the end of a series. Pick about three to five for any given evaluation, and change it up for each one:

- What I learned from the series . . .

- What I liked about the series . . .

- What I would've changed . . .

- What are your thoughts on the podcast? Do you use it? How could it be more useful to you?

- What are your thoughts on the youth ministry as a whole this school year (Wednesdays, activities, Bible studies, messages, worship, Sunday mornings, events, communication, and so on)?

- What kind of topics/ideas/formats do you want considered for a future series?

- What's one activity that you'd like for us to do this summer?

- What was your favorite video we watched in this series? Favorite message?

Conclusion

I want to conclude this chapter by going back to the question that we started with, asking youth, "Why are you here?" There are any number of answers you can get at the beginning as to what draws youth to your church and ministry. But over time, hopefully one common theme emerges: I want to grow in my faith, and this is a place where I can do that. Coffee, silly games, friends, and any number of different things may attract young people to your church, but what will keep them there is Christ and Him alone. Teaching the faith is absolutely the cornerstone of youth ministry and it can be tough work, but the end goal is worth it. So we teach the faith in various ways and methods until the day He calls us home to experience eternal life with Him forever. When we get there, I pray that we will see countless youth in heaven who are there because they heard about Christ through our youth ministry and congregations. I also pray we will meet all those who came to know Christ through the witness of those youth as they lived out their life of faith in their various vocations throughout their lives. That's the goal, that's the hope, and now's the work. But know that in the Lord, your labor is not in vain.

Resources

Yancey, Philip. *What's So Amazing about Grace?* Grand Rapids: Zondervan, 1997.

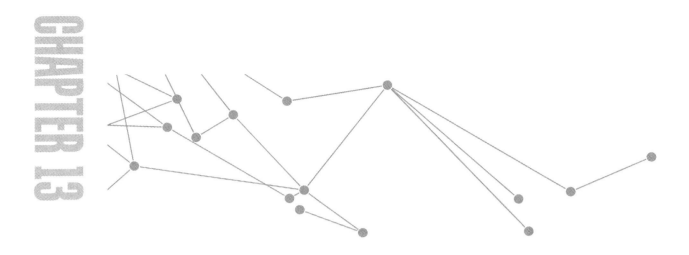

CHAPTER 13

BUILDING COMMUNITY ONE YOUTH AT A TIME

BY MARK COOK

"Trinfam" was the moniker some of my high school youth came up with during one of our events. They decided to slap together the name of our church and the concept of family into a slang term, and it was beautiful. I loved it—the connotation, the sound, the warmth, the fact that the youth came up with it. And they latched onto it on their own. They welcome others as part of the Trinfam. They care for each member of the Trinfam. They reassure one another in times of need by telling one another that the Trinfam cares about them and prays for them. We've all been a part of these moments or had glimpses of true Christian community at some point, and we can echo the psalmist who wrote, "Behold, how good and pleasant it is when brothers dwell in unity!" (Psalm 133:1). It is reminiscent of the Early Church in the Book of Acts, "Now the full number of those who believed were of one heart and soul, and no one said that any of the things that belonged to him was his own, but they had everything in common" (Acts 4:32).

But Christian community does not always work this way. Luke no sooner describes the wonderful Christian community of the Early Church than he explains how sin, death, and the devil attempt to destroy it. Ananias and Sapphira kept for themselves a portion of money from selling their land and only pretended to give all of it to the church. For this, Peter says:

> **Ananias, why has Satan filled your heart to lie to the Holy Spirit and to keep back for yourself part of the proceeds of the land? . . . Why is it that you have contrived this deed in your heart? You have not lied to man but to God. (Acts 5:3–4)**

Both Ananias and Sapphira in turn fell dead after hearing these words from Peter. The very real consequences of sin are present in this world, but so are the very real promises of salvation and communion (community) with all believers.

BARRIERS TO COMMUNITY

To ignore the barriers to Christian community that exist all around us would be to ignore sin altogether. The unfortunate reality is that these barriers exist in the lives of every single one of the youth in your congregation. Sin and Satan do not discriminate as to who gets impacted with these barriers.

The CDC-Kaiser Permanente study on adverse childhood experiences is one of the largest studies on abuse and neglect among children in the United States. Their research looked at the prevalence of abuse and neglect through measuring the following ten items:

- emotional abuse
- physical abuse
- sexual abuse
- emotional neglect
- physical neglect
- mother treated violently
- household substance abuse
- household mental illness
- parental separation or divorce
- incarcerated household member

Of the children studied, nearly two-thirds reported at least one of these ten adverse childhood experience (ACEs), and over one in five reported three or more ACEs. And if that weren't bad enough, the higher the number of ACEs in a child's life, the higher the risk he or she has for a myriad of negative outcomes including alcoholism, depression, drug use, multiple sexual partners, STDs, smoking, suicide attempts, intimate partner violence, and poor academic achievement (to list a few). The effects are very real, and we have an extraordinary amount of our youth who have had a significant event affect their life in a major way.[1]

You may or may not even know which youth have had adverse childhood experiences. Today's adolescents have become very good at putting on facades. They learn to (unsuccessfully) bury emotions and hide feelings. They crumble to pieces on the inside yet post flawless pictures and stories on their social media homepage. In Chap Clark's book *Hurt 2.0: Inside the World of Today's Teenagers*, high schoolers relate the "masks" they wear so everyone else thinks they are living the "perfect" life.[2]

Every one of the youth at your church has something he or she is dealing with in this sinful world. Each one has a wall, a mask, a barrier constructed to hide as he or she seeks

---

1   Centers for Disease Control and Prevention and Kaiser Permanente, "The ACE Study Survey Data [Unpublished Data]" (Atlanta: US Department of Health and Human Services, Centers for Disease Control and Prevention, 2016), accessed March 1, 2018 https://www.cdc.gov/violenceprevention/acestudy/about.html.

2   Chap Clark, *Hurt 2.0: Inside the World of Today's Teenagers* (Grand Rapids: Baker Academic, 2011), 45.

some sort of protection or something to hide behind. Wasn't this the same thing Adam and Eve did after the fall? They tried to cover themselves and hide their shame. The reality of Christian community is that whatever has happened in the lives of our youth, whatever they are scared about, embarrassed about, ashamed about, anxious about—Jesus took that yoke on His shoulders. He forgives that sin and promises new life.

CHRISTIAN COMMUNITY

Dietrich Bonhoeffer tells us that Christian brotherhood is a reality created by God, not some ideal we need to live up to.[3]

It may be easy to think of Christian community as our youth group having a good time together or having good feelings toward those around us. We may even be tempted to think we can create Christian community through laser tag and lock-ins, but the central part of community lies in one of the roots of that word: unity. "Behold, how good and pleasant it is when brothers dwell in unity!" (Psalm 133:1). Jesus Christ alone is the source of our unity and therefore the source of our community. It is that reality that we participate in that makes us a Christian community. It does not come from circumstance, geography, or an ideal, but from our unity in Christ alone as forgiven children of God.[4]

Because of that unity, this is what a Christian community looks like—under a common mission, people worship together, study together, pray together, and serve together.

As Christians, we are all partners in a **common mission**—the Great Commission. We are called to go out into all the world with the Gospel message so people may come to faith, be baptized, and learn to obey everything God has commanded (Matthew 28:19–20). It is fundamental that Christian communities be focused on reaching out to the lost.

A Christian community **worships together**. Paul's instructions to the young pastor Timothy include, "Devote yourself to the public reading of Scripture, to exhortation, to teaching" (1 Timothy 4:13). We receive God's gifts when we worship together through Confession and Absolution, the hearing of God's Word, and Holy Communion.

Study together. "Let the word of Christ dwell in you richly, teaching and admonishing one another in all wisdom, singing psalms and hymns and spiritual songs, with thankfulness in your hearts to God" (Colossians 3:16). Christian communities spend time in God's Word. They are united through the Holy Spirit speaking to them in Holy Scripture.

Christian communities **pray together**. Not only do they pray together, but they pray for one another and for others. Just as Paul lifted up in prayer the congregations he wrote to, so we, too, should pray for our brothers and sisters in Christ. In addition, we are commanded to pray for all people (1 Timothy 2:1) and to pray for our enemies and those who persecute us (Matthew 5:44).

---

3   Dietrich Bonhoeffer, *Life Together* (New York: Harper & Row Publishers, 1954), 30.
4   Bonhoeffer, *Life Together*, 26–30.

Lastly, Christian communities **serve together**. Jesus set the example by serving not only His friends and disciples, but others He came into contact with. After washing His disciples' feet, Jesus gave a new commandment, "Love one another: just as I have loved you, you also are to love one another. By this all people will know that you are My disciples, if you have love for one another" (John 13:34–35). Christian communities seek to serve the members of that community and "count others more significant than yourselves" (Philippians 2:3). This love through service is carried over into the community and world to reach those outside a Christian community.

These aspects of a Christian community truly are a participation in the commands and promises of Jesus. A youth group's community is built first and foremost on unity in Christ through mission, worship, study, prayer, and service. We build upon this foundation and deepen the bonds of community, but without a foundation of faith, our man-made attempts at community are simply a temporary construct.

In Practice (Individually)

We called her "Granola." We cracked jokes incessantly about her age (she was only 58), "Hey, Granola, did you get the senior discount when you came to my football game?" We also loved her dearly, and she loved us. She was my small group leader in confirmation class, and an adult leader at my church for my entire time through junior high and high school. She came to youth events, fundraisers, sometimes even to one of our high school games. One time we even coerced her into riding the biggest rollercoaster at Six Flags in Gurnee, Illinois. She grasped the restraint white-knuckled, completely silent, never opening her eyes for the entire ride. Whether or not she knew it, Granola was the perfect example of building community. She participated in the fundamental list, and then she heaped on top of that foundation these other key skills:

Genuinely care about your youth. If I had to reduce everything in this section to one key point, it would be this. Every time we have new members join our board of youth, I tell them this is their job—the youth in our church need adult members of the church to genuinely care about them and have a relationship with them. No matter what their words or body language convey, young people want to be heard and cared about. The resistance a child puts up to being cared for and heard does not reflect their need for being loved; it reflects the barriers and walls they constructed from past experiences of being let down. These children of God, maybe even more than others, need to be genuinely cared for and heard.

So how do you do this? It starts with knowing their names. Every adult leader must learn the names of every youth in the group. Then, be intentional about questions. The mistake I see most often is leaders who ask one, two, or three questions, and then just end the conversation because the only answers they got were "fine," "good," and "okay." If a youth gives you those answers, see it as a personal challenge to find a subject area where their eyes light up and they start talking. One of my youth gives the typical one-word answers in conversation, but once you mention hockey, then he suddenly realizes his vocal chords are functional! At first, it might feel like an interrogation to you (and it might to the youth as well), but they will walk away from the conversation knowing that someone is actually interested in them and their life. There is someone who genuinely cares about them.

Spend quality time with them. Sit with them, play with them, and be present with them. Our junior high youth go on a mission trip each summer, and there are typically a few other youth groups attending the same week as us. Every single year I have been baffled by the same thing—whenever the whole group gathers for Bible study or devotions in a larger meeting room, all the kids sit on the floor in small clusters of friend groups, and the adults always, always, sit along the outside, in the back, or on chairs totally separated from the youth. It's a swimming pool of youth with adult leader lifeguards perched on the wings. Go for a swim! I tell every one of my adult leaders their job is to sit with a group of young people. Show them you want to spend time with them. Set an example of attentiveness in Bible study. Spend quality time with them.

Another pet peeve of mine is the concept that adults ride in the front and youth ride in the back on van or bus rides. That is a chance for precious quality time, conversation, and interaction with your youth! If we are in a twelve-passenger van, I nearly always have a youth sit shotgun and have adult leaders sitting with the youth in back. On a bus, always choose to sit among the young people instead of separating the adults into the front seats. Some of the deepest and most meaningful conversations I've had with my youth have been sitting alongside them on a bus, train, or van.

You have permission to participate with your youth and play with them without being afraid of looking stupid. Anything they do at your Bible study, event, retreat, or mission trip, you can do alongside them. Don't watch from the sidelines. Dive in, participate, and play!

Downtime is primetime. I've also had many deep and meaningful conversations with youth between 10:00 p.m. and 2:00 a.m. Late-night conversations on retreats and mission trips are when the walls come down and the kids open up. Be respectful of those getting some much-needed sleep, but be flexible with those who want to stay up late just to talk, and make that extra effort to stay up with them. Besides late-night talks, schedule downtime or free time on retreats and long trips. Scheduling every minute of every day gives no chance for spontaneous conversation and community building. Youth need that time to relax and play, and it gives a great opportunity to build relationships one-on-one.

Be a Mary. In Luke 10, Luke records the interaction where Martha is busy cooking and cleaning to wait on her guests while Mary sat by Jesus' feet and listened to Him (Luke 10:38–42). While showing hospitality was necessary, the time Mary spent at Jesus' feet was invaluable. The time we have with our youth is also precious. If we are so consumed with the logistics and planning that we neglect to spend quality time with the people around us, we have missed an opportunity. Certainly there is a need for planning and leading, but the time we spend interacting with our youth has a lasting impact.

Mentor them. Youth will only respond to a mentor if they know first and foremost their mentor cares about them and they can trust them. Chap Clark describes abandonment as *the* issue for contemporary adolescents.[5] He goes on to describe how youth today have not turned their back on the adult world; rather, they feel the adult world has abandoned them. Their area of refuge is an escape to the constructed adolescent world and culture.[6] Every youth needs the assurance that he or she has an adult in the church who will do whatever it takes to help them navigate the rough spots of adolescence and the struggles of becoming an adult. They need someone who will not, under any circumstance, abandon them, but will listen to them and care about them. This responsibility is not for parents alone, but for the church to stand alongside and support our parents. In this age, where an increasing number of children come from single-parent households and blended families, it becomes even more imperative for the adults in our church to be faithful Christian mentors for our youth.[7]

IN PRACTICE (GROUPS)

Building community as a whole group, rather than with individuals, takes on another level of complexity. The more youth you add into the mix, the more group dynamics there are to take into consideration and accommodate. The goal with building community in the whole group is to bring a level of comfort and mutual trust among all participants so they can feel safe, accepted, and supported in the group. The growth of the community happens through choice (on the part of the youth) and through good sequencing (on the part of the leader).

Sequence means that as an adult leader you structure everything to go from easy to difficult, shallow to deep, low to high. From the perspective of physical interactions, if you meet someone new, you don't give them a big hug. That would be bad sequencing. You start with a handshake. It takes time to get to know that person before you (or she) would be comfortable with a hug. The same concept applies for our emotional, intellectual, and spiritual experiences. A group will not share close, personal feelings with one another without first sharing casual, surface-level feelings. It is a continual process to move a group from low emotional investment to high, low touch to high, limited spiritual sharing and vulnerability to high.[8]

Choice means that we recognize it should be the decision of a youth whether he wants to participate, answer, or volunteer. Forcing someone to do something may get him to do it, but in the end he will throw up barriers in that relationship. Forcing a youth to follow a sequence from low touch to high touch causes her to retreat and close herself off. But if she makes that step as her own conscious decision, it invites everyone around her to join in this new level of community. It is the same concept as asking a particularly difficult question. There may be silence, but once an individual makes the choice to share his or her own experience, everyone else in the group feels more free to offer their own in return.[9]

---

5 Clark, *Hurt 2.0*, 23.
6 Clark, *Hurt 2.0*, 28.
7 Clark, *Hurt 2.0*, 195.
8 Craig Oldenburg, *Experiencing Safely: Making Good Decisions on High-Risk Programs* (Morrisville, NC: Lulu, 2008), 40–43.
9 Oldenburg, *Experiencing Safely,* 43–45.

Group initiative courses, or as some people know them, ropes courses or challenge courses, use the strategies of sequencing and choice to develop group dynamics. Everything is structured to bring the group to ever-increasing levels of trust, teamwork, support, safety, and inclusion. The group may start the day by playing a silly game throwing a ball around, but by the end they are encouraging and building a community around a student standing on a platform ready to fall backward with his eyes closed into the waiting arms of the youth group. They've moved from low touch (passing a ball to one another) to high touch (catching someone in your arms). They've gone from low trust/emotion (silly tag games) to high trust/emotion (placing your personal well-being in the people standing below you). While I certainly recommend groups participate in group initiative courses with a trained instructor, you can use these same principles in everyday youth group activities.

Bible studies are a great place to employ sequencing. Questions and discussion can be carefully crafted to get the most out of the participants while building community at the same time. Don't lead off with, "What is something you do that is selfish?" Wow! That's a loaded question. If you get any answers, I'd be willing to bet they are joking answers, because any youth answering it would simply be trying to deflect from the real weight of the question. Sequence your questions to build up to a more personal answer. "What is the main point of Philippians 2:3–4?" "What would you define selfish ambition as?" "Where have you seen selfish ambition?" "What is something you do that is selfish?" As students become more comfortable answering deeper questions, they will be willing to share things close to their heart.

Youth events, games, and activities are another opportunity to use good sequencing and choice. As much as some people don't like ice breakers, they actually serve a great purpose when used according to the rules of choice and sequencing. They break down walls and move groups from low to high in physical and emotional boundaries. The other activities and games you do should also follow this path to encourage greater participation and closer team building. The other strategy to use with games is to make them accessible to all levels of skill and athleticism. Games entirely dominated by the athletes in the group quickly become boring to everyone else. Games where players are eliminated and have to wait an extended period of time to join again also can put a damper on the activity. The best games for building community are accessible to all skill levels and allow for continuous or near continuous (quick re-entry) play.

I have described several techniques and skills for developing community within a group, but I cannot stress enough that these things are not in and of themselves what create Christian community! Community maybe, but not Christian. We must remind ourselves each and every time that Christian community is not a man-made structure. Community is not something we create through our own efforts and techniques. Rather, it is a participation of fellow Christians in the reality that we are sinners in need of forgiveness and have a Savior who has forgiven and redeemed us. As an adult leader, you cannot genuinely care for the youth of your church through your own ability. Your genuine care comes only because you know that both you and your youth are baptized and beloved children of God, and you can share in that knowledge. Paul writes to the Church in Corinth:

If I speak in the tongues of men and of angels, but have not love, I am a noisy gong or a clanging cymbal. And if I have prophetic powers, and understand all mysteries and all knowledge, and if I have all faith, so as to remove mountains, but have not love, I am nothing. If I give away all I have, and if I deliver up my body to be burned, but have not love, I gain nothing. (1 Corinthians 13:1–3)

In the same way, if we practice these techniques or strategies, but Jesus isn't at the core, we have nothing but a man-made construction of community. Our actions of genuinely caring, spending quality time, being a Mary, and mentoring youth are governed by the Holy Spirit and are done for the sake of Christ. "We love because He first loved us" (1 John 4:19).

DEALING WITH DISAPPOINTMENT

The numbers game: I've had many people talk to me about how they were disappointed because only (insert number here) people showed up. Numbers can be a helpful tool if you are looking at trends and trying to put quantitative data together to assess a ministry area. But in the moment of that youth event, it doesn't matter whether you have two or two hundred. Isn't our ministry the same? Doesn't having two young people provide an extraordinary chance to really spend some quality time building relationships with those two? I've always been tempted to answer, "You had one kid show up, great! What did you get to do with him?" The ultimate goal isn't how many kids we can get to our youth event; it is how we can connect the kids in front of us (no matter how many) with their Lord and Savior Jesus Christ and walk alongside them in their faith.

When you think something is going wrong: I took a group of middle schoolers whitewater rafting—I have never experienced such a display of whining and complaining. These kids had little experience paddling, so some would zigzag back and forth across the river hitting one bank then another. Sections of the river were shallow and they would inevitably get hung on the rocky bottom and end up walking/dragging their raft for long stretches. In the deep sections of the river, they would somehow get stuck on literally the one and only rock protruding from the surface. All the while, there was complaining about the bugs and being hungry. Oh, and one kid sliced his foot on a rock. It was horrible. The next year when we were talking about plans for the summer mission trip, one of the youth asked if we were going to go rafting again, and I replied with a hearty, "No." Sure enough, several of them chorused in with, "Aww, but that was so much fun!" and "Yeah, it was awesome!" Who are you and what happened to the kids that I was rafting with last summer?

We sometimes think things are awful in the moment, but in retrospect can laugh at them or even see them with fond memory. Some of the events my past youth remember the best are when something was "going wrong." One kid lost a fingernail—had it ripped clean off. Another forgot to open the damper on the fireplace and filled the youth room with smoke. One accidentally hit a pool ball off the table and through a floor-to-ceiling window at a hotel.

The important part is our reaction, because that is what will be remembered—the event and the reaction. As hard as it may be at the time, respond with comfort and grace, and show empathy to that youth. Even if we feel like things are not going according to plan, remember that the success of an event is not measured in how flawlessly it went, but in how our youth grew in faith and knowledge of their Lord and Savior Jesus Christ.

When something is actually wrong: There are times, too, when we've moved past the accidental or inconsequential, and this must be dealt with in a completely different manner. When a youth insults or belittles someone else, when someone talks behind another person's back, when there is sin involved, we must apply both Law and Gospel. Be quick to pull that individual aside and confront her with her sin (following Matthew 18). Community has been broken, and this is not something that will go away with time or be diminished if ignored. Deal with it quickly. We must be ready to reach out with the forgiveness Jesus gives. There is a relationship that must be restored, and forgiveness is the only way it is truly healed. Sin endlessly seeks to break Christian community, but the power of God can not only heal that break, but make a Christian community stronger and closer through the process of reconciliation.

Reconciliation and forgiveness is not a one-time event, but rather an ongoing way of life for Christians. We cover everything with grace and forgiveness because God has covered us with His own grace and forgiveness. "Be kind to one another, tenderhearted, forgiving one another, as God in Christ forgave you" (Ephesians 4:32). It starts with knowing our own sinful condition and the grace extended to us in Christ Jesus (Romans 5:6–8), and continues by extending that same grace to another person. We are given an incredible gift of being forgiven and the ability to forgive others. We don't have to settle for telling someone, "That's okay." Jesus has told us we can say, "You are forgiven!" (John 20:23). The relief of true forgiveness given by God is vital to building community. If we are reluctant or slow to forgive, we leave room for Satan to gain a foothold to tear apart relationships and Christian community. Thanks be to God for His forgiveness, which extends beyond all sin and division!

AUTHOR'S NOTE

I see Granola about once a year when I'm visiting back home and worshiping at the congregation where I grew up. In writing this chapter on building community, I touched base with Granola again, because I truly did not know how old she actually was. I was glad to hear she is still involved with youth ministry, and because you can't make this stuff up: I found out she had a box of old pictures, newspaper clippings, and items that she had collected while I was a youth and now wanted to give to me. I wonder how many times she said a prayer for me as I grew up? I wonder how many times she consciously decided to invest in my life through a conversation, through coming to an event, through just being there with us?

The youth in your congregation also need to know that adults in the congregation love them and care for them. They need to know they will never be abandoned but always welcomed. Even though there are barriers in their lives, they need their family of faith to worship with them, study God's Holy Word with them, pray for them and with them, serve alongside them, and maybe even save some pictures and newspaper clippings in a box. I pray that you, like Granola, grow each and every day in the love of Jesus Christ, and that it pours over into the lives of the youth in your congregation—that you love and care for them as their heavenly Father does.

RESOURCES

Bonhoeffer, Dietrich. *Life Together.* New York: Harper & Row Publishers, 1954.

Centers for Disease Control and Prevention and Kaiser Permanente. "The ACE Study Survey Data [Unpublished Data]." Atlanta: US Department of Health and Human Services, Centers for Disease Control and Prevention. 2016. Accessed March 1, 2018. https://www.cdc.gov/violenceprevention/acestudy/about.html.

Clark, Chap. *Hurt 2.0: Inside the World of Today's Teenagers.* Grand Rapids: Baker Academic, 2011.

Oldenburg, Craig. *Experiencing Safely: Making Good Decisions on High-Risk Programs.* Morrisville, NC: Lulu, 2008.

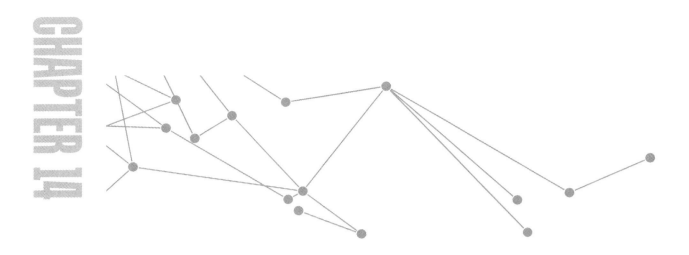

CHAPTER 14

ENCOURAGING YOUTH IN THEIR VOCATIONS

BY CASSIE MOORE

Some people were born for the stage.

I am not one of those people.

In my senior year of high school, I tried out for a role in our school's drama production. Much to my surprise, I was cast in a leading role. I spent weeks memorizing my lines, carefully assembling my costume, learning how to apply stage makeup, and finally stepped out on opening night to a sold-out crowd.

It was in that very moment I realized I hate acting.

As I saw hundreds of faces peering up at me, I had a flash of insight about my personality. I love working behind the scenes, directing people. I abhor hamming it up in front of others.

Despite my chagrin, I learned something helpful about myself. Needless to say, the drama director did not encourage me to try out for the spring musical.

All individuals seek to understand who they are and what purpose they have in life. Our youth wrestle with this same desire to comprehend themselves, which explains the reason for the identity issues we see in teenagers.

God created each one of us with different personalities, unique talents, and varied interests. No matter our gifts, He intends for us to use these traits to His glory. As Hebrews 10:24 says, "Let us consider how to stir up one another to love and good works."

Let's be honest though. Not everyone has the same gift. Some can sashay into the spotlight and belt out a song, while others can counsel a distraught friend. While some of our students may be incredible visionaries, others may serve as encouragers, teachers, or goofballs who make the whole room more relaxed.

A portion of our youth may have natural leadership aptitude, but others will display talent for a variety of other roles. The idea that anyone can do anything is a farce. I'll never be a professional basketball player, as much as I like the sport. The quest for our students to discover who they are and what they're capable of doing is important, and we do them no favors by implying that everyone is a carbon copy of one another.

As for the message to continually keep learning, growing, and striving? That's a truth every one of us needs to learn. We need to be honest and realistic as we work with young men and women who put value on our words and opinions. We must have the courage to speak the truth in love to them as they explore their identity and passions.

Every gift, whether it be a personality trait or skill, is vital to the mission of making Christ known to all. It's our distinct privilege to intersect with youth in this formative stage in their lives as they discover who God made them to be and what He has planned for their futures. We have the opportunity to share why all roles are important, and why every person shares a special piece of the Great Commission as they "go therefore and make disciples of all nations" (Matthew 28:19).

So how do we help youth navigate through their personalities and vocations in a way that honors God?

CELEBRATE AND EMBRACE DIFFERENCES

We're each a matchless masterpiece, created by our heavenly Father. In a culture that quickly judges and slaps a label on everything, we exist as nuanced and complex personalities.

Navigating the long and winding path from childhood to adulthood is difficult, and the teenage years are especially tricky in our rapidly shifting and vacuous culture. Our youth must balance school, relationships, and commitments on top of maintaining identities via social media, keeping up with the constant messages on their phones, and trying to figure out how to finish their homework on time. On top of this, their bodies and brains are growing rapidly, their desire for freedom and independence is increasing, and the pressure to figure out their futures is overwhelming.

Ironically, these chaotic years mark the most formative moments for an individual's personality. In those tenuous years of middle school, especially, students start to make their own decisions and embark on the direction their lives will most likely follow. These years shape a person's character—for good or for bad.

It's vital to recognize, celebrate, and embrace differences in personality and talent with our youth. We do no favors for our students by blindly pretending everyone has the same skills, but we do an incredible service in helping youth discover their passions and abilities.

How do you help youth identify their talents and passions? Pay attention to what a student loses himself or herself in, for the simple joy of doing. Take note of how a teen lights up with excitement while engaging in an activity, displays an unusual talent or skill in a certain area, or shows a natural aptitude for something.

Take time to do personality and spiritual-gifts inventories with young people. Many can be found online and in print, and quizzes such as the Myers-Briggs and DISC inventories are insightful and highly applicable to students.

Watch how students interact with others. Are they comfortable and able to make others feel welcomed and relaxed? Are they the class clown? the organizer who keeps everything going according to plan? the person who has the caring one-on-one conversation with a friend?

Find moments to share your observations with your youth in thoughtful and encouraging ways. Consider places you can use their talents and passions within your ministry or organization. Give opportunities for them to flex their fledgling skills. Be patient with them, and give them helpful feedback as they continue to explore who they are and how they love serving.

A few years ago, I met my match—a miniature, young teenage version of myself. Marenda had undeniable leadership potential, and also no problem flexing her budding leadership muscles against me. I knew I'd have to step out of Marenda's way and let her run full-steam as a leader. I had several heart-to-heart conversations with her about her God-given gift of administration. I issued her a challenge to step up and use her ability to bless others, not derail my classroom. Today, Marenda is running our children's ministry events with as much capability as any adult leader. "Having you recognize me as a leader helped build my confidence and realize that people could see me as a leader instead of putting me into the stereotypical category of a teen who doesn't care," Marenda told me. "I'm definitely stronger as a leader because I know that someone believes that I can help influence others." Marenda sees herself in a new light: someone who can make a real difference in others' lives, no matter her age.

Often, students need a trusted adult or classmate to point out something special they've overlooked in themselves. Perhaps you see a young person who has the heart for pastoral ministry, or someone who has an uncanny knack for leadership. Maybe it's a passion for missions, music, writing, or educating children.

As 1 Corinthians 12:4–6 reminds us, "Now there are varieties of gifts, but the same Spirit; and there are varieties of service, but the same Lord; and there are varieties of activities, but it is the same God who empowers them all in everyone." Each one of us, including our youth, have important gifts to be used to God's glory in His kingdom.

One of my favorite activities to do with young adults is to spend time celebrating their unique qualities. I design many activities to give students the chance to publicly recognize one another's differences, from writing notes about what they appreciate about one another's character to handing out awards for personality quirks to pairing up and verbally affirming one another.

Every person is valued by God—so much so that He sent His Son to die to save us—and every person has a special role to play in this world. Believing this simple truth influences the way we see ourselves and the way we live our lives.

CHANGE THEIR FOCUS

It's natural to be inwardly focused as a teenager. Teens hyper-focus on themselves as their bodies and voices change, brains develop, school stress intensifies, and relationship drama takes center stage. They're intensely concerned about how they look, their popularity and place in the social structure of their school, and what the opposite sex thinks about them.

In short, their entire world is wrapped around *themselves*.

Precisely because teens are so self-focused, we must take every opportunity to focus their eyes on others. Service and exposure to others less fortunate than themselves are key methods. It is in these moments that our students' worlds are broadened, their skills tested, and their hearts opened to the realities that other people are experiencing.

My students regularly serve at cancer centers, nursing homes, and with homeless ministries. They've formed friendships with young people at pediatric nursing facilities, laughing with kids who'll never get out of a wheelchair and praying with children who will never be able to speak a single word. They've cheered for Special Olympics, watched videos of kids with Down syndrome score the game-winning shot in a basketball tournament, and sung karaoke with a teen who lost her hair to leukemia. They've given meals to homeless men who haven't showered in months.

These diverse experiences stretch and challenge them immensely. By overcoming apprehension with uncomfortable experiences, they've learned valuable social skills in addition to learning about their own personalities. New avenues open up, giving them uncharted passions to explore.

Take time to expose your youth to many different things. Share pictures, stories, and videos of men and women of various ages, races, backgrounds, and cultures. Explore unique opportunities to learn, utilizing a range of activities, lessons, and experiences.

I once took students to a controversial science exhibit, in which bodies donated to science were displayed to highlight the intricacies of blood vessels, muscles, and bones. This exhibit drove home the reality of God's design for His creation more than any lesson I ever taught on the subject. It's a lesson that still stands out to those teenagers years later.

Our entire society benefits when we expose youth to diversity and challenge students to look beyond themselves and seek to serve others.

LET THEM GROW FROM FAILURE

Every time I go bowling, I'm reminded about how much I hate failing. Even with helpful instructions from friends, I still won't be joining a bowling league anytime soon.

In those moments of embarrassment over gutter balls, however, I discovered that I do have a skill useful to the sport: I'm resilient. No matter how badly I hurl the bowling ball down the lane, I'll get up and try again, undaunted.

Failure is necessary to our growth as individuals. It alternately humbles, corrects, and drives us. As John Quincy Adams once famously said, "Try and fail, but don't fail to try."

It's illogical to think that we'll be perfect at anything on the first few tries, and this is something we need to teach youth. We must give them opportunities to safely attempt new things, and give feedback and encouragement when they mess up.

Perhaps the biggest challenge for us is to keep our distance when we see our kids messing up. Don't hover and jump in to help right away. The first few times I let my youth lead portions of events, I wanted to close my eyes and pretend it wasn't happening. They were awful, stammering and nervously twisting their hands, failing to clearly articulate anything.

But guess what? I was the same way once.

In time, every one of those students grew drastically from their initial flops in leadership. They became confident and skilled leaders who now show no trace of their initial failures.

We must give our students the chance to try, fail, and learn.

After all, we are raising young *adults*—people who undoubtedly will work in a world where they make mistakes, deal with things that don't go their way, and are challenged by difficult situations. We cannot lose sight of our end goal of faithfully sharing the Gospel and helping our students prepare to find their place in the world as Christians.

Character develops through trying, failing, and trying again. One of the most inspiring phrases I heard in my own childhood was "failure is not falling down, but staying down." I often remind myself that I can learn from all situations, good and bad. This is the same attitude of optimism and perseverance that we must pass on to our students.

As you coach students through failure, be patient with them, unflagging in your encouragement, loving in your critiques, and thoughtful in the opportunities in which you provide for students to test out their fledgling abilities. Start small, and gradually allow them to share bigger roles as they gain confidence and knowledge.

I often start with students leading daily prayers, then opening sessions with announcements or games, explaining portions of the activities, and graduate to letting them co-lead events or discussions. Every step of the way, I give practical advice and ask them what they've learned and how they can do better the next time.

Perhaps most important, I always give them a next time. No matter the mistakes made, a student always gets another chance to learn and grow.

Take Time to Process

One of the most foundationally important activities for students is debriefing, where an experience is discussed and knowledge and life application shared. In our fast-paced, multi-tasking world, we rarely take time to pause and thoughtfully consider how something affected us or how it influences us as we move forward.

We must intentionally carve out time to have these important moments with our students. Physically sit down and hash it out together in the middle of the woods on a camping trip, when you're tired from building a house, as you're standing outside the nursing home, or after you've watched a terrorist attack on television.

Debriefs are vital to help all students process and employ insight to their lives, and necessary for the formation of healthy leaders. It's in moments of reflection that students learn about their Savior, about themselves, and about others. They get the chance to step back objectively and evaluate honestly. Dislikes and irritations become obvious. Strengths and passions are recognized. Goals are set. Resolve for the future formed. And most important, students get the chance to see how the Holy Spirit is at work in the world all around them.

Even though your students may roll their eyes, take time to process experiences and situations with them. As much as possible, allow them the chance to share with one another. Find a quiet place to speak for at least a few minutes, and emphasize authenticity in your conversation.

My typical goal is to speak only about 25 percent of the time when I'm with students, giving my youth the majority of time to discuss, debate, and converse with one another. It's one of the ways they learn best.

Use debriefs as a time to publicly recognize students' different talents and contributions to the effort: "Sarah did such a great job teaching the children today at summer camp, and Angelo really has a knack for making others feel comfortable and connected!"

By pointing out the character strengths and personalities you observe, you simultaneously encourage and educate your youth.

Embrace Conflict

Ever had a couple of youth punch each other in the face in your youth room?

I have. We try to avoid it now, because the paperwork is killer.

Conflict happens, and it's uncomfortable. Whether it's a bunch of boys smacking one another, girls gossiping about peers, cliques restructuring, comments flying on social media, or confrontations building between individuals, we encounter conflict in many different ways.

In college, I served as a dorm resident assistant, monitoring my peers. During that time, I realized conflict is a normal part of life. Spend enough time with anyone, and you'll start to drive each other nuts with all sorts of quirks. Whether you are roommates, co-workers, spouses, friends, a youth group, siblings, or classmates, tensions are bound to build and frustrations eventually spill out.

Irritations boil over online as well as face-to-face. Technology has enabled us to broadcast every thought at every moment with thousands of people, and often the brevity of words or images obscure the actual intention of that individual who posted a message. How many people do you know who have gotten into nasty spats online, or had a falling out with a loved one because of a misinterpreted text message? I'm guilty.

We all have different personalities, backgrounds, likes, and dislikes. Our community is greatly strengthened by varied types of people. It's a positive to any organization to have individuals who think outside the box, play the devil's advocate, and alternately push for action and pump the breaks on activity.

Where the tension crops up is when people get frustrated or disagree with one another. We must remind our students that anger and hurt are a result of living in our broken, sinful world. Being stressed, upset, or embarrassed doesn't justify lashing out at others.

Encourage youth to embrace conflict as a part of life and not let it emotionally derail them. I ask my students to face each other when disagreeing, so they can physically see the impact their words make on each other. In heated moments, I remind them that it's perfectly fine to disagree, as long as they can do so respectfully and while sticking to the issues, and not devolving into character attack. We regularly debate different topics, so they become comfortable with challenging others politely.

I frequently remind my students that I know the teenage years are difficult, but that I'm confident they'll navigate it just fine as they cling to Jesus and let His Word guide their lives. So often, they just want to know that what they're going through is normal and they're not alone in facing it.

That tension with your childhood best friend? Yep, I've been there too.

Your parents driving you crazy? Just another part of growing up and becoming independent.

Feeling on top of the world one minute and totally frazzled just moments later? Yes, it's normal as your brain is still developing.

Helping our students learn to deal with the inevitable conflict they'll face will help them grow to be productive, thoughtful, Christ-following adults who can articulate their faith and not be discouraged when others disagree with them.

GIVE OPPORTUNITIES TO LEAD AND SHOW YOUR TRUST IN THEM

I vividly recall the first moment I had students' lives in my hands, because it scared the living daylights out of me.

I was in college, and my fieldwork supervisor, Kyle, enlisted me to help chaperone a youth event he was taking a dozen middle school students to for the weekend. A few days before the event, Kyle injured himself and was unable to attend the event.

The phone call he made to tell me I was now in charge of the trip stands out in my memory, mainly because Kyle was completely unruffled about handing the young people into my solo care.

"I've never chaperoned a group of kids for an entire weekend," I protested in panic. "I'm just a college student. I don't know what I'm doing; I'm no professional!" He shrugged off every plea, assuring me that I was a great leader and I'd do fine.

Those poor teens put up with me counting and recounting them hundreds of times, as I nervously worried about losing one of them. Thankfully, we made it through the weekend unscathed and enjoyed our time together.

Kyle's confidence in me surpassed the confidence I had in myself at that time, but it dramatically bolstered my leadership ability. In one weekend, everything I'd been learning theoretically in safe, comfortable classrooms became practical. As a veteran leader, Kyle realized that experience is the best teacher, and he allowed me to have that opportunity to thrive. His encouragement and little shove into a tough situation were foundational in my growth as a young leader.

We, too, must be willing to push our youth into positions where they'll learn from hands-on experience. Actively look for every possible way your students can lead and serve throughout your classroom, youth group, church, or community organization. Plugging young people into service automatically makes them more invested in the organization, teaches vital social skills, and creates a mind-set of caring for others.

Allowing our youth to lead sparks a passion within them that will continue to grow and consume their lives. As William Butler Yeats wisely said, "Education should not be the filling of a pail, but the lighting of a fire."

My students can attest to the fact that I constantly look for creative ways to involve them in leadership. Every day, they direct prayer with their peers. They set up our meeting spaces, our television, and our sound system. They choose topics to study, run elements of classes and events, and take turns leading discussion with their classmates. I let them do introductions and announcements, run registration tables, and manage activities for younger kids.

It can be challenging to loosen our own grip on the reins, but letting students lead is one of the surest avenues to provide teenagers with opportunities for growth in life and faith. Your youth will likely forget the specifics of lessons you taught them, but they'll never forget those special opportunities they had to shine Jesus' light.

As 1 Timothy 4:12 reminds us, young people are important workers in God's kingdom too: "Let no one despise you for your youth, but set the believers an example in speech, in conduct, in love, in faith, in purity."

NEVER GIVE UP

As adults, we're a blessing to our students in ways we'll never fully comprehend. God uses each one of us with our unique personalities to reach His children in ways that will challenge and change their hearts.

Our youth need a steady stream of encouragement from us. They need adults who care for them, despite the stupid comments they make, the overhead lights they accidentally shatter at youth events, and the popcorn they throw when you take them to a movie (the first and last movie outing in the same trip, am I right?).

Those of us who work with young people need to cling to the words of Galatians 6:9: "And let us not grow weary of doing good, for in due season we will reap, if we do not give up."

Your patience and unswerving commitment to the youth around you may influence lives in ways you'll never know. Stay grounded in that truth that you can do all things through Christ, who strengthens you (Philippians 4:13). The words you speak and the role model you present are beyond valuable in the eternal lives of young people.

Look to Christ as your foundation and your inspiration in all you do. Pray for the Holy Spirit to work through you to shine the love of Christ through your own cracks and flaws. Continue to be who God crafted you to be: an authentic, imperfect masterpiece redeemed by the blood of Jesus.

Our prayer is that God gives us the ability to equip and encourage young leaders, so we may unleash their untold potential. As an old adage reminds us, anyone can count the seeds in an apple, but only God is able to count the apples in a seed.

Through Christ, you're shaping incalculable students now and for eternity. Though you may never comprehend the immense significance of that, live secure in that humble reality that the Holy Spirit is using *you*, at this very moment.

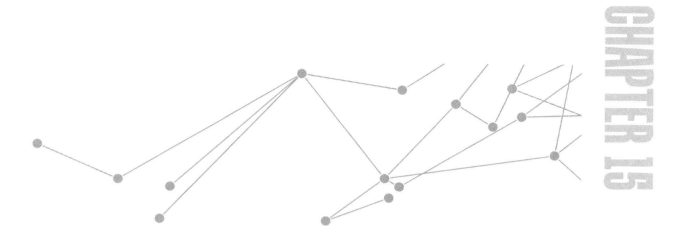

CHAPTER 15

EQUIPPING YOUTH FOR WITNESS

BY JESSICA BORDELEAU

WHY?

As Christians, our identity as loved and forgiven children of God defines every aspect of life. We have been given a gift that sustains us through the hardships of this world and gives us an eternity of peace and joy. God's love in Christ gives us meaning in the present and a certain hope for the future. It changes everything! The hope we have is too good not to share.

The world is full of youth and adults lost in hopelessness. According to the Pew Research Center on Religion and Public Life, only one-third of the world's 6.9 billion people identify themselves as Christians.[1] That leaves billions and billions of people around us who need the message of Christ. The question isn't who should share that message, but how can we best encourage one another to do it!

> **Go therefore and make disciples of all nations, baptizing them in the name of the Father and of the Son and of the Holy Spirit, teaching them to observe all that I have commanded you. And behold, I am with you always, to the end of the age. (Matthew 28:19–20)**

The call to witness extends to all Christians, in every stage of life. No one is too young or too old to be a useful part of the Body of Christ. From the moment of our Baptism, we are filled with the Holy Spirit, who effectively and powerfully works through our actions and words.

---

1   "Global Christianity—A Report on the Size and Distribution of the World's Christian Population," *Pew Research Center*, Religion and Public Life, December 19, 2011, accessed May 2017, http://www.pewforum.org/2011/12/19/global-christianity-exec.

> But you will receive power when the Holy Spirit has come upon you, and you will be My witnesses in Jerusalem and in all Judea and Samaria, and to the end of the earth. (Acts 1:8)

THE CHURCH OF TODAY

INTERGENERATIONAL MENTORING

God calls and equips His people of all ages to live out their Christian faith and share His love. Each member of His Body has a unique set of gifts and opportunities to do God's will. Children, teens, young adults, middle-aged adults, and older adults are all equally valuable and effective in sharing the message of God's love. When we mentor and teach youth to live out their faith, we don't just mold future adults—we equip fully functional members of God's Church in the present.

The individual members of God's Church are all part of a community, a family that needs one another. Just as a family has members of different ages that depend on one another, our church family includes a diverse collection of ages and life stages. A healthy, growing congregation incorporates both age-specific faith development and intergenerational mentoring to prepare its people for witness. By creating opportunities for adults to intentionally interact with youth, we facilitate spiritual growth for the Church as a whole. It's a two-way street. Youth are given the opportunity to see firsthand what Christian care and witness look like. Adults are encouraged and inspired by what the youth have to offer. When we dismiss the contributions youth make to the community, we tell them that their gifts don't matter and they aren't "good enough" to share their Christian faith. It alienates them from the life of the Church and the opportunities to develop their witnessing skills. If youth and young adults continue to hear the message that they aren't contributing members of the congregation, that's what they become.

Shared service is one of the most effective ways to build relationships. As congregations, we are placed within the larger context of the community around us. We love and care for those inside the family and as a family reach out to love and care for the larger community. Our call to share the Gospel is a call to serve. As we serve together, we also grow together. When individuals of all ages join together to look outward into the community, they develop a sense of common purpose. As individuals learn to work together, authentic friendships are developed. The natural relationship building that occurs through shared service can't be replicated in any other environment.

When we give teens actual responsibilities in real-life settings (and allow them the space to succeed or fail), we acknowledge the significance of their contributions and the work of the Holy Spirit in their lives. This experiential learning enables them to realize that the call of the Great Commission includes them. They may have been taught that faith in Christ isn't just for "when they grow up," but authentic service opportunities give that message credibility.

The Lord sends all of His people, both young and old, to share His love in a world desperate for His message of peace and hope. "Jesus said to them again, 'Peace be with you. As the Father has sent Me, even so I am sending you'" (John 20:21).

PEER POWER

The influence of intergenerational mentoring is vital. In fact, the most powerful indicator of whether youth will retain their religious faith is the involvement of adult Christians in their lives.[2] That doesn't discount the incredible value of peer ministry and peer witnessing. Teens have their own culture and language. They communicate with one another in ways that elude (and sometimes baffle) adults. Teens speak to one another in ways adults just can't.

One of the most common ways teens communicate is through social media. Posting, texting, and messaging are a part of their daily life. Whether the impact of digital communication is positive or negative is a separate discussion. It's the ocean in which they swim. Social media is a tool that can be used to help or to harm. Let's teach youth to use it for the good of those around them. As youth learn to live out their identity in Christ, their Christian worldview spills over into all aspects of their lives. Teens learn to express their faith in Christ digitally and communicate God's love through their native language of technology. That shared language is a unique gift that can be used to God's glory.

Peer influence is a significant form of accountability. Youth support and encourage one another in their Christian faith and witness. Most media messages bombarding teens every minute come from a secular worldview. They find themselves immersed in a culture that devalues and marginalizes Christianity. The value of a friend who shares their common faith in Christ is immeasurable. When teens know they are not alone, they have more courage to live out (and speak out) what they believe. When we help cultivate those kinds of friendships, we give teens a powerful ally in their struggle to remain faithful. "Iron sharpens iron, and one man sharpens another" (Proverbs 27:17).

Many unchurched teens feel that religion is for "older people." They don't necessarily think that Christianity is good or bad; they haven't even thought about it at all. It's something to think about later, like life insurance and retirement plans. That perception changes when they see other teens living out their faith. Suddenly, Christianity becomes something potentially possible. The desirability of that possibility depends on the example. If Christian teens project an exclusive, self-righteousness attitude about their faith, they alienate their peers and build walls of resentment. The other extreme isn't any better. When teens who profess to be Christians act in selfish and immoral ways, they send the message that religious faith is powerless or even harmful. When we guide teens to live out their faith, we also help influence their non-believing peers in positive ways. The next question is how.

---

2   Christian Smith with Patricia Snell, *Souls in Transition: The Religious and Spiritual Lives of Emerging Adults* (Oxford: Oxford University Press, 2009), 286.

How?

It's a Skill: Instruct, Apply, Reflect, Repeat

Witnessing is a developable skill. Too many people operate under a "you've got it or you don't" mentality concerning sharing their faith in Christ. It isn't easy and it doesn't come naturally, but it can be learned. It's important to get that message across to youth. It's okay for youth to feel uncomfortable sharing what they believe as long as they see it as a stage in the process. It may be a repeating stage, but those feelings don't need to hinder their witness. A helpful cycle of witness development looks like this: instruct, apply, reflect, and repeat.

Instruct: The Why

Make use of formal instructional time (Sunday School, Bible study, confirmation class) to explore the motivation and necessity of reaching out with Christ's love. The instructional content begins with "Why." Why should Christians share their faith? Some key points to convey:

- **It's our response:** God has saved us from sin and death by sending His Son, Jesus, to die in our place. We get to spend eternity in heaven with Him. We don't share what we believe because it secures our salvation; Jesus already did that. We don't do it because it will make God love us more; He already does. Our response to that incredible gift is the desire to live a life of obedience to God and love to our neighbors.

For by grace you have been saved through faith. And this is not your own doing; it is the gift of God, not a result of works, so that no one may boast. (Ephesians 2:8–9)

- **In obedience to God:** God calls us to share the Good News. He loves all mankind and wants all people to be saved.

For God so loved the world, that He gave His only Son, that whoever believes in Him should not perish but have eternal life. (John 3:16)

This is good, and it is pleasing in the sight of God our Savior, who desires all people to be saved and to come to the knowledge of the truth. (1 Timothy 2:3–4)

- **In love for our neighbor:** We are surrounded by hurting, hopeless people lost in the darkness of sin. Their future is worse than their present as they face eternal separation from God. Christ offers the light of forgiveness and hope. Our neighbors need that message!

And there is salvation in no one else, for there is no other name under heaven given among men by which we must be saved. (Acts 4:12)

INSTRUCT: THE HOW

The next area of instructional content is the "How." How can we effectively share our faith in Christ? When it comes to outreach, the "Why" is straightforward and clear, but the "How" is broad and varied. There are many ways to bear witness to Christ. This portion of instruction should be practical and interactive. Some key points to convey:

- **Actions:** Personal witness begins with actions. The way we live influences what others think about Christians and about Christ. When we care for the needs of others and serve our neighbors, we point to the truth of God's love. When we build healthy relationships with those around us, we create an authentic context in which to share the message of the Gospel. They won't care what we know until they know we care.

You are the light of the world. A city set on a hill cannot be hidden. Nor do people light a lamp and put it under a basket, but on a stand, and it gives light to all in the house. In the same way, let your light shine before others, so that they may see your good works and give glory to your Father who is in heaven. (Matthew 5:14–16)

- **Words:** When you speak about your faith, it's natural to feel nervous. Taking steps to prepare for the opportunity will give you confidence. As you study Scripture, your spiritual vocabulary will grow and mature. Writing out what you could say and practicing saying it will help you learn to articulate what you believe. Go into witnessing situations with prayer and be assured that the Holy Spirit works through flawed people!

For God gave us a spirit not of fear but of power and love and self-control. (2 Timothy 1:7)

But in your hearts honor Christ the Lord as holy, always being prepared to make a defense to anyone who asks you for a reason for the hope that is in you; yet do it with gentleness and respect. (1 Peter 3:15)

- **Attitude:** Our goal is to share the Good News of God's love, not to win a debate or show how good we are. We may not agree with the viewpoint or lifestyle of those we are witnessing to, but we are still called to treat them with respect. An attitude of self-righteousness has no place in the life of a Christian. Our attitude should be that of a humble servant, putting the needs of others first.

Have this mind among yourselves, which is yours in Christ Jesus, who, though He was in the form of God, did not count equality with God a thing to be grasped, but emptied Himself, by taking the form of a servant, being born in the likeness of men. (Philippians 2:5–7)

APPLY

The next step in the cycle is application. Facilitate opportunities for youth to put what they've learned into practice. In many big and small ways, you can provide ongoing opportunities. Start by helping teens identify specific friends who need to hear the message of God's love and pray for that person together. Prepare students to speak up about their Christian faith by helping them plan the words they use to articulate what they believe. Go with your youth to a preexisting community service project. Join with other groups in your congregation (e.g., adult Bible study group, elders, board of trustees) to plan a service day of your own. LCMS Servant Events—found online at lcms.org/servantevents—offers a listing of events around the country as well as resources to plan your own.

REFLECT

An often skipped step in the cycle of witness formation is reflection. To truly glean all the benefits of an experience, it's important to intentionally discuss and process what occurred. Lead teens through a progression of thought that helps them learn from the experience. Begin with questions that help them remember what happened. Then move to more analytical questions about what they learned from what happened. Finally, guide them to set goals for next time and plan specific steps they will take to accomplish those goals.

Questions that help youth remember what occurred at a witnessing opportunity:

- What kind of work did you do at the service project?
- How did the conversation with your friend go? What did you say?
- Did anyone at the event ask you why you were serving? What did you say?
- Describe an interaction you had with a non-Christian this week.

Questions that help youth process what they learned from a witnessing opportunity:

- What was the greatest challenge you dealt with today during the community service project?
- Were you effective in your goal of having a humble attitude?
- Which part of the conversation was easiest for you?
- Describe a meaningful interaction you experienced or witnessed while serving.
- What was something you admired in someone else's actions yesterday?
- What do you want to remember from this experience?

Questions to guide youth to set specific goals and plan intentional steps they will take to accomplish those goals:

- What would you like to do differently next time?
- How will you determine what to say in your next conversation with that person?

- What's one thing that went well with your experience today? How can you help make it happen again?

REPEAT

The final step in the cycle is to repeat the cycle. Don't stop! Encourage teens to continue living out their faith in Christ and sharing God's love. Both teens and the adults who mentor them will experience struggles, challenges, and what feels like failures. There will also be the incredible joy of seeing the ways God works through His people to show His love. We can rely on the Holy Spirit to guide our witness and work despite our weaknesses.

Developing witnessing skills is an ongoing process in the life of every Christian. The cycle of instruct, apply, reflect, and repeat serves as a helpful tool, but the process is never perfected. Youth and adults alike are in a lifelong journey of faith and witness. As we encourage teens to live out their faith, we grow and learn as well. Make use of resources to guide your mentoring and look for team members to work along with you. Most of all, be encouraged by the fact that the Holy Spirit works through Scripture and the Sacraments to strengthen us. As He guides and equips us, we and the teens we mentor become more and more like Christ and shine His light to the world.

And God is able to make all grace abound to you, so that having all sufficiency in all things at all times, you may abound in every good work. (2 Corinthians 9:8)

A RESOURCE ALREADY READY: LUTHERAN YOUTH FELLOWSHIP

The Lutheran Church—Missouri Synod offers resources to help equip teens for leadership and peer ministry. Lutheran Youth Fellowship (LYF) is a leadership development ministry for teens. It strives to equip teens to use their leadership skills as they serve Christ within their congregations and communities. LYF develops its own resources and facilitates training events that give teens tools to mature in their faith, become leaders in their congregations, and reach out to their peers with the love of Christ.

A unique aspect of LYF is the use of teen leadership within the program. Not only do the topics of the curriculum resources focus on peer ministry (see the list of resource topics below), but teens are also equipped to use the resources to facilitate the curriculum units with other teens in their congregation and district. The national LYF Leadership Training event is facilitated by a team of teens who receive intentional mentoring for the task. This team of teens equips youth participants to lead a training session with other teens back home. Teens are encouraged to partner with an adult mentor to facilitate a leadership training experience for other youth. Adult mentors take the initiative in the logistic arrangements for the training experience, while teens facilitate the training sessions using the multimedia curriculum resources. The training experience can be as simple as leading a Bible study with their friends or as expansive as a district youth event. The goal of this ministry model is like a ripple in a pond. The use of the pattern to instruct, apply, reflect, and repeat makes it possible for teens to incorporate what they've learned and pass it on to other teens. The circle of influence spreads as teens lead one another. In this way, teens are given the opportunity to model leadership, inspire other teens for service, and live out their role as an active part of the Church.

The topics of the curriculum resources are also developed by teens. Each year a new Lutheran Youth Fellowship curriculum is developed around themes determined by the participants of the national LYF Leadership Training event. The curriculum is then used as the central resource for the next training event. The most recent of the curriculum units makes use of video segments, but all of the units incorporate the instruct, apply, reflect, and repeat pattern through interactive processing activities and group discussion.

LYF FOR YOU

Lutheran Youth Fellowship resources help incorporate peer ministry and witness into the lives of teens as individuals and in their youth group as a whole. By sending one or two youth you've identified as having leadership skills to an LYF training event, you help them develop a passion for peer ministry. The passion and skills develop as teens participate and grow at the leadership training. The entire youth group will benefit from the example and leadership they bring back as they apply what they've learned.

The curriculum units can also be used as stand-alone resources for weekly Bible study or as part of an intentional peer ministry training in your congregation. When combined, the Leadership Training event and curriculum resources offer practical ways to prepare youth to support one another in their Christian faith and reach out to their friends with the love of Christ. The resources are inexpensive and available online.

LUTHERAN YOUTH FELLOWSHIP LEADERSHIP CURRICULUM RESOURCES

Available at lcms.org/lutheranyouthfellowship

Teen Leadership

This five-part curriculum gives teens the tools to identify their own leadership style. Dr. Mary Hillgendorf equips participants to learn from biblical examples of faithful leaders and develop an understanding of their leadership gifts in a way that focuses on Christ and His eternal life-saving message.

Teens Answering Teens

This content-rich, apologetics-focused training was written by Brad Alles, well-known speaker and author of *Life's Big Questions, God's Big Answers*. Teens are given the tools to help explain and defend their Christian beliefs.

Bridge Building

In a culture where generations are often separated by miscommunication and distrust, this resource focuses on bridging the gap. Jessica Bordeleau offers a guide to initiate intergenerational relationship building. Participants are given practical tools, including a step-by-step guide that leads teens through the process of writing a devotion they can share within their congregation.

Teens Reaching Teens

It can seem intimidating for teens to share their Christian faith with others their own age. This resource, written by Rev. Jay Reed, walks teens through the process of developing a witness plan that includes the key components of the Gospel message and their own faith story.

Teens Stand Strong

This multimedia training equips youth to stand strong in their Christian faith in the midst of a secular world where people in authority often dismiss or ridicule Christian beliefs. In the video portions of this training, Dr. Joel Biermann encourages teens to remember who they are in Christ and equips them with practical advice to guide their walk of faith and Christian witness. The written portions of the resource were developed by Jessica Bordeleau to help teens apply the content and create a personalized action plan.

Teens Reaching Teens in the Digital Age

This multimedia training offers teens the tools to point to Christ in an age of religious pluralism defined by technology and social media. This four-part curriculum makes use of video segments that include *Why Jesus? Colliding Worldviews and Witness in a Digital World* with speakers Dr. Bernard Bull and Pastor Jeff Cloeter. The written curriculum, developed by Jessica Bordeleau, contains discussion questions, processing activities, and a guide for teens to develop their own personal strategy to implement what they've learned.

Faith during Times of Transition

Life changes. God doesn't. The storms of change can hit hard, but in Christ we are able to weather the storm. This four-part resource helps teens see the ways that God uses difficult situations and equips them to point their peers to His love. The written curriculum was developed by Jessica Bordeleau with video presenters Micah Steiner and the authors of *Loaded Words: Freeing 12 Hard Bible Words from Their Baggage,* Leann Lutchinger and Heather Davis.

RESOURCES

"Global Christianity—A Report on the Size and Distribution of the World's Christian Population." *Pew Research Center,* Religion and Public Life. December 19, 2011. Accessed May 2017. http://www.pewforum.org/2011/12/19/global-christianity-exec.

Smith, Christian with Patricia Snell. *Souls in Transition: The Religious and Spiritual Lives of Emerging Adults.* Oxford: Oxford University Press, 2009.

SECTION 4

SPECIAL CONSIDERATION FOR WHOLE CHURCH AND YOUTH MINISTRY

Connections go both ways. When a congregation reaches out to adolescents with care and respect, it receives an often-unexpected bonus. The youth ministry benefits from the church. Even more, the youth benefit the congregation and Church at large. In the Body of Christ, we are all loved and needed. We all have roles and vocations as we serve one another. This is no different for children and youth! Again, young people are not only the Church of the future, but they are also the Church of right now. If children and teenagers truly feel valued and needed in their church community, their likelihood of remaining in the congregation increases exponentially. While you make youth ministry the best it can be, don't forget that the policies you put in place can benefit your entire congregation both in how you serve and in whom you equip.

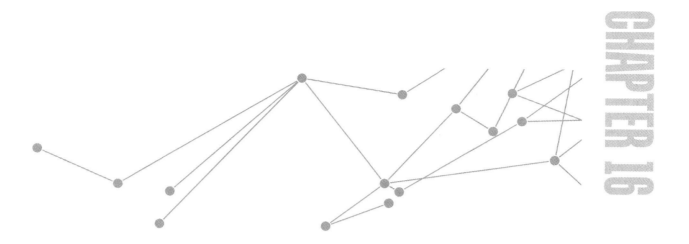

CHAPTER 16

COMMUNITY YOUTH MINISTRY

BY DEREK BROTEN

"How are you going to get more youth to show up to stuff?" It was the driving question when I started interviewing for youth ministry positions. Youth ministry was experiencing its own Jerusalem Temple collapse after confirmation as youth scattered into the community but didn't come to church.

As I started my first job, I wanted to get familiar with both my new church and the surrounding community. It didn't take me long to realize there were two churches known for their youth ministry in our community. Several parents expressed to me that it was a weekly struggle to force their kids to come to our church because they would rather go with their friends to one of those two churches. I spent time that year asking questions and doing research and started to put together a plan that basically tried to out-attract and compete with these other ministries and start our own reputation in our community. We planned fun and big events with special enticements for them to bring their friends. We planned big trips. It started to work, and we saw our numbers grow.

Three years later, we had a youth program that experienced great growth, but our leadership team was exhausted and worn down. And even though our reputation in the community was growing, so was an inner discontentment inside of me. I was worn down and questioning if we were really focused on the things we should be focused on. It was during my second call in Minnesota—about six years into ministry—that I knew something within our process had to change. I started going to conferences, reading books, and having conversations with veteran youth workers trying to figure out a better process of discipleship and a ministry centered on and following the heart of Jesus.

Somewhere in that process, I stumbled on these four verses from 1 Timothy 2:1–4 that would play a central role in a shifting of youth ministry philosophy in my ministry:

First of all, then, I urge that supplications, prayers, intercessions, and thanksgivings be made for all people, for kings and all who are in high positions, that we may lead a peaceful and quiet life, godly and dignified in every way. This is good, and it is pleasing in the sight of God our Savior, who desires all people to be saved and to come to the knowledge of the truth.

Our ministry at that time could be described more like this:

First of all, I urge that big events and special promotions be made for all youth, that we may lead with high attendance, crazy and talked about in every way. This is good and is pleasing in the sight of the youth board and church leadership, who desire all of our kids to love their church and know Jesus as their Savior.

What would youth ministry look like if we modeled it around the desire of God for "all people to be saved and to come to the knowledge of the truth" in 1 Timothy 2:4? What if we spent more time lifting up supplications, intercessions, thanksgivings, and prayers, developing a heart for all the young people in our community? What would it look like if our youth were to live and model godly and dignified lives in every way in their schools, during their games, and at their activities? What if we spent more time preparing them to go out instead of all the time we spent marketing to get them to come in?

Isn't that what Jesus did with His disciples? *Drop your nets and your personal agendas and come live life with Me so that I can equip you for the day when I leave and you will be sent into the world.* Throughout that equipping process, it seems that Jesus' harshest critics were those who were temple-centered leaders.

SHIFTING PERSPECTIVE

So I gathered a group of adults, with incredible hearts for youth, to join me in that struggle. We spent the next year praying, researching, interviewing, and praying some more around the stories of Jesus and how He prepared His disciples. In that process, a major shift happened in the questions we were asking. *What if we were known in our community as a church who cared as much for the youth who didn't come to our church as the ones who did?* What if we were to discover the gaps and needs within our community around youth and serve in those areas with joy? What if we were the church that people in our community called first in times of crisis and need because we were known for showing up and caring?

We knew we needed to shift our focus from an attractional approach to a community approach. It would take time to re-teach our leadership, adult leaders, and youth away from its primary focus on attendance to an equipping to go out. Instead of a complete focus on bringing people to the temple, we would focus on living out the reality of 1 Corinthians 6:19–20 as portable temples filled with the Holy Spirit, bought at a price, and on a mission to glorify

God. What if we stopped stressing temple-focused attendance and sent youth as portable temples to schools and activities? What if we spent more time preparing them to honor Christ in their hearts and to prepare them to always be ready to give a defense for the hope that they have in Christ (1 Peter 3:15)? We knew we needed to spend more time preparing them to go out into the world.

We got a lot of support from key church leaders but were surprised that our biggest opposition was from the youth themselves. The majority of our youth were more comfortable in the expectation of attendance than the challenge of bringing the Gospel to their schools. We discovered that one of the things we needed to do was re-define what it means to live out the Gospel in their schools. There were some youth who wanted a youth group like the disciples had in the locked room after Jesus' crucifixion. Youth group was a refuge and safe place for them. Others grew accustomed to keeping church life completely separate from everything else. It reminded our leadership team of the many stories where the Jews struggled to bring the Gospel to the Gentiles.

To make this major shift in our community, we knew we needed to shift the way we taught and communicated with our youth. We started to tell more stories of the impact other people had on our life in everyday situations. It started with my story from seventh grade, and how the Holy Spirit used a guy named Ken and a love for racquetball to create a meaningful and life-changing relationship in my life. I shared how the Holy Spirit used Ken to create and develop a deeper Gospel understanding as we lived life together jet skiing and eating caramel malts at Hawley's. Ken cared enough about me to show up to meaningful events that mattered to me.

Others in our church shared stories as well. We brought in different adults to tell their ordinary stories of interactions with others that helped them see the love Jesus has for them. We used small group time focused on observation and reflection to help them see the Holy Spirit's power and plan in everyday life interactions and relationships.

During that year, we also reshifted our strategy for both adults and youth to community-directed youth ministry. We live in a very diverse youth culture and knew that our approach needed to reflect that diversity. We drew wisdom from the apostle Paul and his heart and focus toward many different youth communities with the heart for the Gospel. One of the passages we came back to often in developing this strategy was 1 Corinthians 9:19–23:

> **For though I am free from all, I have made myself a servant to all, that I might win more of them. To the Jews I became as a Jew, in order to win Jews. To those under the law I became as one under the law (though not being myself under the law) that I might win those under the law. To those outside the law I became as one outside the law (not being outside the law of God but under the law of Christ) that I might win those outside the law. To the weak I became weak, that I might win the weak. I have become all things to all people, that by all means**

I might save some. I do it all for the sake of the gospel, that I may share with them in its blessings.

THE APOSTLE PAUL'S YOUTH MINISTRY JOURNEY

I asked our leadership team, if the apostle Paul were to embark on a missionary journey to our youth culture, what would it look like? How would he keep the freedom of diversity and at the same time keep tight focus on his intentionality? Our team developed four key areas (mission stops) that we believed the Holy Spirit was leading us to focus on: friends, school, community, and service.

MINISTRY STOP 1: FRIENDS

This mission stop was an area we already saw as a strength that we could build on. At every event, we encouraged and celebrated friends who were brought. We saw this as one of our foundational starting points into our community because our youth already had relational connections and influence with their friends. But we also knew that this area was crucial because if they didn't have a heart for their friends having a relationship with Jesus, what was the likelihood that they would have a heart for the rest of their school? We also noticed that the majority were playing it safe by inviting their friends who already had a church connection. We had built a culture in which the ultimate goal was inviting people to come to us, but then it was the professional's job to share the Gospel. This was a behavior being passed down from the adults in our church.

We knew we had to be bolder in our teaching to create an urgency in our youth to have a heart for those who didn't know Jesus, to understand what was at stake, and to know God's desire was for all to be saved. We wanted them to understand that they were part of His kingdom work in our own community. Our leadership team studied and highlighted different research from Barna that talked about the importance of kids at a young age establishing the foundation for what they would believe the rest of their life. We took to heart that the older people got, the less likely they would have a relationship with Jesus. We challenged our students to see that God helped to establish their friendships not for a passive invite but for them to be an active part in reaching their friends with the Good News of Jesus.

One of the activities we did early in the year was to make a list of all their friends and to divide them into inner-circle and casual friends. We had students write a sentence about each friend on their list and what they knew and believed about Jesus. This exercise was eye opening for us as we discovered most of the students had never really thought about this with their friends. We had them highlight the friends they believed would never step into a church. We were trying to help students see the need and urgency to go beyond inviting friends to the temple and to instead bring the temple to their friends at school. We spent a lot of time in our small groups discussing what it looked like to bring the church to their friends, and we started to see a small shift in conversations we were having with our youth.

I also spent a lot of time with our adult leaders creating a more friend-focused culture. When someone brought a friend to an activity, our adults knew that friends got our primary focus. We worked hard at getting to know their names and what was important to them. I bought friend journals for our adults so they could write down names and interests and pray for those friends. I reminded them monthly to check back in and ask our youth about their friends and to greet their friends for us. It also helped our youth be more intentional about following up and staying connected. When that friend came back, we made a big deal about it, making sure we greeted him by name and he felt noticed. Our adults created that friend-friendly atmosphere, and when friends felt noticed and cared about they spoke positively about our church at their school, which was the second mission stop.

MINISTRY STOP 2: SCHOOL

We knew this could be the most difficult mission stop because many of our youth wanted to keep church and school life separate. For some, school was not a safe environment. We wrestled with how to have a more visible presence in our school community. We knew we needed to take some bold first steps to help our students shift into seeing school as a mission place. We knew that this stop proposed the biggest risk for our students. We had a bigger presence in the school when I first came to Minnesota. At that time, we were allowed to eat lunch with our students and connect with their friends as well. But that opportunity closed when a local youth minister starting using that time to proselytize and some parents complained and shut it down.

It was now two years later, and we saw an opportunity to strengthen our relationships with the school. We set up a meeting with four of our leaders with the principal of the high school to encourage her for the great job the school was doing with our students. We acknowledged past boundaries that were broken and an understanding for those boundaries. We then asked if there were any areas or gaps in her school where local churches could come alongside and help support these youth while following the boundaries established. The principal quickly named five areas that were needs and gaps for the school. We saw two of those areas as great ways for us to increase our presence within the schools.

The first area was helping out with different school events and activities. The teachers were pushed and stressed, and providing chaperones for things like school dances was an easy way to help. It gave us opportunities to learn some new dance moves, at least the ones appropriate and physically possible. It was also a great way for us to connect with our youth and their friends in another environment. It's important to note that some of our youth were not thrilled by our increased presence in their school because they acted different at school than when they were at church and didn't like the exposure.

Another idea the principal mentioned was the one that weighed heavily upon her and the one that I became most excited about. There was a group of students who would just hang out in the park after school, which often led to trouble. They had increased police presence because of fights and other risky behaviors. So we decided to check it out the following Thursday. We grilled hot dogs and gave away Mountain Dew as a connection point. We had no idea the opportunity that was about to come our way.

That first Thursday we had about ten students brave enough to come and eat free food with these three adults they had never met. Most of the students were skeptical and tried to figure out our motivation and openly questioned us. One of the youth, Tyus, asked us straight out, "Are you with the cops? Why are you doing this?" We told him and the other students that we worked with youth in our community at local churches. We said we had a heart for students, and not just for the ones who go to our church. We had a few of our students there to vouch for us. We told them we would be back next Thursday and to let their friends know. That is exactly what they did.

Next Thursday, thirty students showed up. The week after that there were forty. Within two months, we had around sixty to seventy-five students who would come and hang out for an hour and eat free food. Each week there were new people who were skeptical about our intentions, but there were about twenty-five core youth, mostly non-churched, who would respond for us. I still remember Tyus's response to one of them: "They are not cops. They work at a church and just want to show us a little love." I got emotional that day because one of the hopes we had for our youth program was that youth who didn't go to our church would know we care about them as well.

The beauty of that opportunity is that the majority of those young people would never step foot into the church, and those conversations in the park were some of the most real, raw, and honest conversations I have had in ministry. We took what we learned in the park and expanded our presence by tailgating before big rival sporting events as another opportunity to practice presence. I found it fascinating that the story most people were talking about in our church was the hot dog ministry that was going on at the park, which was simply a ministry of hospitality and presence.

I remember getting the phone call from Linda, the principal, thanking us for getting involved and helping transform what was going on in the park. She was noticing a difference, and students were talking about it in school. It was also an opportunity for us to connect with some of our fringe kids who stopped coming regularly after being confirmed. Even though it was not our intention, we were thrilled that some of the youth from the park started showing up at our church events, and some of them even joined small groups. But our focus remained on bringing the presence of the church to the school. The next year the high school experienced the grief of a student suicide, and one of the first calls was to us, asking us to come and be with students in the school for the week. This established connection continues to bring calls asking us to fill gaps and needs and be a Jesus-like presence in our schools.

MINISTRY STOP 3: COMMUNITY

We were careful to respect the boundary of the schools and the no-proselytizing boundary, but we had a heart for deeper conversations in a safe atmosphere. We decided to mark out key spots in our community where we knew youth naturally hung out. We also shifted some of our programming to meeting out in the community. On Tuesday afternoons, I hung out at one of the local coffeehouses, and students would just drop by for conversation. Several would bring a friend. We also had small group leaders who did outings with their group to see a movie together, which is also a great place to run into other youth. We had other groups that would eat together and try new restaurants.

At that time, there was an increased presence of youth on chat sites and hanging out on the internet. So we had one of our adults available to chat online on Thursday evenings. We were amazed at some of the things youth were willing to discuss online that they were too afraid to talk about in person. Several of those conversations walked them through difficult situations with their friends and how to bring the church into their friends' lives. We did a lot of different experiments, like hosting a fantasy football league but leaving one-third of the invite spots for friends only. There were several friends who got hooked on our weekly trash talking and started showing up to different activities. One of those friends, a once non-churched kid, is being ordained this spring as a pastor with a heart for reaching other youth like him.

The questions we asked on how to have a better presence in our youth community started to catch on with many of our parents. I had four adults who made their basements a teen haven for their kids to encourage their friends to come over. They made sure favorite snacks were on hand and favorite sodas in the fridge. We learned that the majority of the deeper conversations youth have with one another happen in this mission stop. So we helped our youth see these moments as a great opportunity to bring the love of Jesus to their friends, to keep their eyes open for moments of struggle within their friends, and to be more intentional in their efforts to spend time with their friends with a deeper purpose in mind.

MINISTRY STOP 4: SERVICE

As our youth program expanded, we noticed our youth had a heart to serve others. Each summer we went back to the same ministry site in Mexico and would quickly fill a bus. We noticed significant transformation in developing and shaping disciples of Jesus. Barna and Search Institute were also doing several studies showing the inclination of that culture with a bent toward serving. These youth wanted to have a positive impact on the world.

We thought this could be an area of common interest and would increase a positive presence within our community. We wanted to be known as a church with a servant's heart to make an impact in our own community. It was also easier for our youth to invite their friends to a project where they were serving others. We even wove it into our programming by having a serve night for our small groups every sixth week. Each small group researched and selected a service project. We experienced high friend ratios on those nights. Some groups prepared and served meals at a homeless ministry, some served at a food shelter, one played games at a nursing home, another group watched children at a women's shelter to give their moms a night free. We had some groups who rotated to different sites because different youth had different passions.

We also looked for ways to be a serving presence to our larger community. During our annual community parade, a group of youth hands out water and others pick up trash along the route. They also hand out full-size candy bars to the little children with a sticker telling them that Jesus loves them. At one of our campuses, we intentionally connect our youth with a refugee family of a single mom and her six kids, which breaks down barriers for those six kids and expands the world of our youth. We are working with an organization to bring a 6K run/walk into our community, and for every person who runs the race, it will bring clean water to one child in Africa. We have big plans for our youth to promote this at their high school. Each year as a church we bring in a packing event with Feed My Starving Children and dedicate the whole first night to middle school and high school students with half the room spaced for them to invite their friends. This mission stop is a common ground mission stop within our youth community as many of them want to make a difference with their lives, and it has been a great opportunity for our youth to reach out and connect.

HAVING A HEART FOR YOUR COMMUNITY

What I have learned in this journey about having a heart for your community is that it has to start with you. If you don't have a heart for your community, don't expect your youth or your leaders to. It starts with having eyes wide open. It starts with wondering if the youth playing basketball, starring in the school play, hanging out in the park, or ordering coffee in front of you has the hope of a relationship with Jesus. It's also important to realize that God has placed many people in key positions of influence within your youth culture who also have a heart for what they do.

As we developed this focus, we spent a lot of time in prayer. We wrote down the positions and names of all those we believed played a key and influential role on a regular basis within our youth community. That list was well over 1,500 collective names and positions, and in particular there were thirty people in key positions to make culture change. With our adults, we prayed for those thirty specific names on a regular basis. We looked for ways to encourage and thank people like teachers who daily invested in youth. We had students write down the names of their current teachers, and our adults sent handwritten notes thanking them and praying for their role. I send an encouraging note several times a year to the principals, thanking and letting them know our leaders are praying for them. So many of these ideas came out of our time of supplication, intercession, thanksgiving, and prayers for the principals, teachers, counselors, youth workers, bosses, superintendents, coaches, and athletic directors in these high positions (1 Timothy 2:1–2).

As we spent more time praying, teaching, and preparing our youth for a heart toward their community, I started to notice significant shifts in our leaders. They were also sharing with their friends the stories of the changes they were seeing and were more aware of the youth issues in our own community. They were more willing to sacrifice, give generously, open their homes, and look for ways to make a difference. Word was starting to spread, and our presence in the community was starting to be noticed.

I believe one of the reasons Paul had such a great impact on those missionary journeys is his heart for those in each community. He researched and knew what was going on so that he was prepared to give a defense for the hope he had. He did not wait for people to come to him but set his heart and mind to bring the temple to the community. We discovered this is not easy and is a slow developing process. You will be questioned by people both inside and outside of your church and community. Some will question your motives, philosophy, and desired outcomes. This is not a journey centered in one's comfort zone but with an explorer's mentality of discovering new land. There are moments of prayer where you feel like you're in the Garden of Gethsemane and far away from the discovery on the road to Emmaus.

But this journey has been powered and inspired by the Holy Spirit and has shifted my heart and focus to see our community quite differently. He removed the scales from our leaders' eyes to the diverse opportunities and people within our community. We have the joy of experiencing the stories of individuals transformed by the love of Jesus that started through presence in our community. We watched the hearts of our youth challenged by having a heart for their friends, school, and community. They thought differently about what it looks like to bring the church and the Good News of Jesus to people they care about. We constantly fight against the temptation of focusing on ourselves and building a bigger "come to us" program. I am encouraged by the wonderful and rare fruit that comes from the Holy Spirit working through the Word in our community.

I think back to those questions we asked fifteen years ago, and I am thankful for the Holy Spirit's nudging in that direction. We are known as a church that cares for youth whether they go to our church or not. We stepped into some of the gaps and needs of the community and are looked upon by community youth champions in a positive light. Both our school and city officials call us in times of crisis, seeing us as a resource and not an obstacle. We are known as leaders who show up with care and joy when a youth need in our community presents itself.

We follow in the pleasing sight of God our Savior, who desires all youth in our community to be saved and to come to the knowledge of that truth (1 Timothy 2:4).

Discussion Questions

- How much time do you spend in prayer for the youth in your community? What could this discipline look like personally, as adult leaders, and as a church?
- How can you help your youth and adult leaders incorporate a discipline of prayer for all the youth in your community?

- How can you help youth and adult leaders focus on how God desires all the youth in our community to be saved and to come to the knowledge of the truth (1 Timothy 2:4)?
- What specific ways can you start caring for youth who don't come to your church?
- Who are the key leaders in your youth community that you can pray for and encourage?
- How can you discover some of the gaps and needs within your own youth community that can lead to a great ministry opportunity?
- In what ways can you help prepare your youth to be ready to give an answer for the hope they have in Christ (1 Peter 3:15)?
- What is one identifiable "mission stop" that the Holy Spirit is directing you to focus on in your community?
- What are some ways you can focus more on caring for the friends of your youth?
- What are some different ways you can encourage and support your community's high school and middle school principals?
- Is there a group of youth in your community that few people are paying attention to and could be a possible "mission stop"?
- The vast majority of the youth in your community will never step foot in your church. How can you bring the church to their doorstep?
- What is one place in your community where youth hang and could be a "mission stop" where relational connections can be made?
- What are some service opportunities within your community that create an easy invite for your youth to bring their friends?
- Are there serving opportunities that will make bigger impressions within your community?
- What do you want your youth ministry to be known for within your community?

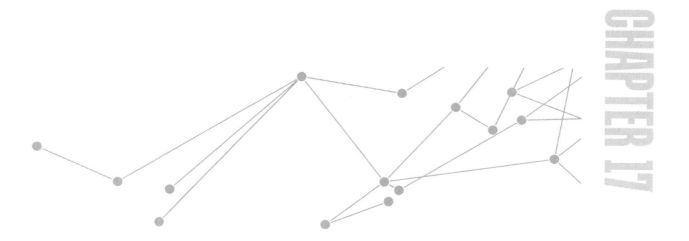

CHAPTER 17

DIVERSITY AND INCLUSIVITY IN YOUTH MINISTRY

BY ASHLEY PAAVOLA

I stood in front of a classroom of girls, most of whom I'd never met before, all of whom were a different race than me, and I thought carefully about my words before I began to speak. As Director of Youth and Family Ministry at a new church plant called All Nations, I jumped at the opportunity to lead a Youth Development and Education Program for girls at our local high school.

Thankfully, I had read Mark DeYmaz's book *Building a Healthy Multi-Ethnic Church* and was holding on to one of his many powerful takeaways: we cannot assume trust will come easily, especially in cultures different from our own.[1] When we serve people whose culture is familiar, whose life experiences we understand, we can earn their trust relatively easily by proving our competency and consistency. But earning trust from someone who is different than you looks and feels very different.

As a blonde-haired, green-eyed white woman, I was foreign in a room of black and multiethnic young women. Many of the girls grew up in a different socioeconomic status than me. Many of them will be first-generation college students; I am a third-generation college student. They were born and raised in our city; I grew up moving constantly and even lived internationally the majority of my elementary school years. We are different. In lots of ways. To pretend otherwise would be ridiculous.

When I finally spoke, I shared that my goal was to do everything I could to learn about them and love them well. I was not going to pretend to be an expert on their lives. It was my hope that through laying out this intentional shift in focus, I would eventually earn their respect and, thereby, the right to be their mentor. In admitting that I wasn't an expert, I moved

---

1   Mark DeYmaz, *Building a Healthy Multi-Ethnic Church: Mandates, Commitments, and Practices of a Diverse Congregation* (San Francisco: Jossey-Bass, 2007).

from a place of proving my competency to admitting that I needed to listen and learn.

Perhaps one of my most treasured moments of the year came several weeks after that first meeting. A few of the young ladies were taking down another student's hair extensions at the end of our after-school meeting, trying to hurry before the activities bus came. I went about my business cleaning the room, knowing better than to interject myself into the world of black hair culture. Then it happened; one of the girls said, "Hey, Ms. Ashley, come help us! Don't worry, we'll teach you how!"

This moment will be etched in my heart for the rest of my life. It meant so much to me, not only because they invited me into their world, their culture, and their experience, but because they *got* it. They *got* that I am there because I love them and want to *learn* about them. They *got* that I am okay with not being the expert on their lives and that I'm not above asking, "What do you mean?" or, "Will you teach me?" They understood that I am not only there to impart my knowledge or lived experiences, but that I believe they offer just as much knowledge and experience to me. The learning is reciprocal.

Let's face it, the famous quote rings true: "People don't care what you know until they know that you care." (This quote is often attributed to Theodore Roosevelt, John Maxwell, or any number of other people, but no one can confirm who first said it or where. Nevertheless, the sentiment is true.) When you didn't grow up in the same neighborhood, aren't the same skin color, aren't the same age, aren't the same socioeconomic status, aren't the same sexual orientation, or aren't the same religion as someone, swooping in to give your prepared answers to any perceived problems is self-focused. It's like waving a giant red flag that says, "I'm here for myself, not for you. I'm here because I want to make myself feel better about my situation and remember how blessed I am. I'm here because I want to be a hero. I'm here because I want to be important and do something big with my life."

But when we examine the life of Jesus, His actions speak the opposite. What He demonstrates in the Scriptures sounds more like, "I'm here for you. I'm here because I love you. I'm here because I think you are valuable and worth it. I'm here to eat dinner with you. I'm here to celebrate a wedding with you. I'm here to serve you. I'm here to wash your feet. I'm here when you are hurting. I'm here when you are sick. I'm here when you are blind. I'm here so you can have living water and stop being thirsty. I'm here because God so loved you."

Diversity

Dear ones, Jesus' opinion, His call, His purpose, is the only one that matters when you are building a youth ministry. He has shown us that pursuing diversity is not just good or important, but it is the heart of the Gospel.

In Ephesians 2, we see a mandated unity, a reconciliation of people and races, possible only through the cross of Christ that reconciles us not only to God, but to one another. We are given a powerful visual of one, new humanity:

For He Himself is our peace, who has made us both one and has broken down in His flesh the dividing wall of hostility . . . and might reconcile us both to God in one body through the cross, thereby killing the hostility. (Ephesians 2:14, 16)

This reconciliation between all people is so central to the heart of the Gospel that when an unbelieving world doesn't see the races reconciled beneath the cross of Jesus, it undermines our confession of what Christ has done. But when the races are reconciled to one another because of Christ, it is so abnormal, so profound, that an unbelieving world takes notice and our confession of Jesus is validated.

ASSESSING WHO YOU ARE

We've discussed diversity as a theoretical concept, but what does this mean for your specific setting? And even more important, how do you broaden this discussion to include others in your ministry? One simple and nonthreatening exercise is a "Six-Box Diversity Assessment Tool" that serves as a confidential and personal reflection device.

Create a six-box chart (see figure 1). At the top of each box, write a racial or ethnic group represented in your community (e.g. black, white, Asian, Hispanic, Native American, Syrian/refugee, Middle Eastern). Give each participant in the activity three copies of the chart.

On the first sheet, have participants write down their extended family's perceptions of each listed group in the space provided. Prompt them to consider things they've heard said about those particular groups of people in passing, casual conversation. At this point, you'll want to remind students that their answers will remain confidential. This activity is only for personal reflection, not to be shared with a group. Give them five minutes to complete this sheet.

White	Black	Asian
Hispanic	Middle Eastern	Native American

FIGURE 1

Next, on the second sheet of paper, have students write the names of their friends and acquaintances in the box representing their corresponding category. Give them five minutes again. Once everyone has completed the exercise, have them underline their top ten friends. Now have them draw a star next to their top three friends from within their top ten (see figure 2).

Most likely, they have noticed that the majority of their friends, especially their close friends, fall into the same racial category as themselves. Encourage students to wrestle with how their family's racial perceptions have or have not influenced their friendships.

White	Black	Asian
*Joe Carl		
Bob *Suzy	Te'Ara	Julia
*Lisa Jeff	Jerome	Yao Wen
Steve Jen	Monique	
Claire Greg		
Hispanic	Middle Eastern	Native American
Maria	Behnaz	

FIGURE 2

Finally, on the last sheet, have participants write down their estimates of the percentage of each category represented within your ministry. If desired, participants can discuss their estimates of percentages and compare with statistics if available.

Suggested journaling or group discussion question:

How would an outsider assess your racial relationships?

ASSESSING WHERE YOU ARE

Now that you have an informal understanding of your current ethnic makeup of personal and ministry relationships, it's time to turn your eyes outward and consider your surrounding neighborhood and community. There are two websites helpful for this discussion:

- The Racial Dot Map shows the geographic distribution of racial diversity in the United

States using data from the 2010 census. On the map, every American's race and ethnicity is represented with a color coded dot[2] (https://demographics.virginia.edu/DotMap/index.html).

- Your city's racial data is likely listed in the online United States Census Bureau to corroborate some of the data found in the Racial Dot Map (www.census.gov).

These exercises do more than expose us to our faults; they become a catalyst to help us discover both the lack of diversity in our lives and the opportunity for diversity near us.

Jesus tells a story of similar opportunity. There was a guy on the side of the road. He'd been robbed and beaten. People passed by him—no one helped. But then, someone saw him. That someone, whom we call the *Good Samaritan*, saw that the beaten man didn't look like him. He was a different ethnicity. But he saw him, saw his hurt, saw his need. He went even closer to him. He crossed the street and showed himself trustworthy by assessing the wounded man's needs, caring for him, and giving of himself for the needs of the other (Luke 10:25–37).

Friends, we are called to cross the street, to see the other. We are called to value all because all are bearers of the *Imago Dei,* the image of God. It's vital to take active steps to connect, empathize, listen, and invest so we can build trust as we grow to understand their pains and celebrations.

Suggested journaling or group discussion question:

Read Luke 10:25–37. How can we cross the street and enter into relationship with people who don't look like us?

INCLUSIVITY

As we strive to build youth ministries that value diversity, we have to first understand what stands in the way of an inclusive vision coming to fruition. Pastor Bryan Loritts, in his book *Right Color, Wrong Culture,* says churches (black, white, Asian, Hispanic) tend to stay homogeneous because there is a majority culture in place. There is something the majority culture in the church does, intentionally or unintentionally, that says to a minority person, "You can't belong unless you change the way you dress or talk or behave or sing in order to fit in here."

Even if a minority person does become part of the majority culture, it's actually assimilation, where the culture of the minority is swallowed up into the culture of the majority. But assimilation is not scalable to the general population of minorities. Most people don't want to change their culture, nor should they be given that expectation. Integration, on the other hand, is scalable and desirable.

Pastor Loritts uses the classic TV show *The Fresh Prince of Bel-Air* to show the difference

---

2   "The Racial Dot Map: One Dot per Person for the Entire U.S.," accessed March 1, 2017, https://demographics.virginia.edu/DotMap/index.html.

between assimilation and integration.[3] Carlton Banks, the preppy Ivy League prospect, is a picture of assimilation. Ethnically black, but culturally white. He listens to Tom Jones and dresses in khakis. Juxtaposed with Carlton's character is Will Smith. Representing cultural isolation, Will does urban handshakes with politicians and wears his school uniform inside out. Between these two characters is Philip Banks, Uncle Phil. He is truly integrated. He grew up listening to James Brown and Malcolm X, but attended Princeton and liked Ronald Reagan. Because he was relatable to the majority culture, he was able to bring his black perspective into the courtroom.

According to Lorritts, in order for a church to move from assimilating or isolating diversity to integrating diversity, the majority must be willing to give the minority—keyword—*influence* in the overall culture. The majority culture must set aside its power, preference, or privilege and give power, preference, and privilege to the minority.

I asked some personal friends to share their experiences, positive or negative, with inclusivity. While no person of color should carry the burden of speaking for an entire people group, they were happy to share their own individual stories.

A minority author and professor shared this:

> **As an educated and professional African American male, I often find myself in predominantly white contexts for after-work events or as a representative for my employer. While I have been in many of these contexts, I still find it uncomfortable. It is uncomfortable because whites typically do not meander over to speak; I often must take the initiative. It is uncomfortable because most African Americans can sense when someone of the majority culture is thinking, "Why is he here?" It is uncomfortable because when I do engage in conversation with whites, invariably someone will say, "You are very articulate." I recall a white female engineering peer once saying to me, "You are not like other blacks." Another white male engineering peer once said to me, "You know you're the token."**

A minority lay member and leader in my congregation told a story from her high school days:

> **I was part of a desegregation bussing program that bussed students from the city schools into the more affluent county schools. As an African American female, I was an outsider in the predominately white school. One day a girl named Beth, who was white, invited me to sit at her lunch table with her white friends. I felt noticed and accepted because Beth made a seat for me. We sparked a friendship that diversified my high school experience.**

---

3   Bryan C. Loritts, *Right Color, Wrong Culture: A Leadership Fable: The Type of Leader Your Organization Needs to Become Multiethnic* (Chicago: Moody Publishers, 2014).

Consider again the words of Jesus. He tells the greatest to make themselves least (Matthew 20:26) and for the first to make themselves last (Matthew 20:16), all terms that are synonymous with a *majority* making themselves as the *minority* for the sake of the minority. Ultimately, this is what Christ demonstrated for us when He set aside His power, preference, and privilege:

> **Though He was in the form of God, [He] did not count equality with God a thing to be grasped, but emptied Himself, by taking the form of a servant, being born in the likeness of men. And being found in human form, He humbled Himself by becoming obedient to the point of death, even death on a cross. (Philippians 2:6–8)**

Three Steps Forward

If everything we've discussed on inclusivity is true, the initial burden of becoming a multiethnic ministry begins with the majority culture—a majority culture setting aside its preferences, power, and privilege for the sake of the preferences of the minority culture.

Pastor and author Mark DeYmaz offers three memorable and effective steps that are practical regardless of where you are as a ministry.[4]

1. ***STATE a Multiethnic Vision***—Utilize the diversity activities earlier in this chapter to host a leadership meeting or retreat focused on creating a multiethnic vision statement. Use a demographic report of your community, pore over God's Word, and pray for wisdom. Then craft a memorable, articulate vision of becoming a multiethnic church. Later, when you begin implementing the vision and make inclusive changes in your context, you will meet resistance from those in majority positions who are accustomed to their preferences. When you encounter this resistance, it's helpful to remind everyone of your vision.

2. ***STAFF a Multiethnic Vision***—Staff is not simply paid employees, but anyone who has leadership and influence in the ministry. If the only minorities on staff in the church are on the cleaning crew, we miss the point. Minorities should be serving in prominent, influential, formative roles such as directors, leaders, deacons, elders, and pastors. Don't get hung up on a quota or percentage of a population, but focus on giving influence to underrepresented people groups in your ministry.

3. ***STAGE a Multiethnic Vision***—Stage is not simply referring to a space where you stand. Instead, think of the metaphor of a stage where props and symbols suggest an atmosphere of a multiethnic church.

Think of every printed word in your ministry, like signage, handouts, screens, and the

---

4   Mark DeYmaz, "Leading a Healthy Multi-Ethnic Church," (Workshop lecture, Exponential East Church Planting Conference, First Baptist Church, Orlando, FL, May 1, 2014).

website. Every written word provides an opportunity to also speak in the heart language of someone whose first language is not English. Visit another country and see what it feels like to finally see a sign in English. You can't help but be drawn toward it. We can create the same visceral reaction in our ministries that not only communicates to minorities, but sends a powerful message to the majority culture as well.

Another opportunity for staging is found in colors. Consider displaying flags representing countries of origin in your community. Be mindful of the skin colors of the people in your stock photographs.

Staging a multiethnic vision can also be done with what you celebrate. Cultural holidays such as Chinese New Year, Cinco de Mayo, and MLK Day could be powerful occasions to celebrate with your greater community. Traditional foods and activities give cultural natives the opportunity to share their personal experiences and values with others.

Finally, music is the ultimate gesture of culture. One helpful group exercise is to listen to the top ten pop music hits and write down the cultural music cues you hear. This can lead to a powerful discussion on how your ministry could incorporate those cultural elements into your music.

Suggested journaling and discussion question:

How can we make space for significant and influential leadership from people who don't look like us?

This will not be an easy process, but I believe any and all ministries can use these tools to take steps forward as they work to achieve racial reconciliation in their context. As we experience this reconciliation, the effects are beautiful. Last Christmas, I smiled through tears as a group of children in our church participated in a live telling of the nativity story. On the stage were children of a multitude of races and ethnicities—black, white, Hispanic, Polynesian—while the Good News of great joy was read in English, Spanish, French, and Chinese. And the heart of the church grew closer to the heart of God. This is the beautiful reconciliation God wants for all of us—reconciliation to Himself through Jesus and reconciliation to one another.

Resources

DeYmaz, Mark. *Building a Healthy Multi-Ethnic Church: Mandates, Commitments, and Practices of a Diverse Congregation*. San Francisco: Jossey-Bass, 2007.

DeYmaz, Mark. "Leading a Healthy Multi-Ethnic Church." Workshop lecture, Exponential East Church Planting Conference, First Baptist Church, Orlando, FL, May 1, 2014.

Loritts, Bryan C. *Right Color, Wrong Culture: A Leadership Fable: The Type of Leader Your Organization Needs to Become Multiethnic*. Chicago: Moody Publishers, 2014.

"The Racial Dot Map: One Dot per Person for the Entire U.S." Accessed March 1, 2017. https://demographics.virginia.edu/DotMap/index.html.

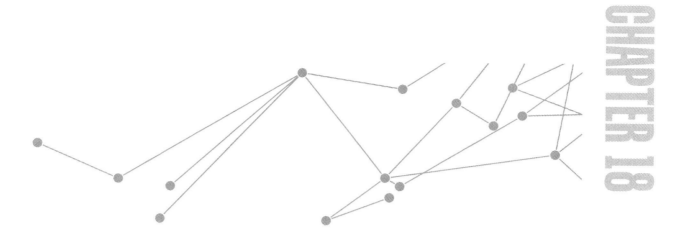

CHAPTER 18

TECHNOLOGY AND SOCIAL MEDIA IN YOUTH MINISTRY

BY JULIANA SHULTS

I am not quite a digital native. My family got our first hulking desktop when I was in middle school. I remember sleepovers where we would gather around the big box screen and double click to begin the screeching dial up of AOL. Once online, we could search randomly for screen names of boys who said they were "13–15." Giggling and taking turns typing, I still have no idea if the boys we talked to were who they said they were. I do know that it was the first time I saw a glimpse of just how powerful technology could be.

Years later during my DCE internship, my ministry team and I faced the big question of how to use Myspace for youth ministry. What was this new platform where all our teens were spending their time? How could we use it to connect with young people? What precautions needed to be taken to keep young people safe? How would adults keep appropriate personal and professional boundaries on this new social media?

At the 2016 LCMS Youth Gathering, 1,359 teens took the Lutheran Youth Fellowship Youth Poll.[1] In that poll, teens admitted to spending a lot of time on social media:

- 28.2% of females and 18.1% of males use Facebook "too often" or 5–10 times per day

- 24.7% of females and 13.8% of males use Twitter "too often" or 5–10 times per day

- 52.5% of females and 32.5% of males use Instagram "too often" or 5–10 times per day

- 67% of females and 46.1% of males use Snapchat "too often" or 5–10 times per day

- 12.2% of females and 12.7% of males use other social media "too often" or 5–10 times per day (Pinterest most popular for females, YouTube most popular for males)

---

1   Paula Schlueter Ross, "LYF Youth Poll Results Reflect Headlines, Scriptural Stance," *Reporter*, January 24, 2017, updated February 1, 2017, https://blogs.lcms.org/2017/lyf-youth-poll-results.

Pew Research shows that nearly three-quarters of teens have or have access to a smartphone. Nearly all of these with smartphones access the internet daily via their phone. Ninety percent of teens with a phone exchange texts, and a typical teen sends and receives around thirty texts per day.[2] That number doesn't include messages through other social media platforms like Snapchat or Facebook Messenger. As teens become busier and busier with school, sports, and other extracurricular activities, technology allows youth ministries to reach all of them wherever they are.

Technology has changed from bulky desktops to tiny screens in our hands. The social media platforms have changed but the questions are still the same. Youth ministries can no longer avoid technology or social media. They have become necessary to our everyday lives and the lives of the teens we serve. Through the work of the Holy Spirit, technology and social media play a powerful role in sharing the Good News of the Gospel.

Using Technology to Teach

Youth ministry with digital natives must integrate technology into Christian Education. There may be important times to keep ministry a tech-free zone, but learning to incorporate technology helps teens take God's Word into their everyday life. Missionaries around the world can speak to students via video chat. Platforms like YouTube, Instagram, and Snapchat allow students to share their faith with the larger church community, friends, and family. This, in turn, gives them a way to start faith conversations with people in their lives who are not yet believers. Poll Everywhere lets individuals in a large group share their thoughts or questions. These innovations opened a floodgate of new ways for youth ministry to connect with your congregation, community, parents, and teens.

Youth now carry multiple Bibles with them wherever they go. Using their phones and tablets, they can access every translation of Scripture, highlight and note with a swipe of the finger. For non-digital natives, this may seem like an excuse to Instagram during Bible study. However, using technology for Bible study and personal devotions engages students on a familiar medium and encourages daily Bible readings. Apps like PrayNow provide structure for youth to engage in personal Bible study.

Technology can help engage and encourage families in faith development. A number of sites allow you to create digital sign-up sheets that send their own automatic reminders to volunteers. You can quickly send an email or group text to parents with questions to ask their youth at home following an event. Church staff and volunteers can communicate quickly and personally with parents to encourage, answer questions, and voice concerns. Your youth ministry only gets a few hours with teens each week. Taking the time to use technology to connect with parents helps encourage faith development throughout the week.

Technology creates teens who know how to get information within seconds. They find

---

2   Amanda Lenhart, "Teens, Social Media & Technology Overview 2015," Pew Research Center, Internet & Technology, April 9, 2015, http://www.pewinternet.org/2015/04/09/teens-social-media-technology-2015/.

themselves inundated with information all day, and they are figuring out how to filter that information. It is vital to train up digital natives in the "Why?" and "What does this mean?" of what we believe. This information helps them filter through the millions of messages they receive every day. Remember youth are no longer going to take your word as the final answer; they may turn to Google. Instead, teach them to dig into Scripture to compare what they hear directly to God's Word. They have the world's information in their pocket and they will use it to verify what you say. Resist the urge to be offended by their curiosity and shut down those conversations. Instead, help them learn to take their Christian Lutheran lens to all they see and hear.

All these new platforms and ways to communicate can overwhelm anyone and look difficult to do on an already overstrapped schedule. You don't have to do it all. But try something. If it doesn't work, then don't be afraid to scrap it and try something else. Technology is ever changing, and sometimes it takes a bit for a new attempt to take hold. In many cases, you can find someone who loves technology and is willing to help you navigate the early learnings until you discover what works for your ministry.

USING TECHNOLOGY TO COMMUNICATE

More than ever before, there are innumerable ways to communicate about ministry opportunities and encourage faith growth in youth. From face-to-face invitations to texting, the medium you use to communicate about your ministry says something about your ministry. Verbal announcements during Sunday morning worship services can't be heard by those who aren't in attendance. Spending the money on a bulk mailing to the community can elevate the importance of the wording and look of a postcard. The ways in which we communicate hold a message all their own, so we should choose them wisely.

Every era in history is in some way defined by the communication methods available at the time. With the creation of the personal computer, we entered an era of interactive communications and social media. Today we can communicate vast amounts of information with people across the globe instantly. Interactive communication is participatory in nature and allows for collaborative relationships and communities to develop without physical interaction. Interactive media allows for people to encounter information in a way that transcends time and space.

The unique natures of Facebook, Twitter, YouTube, Snapchat, and others have created new and exciting possibilities for connecting people and their church. Youth ministries cannot afford to ignore or misuse social media. By understanding the medium and the messages it carries, new ways of sharing information and creating community can be used to further the Gospel.

Technology is moving at a dizzying rate. By the time this chapter goes to print, there will be yet another platform on which to put your ministry message and another device on which to interact with it. Instead of speaking to specific platforms, this section will walk you through steps to strategically use existing and new technology to best share about the Gospel and your youth ministry.

STEP 1: GET THE BASICS

Make sure that your church has a working, accurate website. If not, this is the place to start. If a parent, teen, or young adult Googles the name of your church and comes across nothing, immediately red flags go up. If your existing website is out of date or impossible to navigate, this says something about how seriously you take this generation of digital natives. It doesn't need to be fancy. You can even engage teens in creating and updating the site. All other social media platforms should complement to a static online presence and to other regular communication with your youth and families.

STEP 2: KNOW YOUR AUDIENCE AND YOUR PURPOSE

It's easy to want to jump in with both feet and engage every social media platform you can find. Before you create another username or revitalize a Twitter account with a hilarious GIF, you need a strategy to long-term, positive social media presence. This starts with knowing who you are talking to and what you want to communicate. A long-term plan will push your current use forward and help decide which social media platforms you should be using to create a positive, healthy social media presence

Start with a clear idea of who your ideal audience will be. Students? Parents? Your community? Once you have this group clarified, you will be able to craft your message on media that connects best with this audience. For example, if you are trying to reach students, consider setting up an Instagram account alongside your Facebook. Teens are more likely to interact with images than just text. If you are trying to reach your neighborhood, are there smaller social media groups specific to that area where you need to have a presence?

Along with your audience, you should consider what you want your message to be. Is it static information or are you wanting to start a conversation? Are you sharing pictures or stories of your ministry? Do youth need to sign up for an event? Is there paperwork involved? The purpose of the information helps you to pick the best platform for the information. The purpose and audience of your communication helps you to choose the right media and allows you to focus your work toward a specific kind of presence. It also keeps you away from platforms that aren't going to work for you and are simply going to waste time.

STEP 3: CHOOSE YOUR PLATFORM

Once you know who you are communicating to and your purpose, you need to choose the types of social media you would like to invest time, energy, and resources in. No two social media platforms are exactly the same, and finding the right one will give you the best return on your investment. Do not get caught trying the newest innovation simply because it is new. In the same way, don't limit yourself to only using those social media platforms you know. It's likely your church has already created some social media presence through

Facebook, Twitter, or blog accounts. Below is a small chart of current social media platforms. While this information is by no means comprehensive, it gives you an idea of what you need to be looking for as you decide what social media will meet your needs.[3]

	Types of Posting	Positive Connections	Potential Drawbacks
Facebook Page	Status updates; photos; videos (including live streams); events	Millions of potential viewers of all kinds; connections to other churches/districts; versatile; allows you to post paperwork	Regular posting 1–5 times a month; lots of social media noise makes it difficult to connect; algorithms may mean that your target audience doesn't see your post; many young people less active than before
Facebook Messenger	Instant messages	Often more viewed than email by a younger audience; allows for youth to message your church or ministry's page rather than an individual	Messages get missed if not checked regularly or by multiple administrators; messages missed by those not active on Facebook
Twitter	280-character messages that may include photos and GIFs	Users are very active; quick and easy to update; platform to promote other media	Active use requires posting at least daily; smaller and typically older user base
Texting/Group Texts	Text messages	Allows direct personal conversation; often the preferred method of communication for teens; allows you to see if it has been read	Requires you to know their number; group texts can be difficult to manage; best used for conversation rather than for advertising ministry events
Instagram	Photos with short captions	Connects visually with those who are less likely to read long pieces; can be consumed quickly	Requires you to regularly post or algorithms may mean that your post isn't seen right away; requires finding and editing pictures
YouTube	Videos	Allows for community building in comments; creates a visual connection to your work	Videos require equipment and software; must commit to maintaining comment section
Snapchat	Pictures or short videos	Stories give you a chance to show off several pictures/videos in a row; can get information to younger teens who aren't on Facebook	Content directly to people is only visible once; messages delete, which can be a concern when speaking with minors

---

3   Facebook information from Neil Patel, "How Frequently You Should Post on Social Media According to the Pros," Forbes, September 16, 2016, https://www.forbes.com/sites/neilpatel/2016/09/12/how-frequently-you-should-post-on-social-media-according-to-the-pros/#75dc3f3f240f.

Investigate each social media platform, and then commit to the ones that are going to meet your audience and the interaction you are looking for. Social media changes all the time, so you must keep up to date on any major changes on the platform that might affect how your message is received.

Most social media is easy to set up. You can increase your impact exponentially if you do some very specific and easy things.

- Use the exact same simple username for your ministry on all social media platforms. This might mean that you need to use your location or a slightly shortened version of your church name. Making it uniform across sites makes it easy to remember.

- Create a single picture or logo for your profile picture on each site. This will allow people to quickly connect your content to your organization.

- Consider investing in software or online tools that will help you schedule posts ahead of time and will help track important metrics. While these tools shouldn't replace you logging in regularly to Facebook or Twitter to build community, they can help you post regularly when time doesn't always permit.

STEP 4: FIND YOUR VOICE

The sheer quantity of information being posted on social media every day is staggering, and has instilled in most social media users a keen sense of when content is fake or simply publicity. Emails have spam filters, but social media depends on individuals self-selecting what sounds like a sales pitch or another computer-generated tweet. If you simply copy and paste your bulletin announcement, youth will pass on by like it's just another ad. Engaging on social media requires that you have an authentic voice.

Finding your voice is not simply using a more casual tone. It means tapping into your experiences, perspectives, and faith story to share what is uniquely your ministry. Post a Scripture verse directly connected to your last Sunday-night lesson and add a note of reminder. Tag specific students who attended that lesson. Use inside jokes (sparingly). Share successes of youth on your ministry page. Find pictures from years past for a #tbt post. The more people who create content, the more muddled the voice becomes so ideally find a person or two who are going to take a little time each week to post and interact.

Social media content should not simply be additional ad space. It is a place where we share ourselves to create community and celebrate how God is at work through us.

STEP 5: FOSTER COMMUNITY

As your presence on social media grows, hopefully you will begin to have people inside and outside your church who follow, comment, and connect with you. One of the easiest ways to grow your community is to create opportunities to interact. Ask them questions. Have a caption contest for a photo. Have them take pictures and share them. These connections help people to tie themselves to your ministry, and help them to give you valuable input. When they do, engage with their response so their connection is validated.

Encourage people to comment and communicate positively with one another if the media allows. When, and not if, there are comments that are off topic or destructive, you must delete them. This is a difficult task, because you want to facilitate communication, even when it isn't always positive, but allowing people to get verbally knocked around will only succeed in getting people to disconnect. The more you foster community, the easier it is to share the Gospel and engage people in active face-to-face ministry.

As you work through these steps, there are very few set-in-stone rules for social media. But there are a few pitfalls you can avoid. Especially as a church struggling with new technology, there are a few things to keep in mind.

Do Not Be Overly Rigid and Structured

In a world where spam and auto-replies are fodder for jokes, you must interact and react to your community of followers. Allow those who participate in your discussions, post on your Facebook, or retweet your Twitter to help you direct and refine your social media plans. I may have a specific plan for posting the picture of our youth servant event team, but if a mom gets to it first, use that instead. In fact, I found a very helpful team of parents who forced me to adjust my planned rollout when they put out pictures and information for me.

Creating a highly structured plan for how you will use social media and rigidly sticking to it is akin to attempting to preplan your conversation around the dinner table. It fails to allow for the back-and-forth communication in which social media is based. It is important to have a plan for how your ministry will connect online, but be flexible as interactions start to happen. Let your voice and goal guide your work, but allow for natural shifts as you engage.

Do Not Re-Create the Wheel

At any one time, there are thousands of churches who are using social media to engage people around their ideas. Many of these ministries have been working in social media for years and have found great success. One of the best ways to learn is to watch and interact with other people and groups who are doing what you would like to be doing. The idea is not to mimic their work exactly, but rather to glean what is most successful about what they are doing. Use their understanding and discoveries and then do it in your own way with your own voice.

Be connected to national, district, and circuit youth ministry social media. They will have helpful content you can share to your own groups. There are also places like Concordia Publishing House that will often put out content for Instagram or Facebook based on the liturgical calendar. Even school districts and teachers are now using more technology to communicate. Find out what your local schools are doing. Don't be afraid to use these sources to help engage teens in your ministry.

Don't Be Afraid to Try

The world of technology can be intimidating to those who have not used it or have only limited personal use. It requires a commitment of time and resources, and it may seem that only large groups with vast resources can use social media to create change. Yet, the worst thing a church can do is abdicate its social media presence because it isn't sure if it will amount to anything. Fear of failure or the unknown can keep your ministry from reaching people with the Gospel.

Social media is not something that must always be polished and perfected. Some of the most interesting and engaging efforts in social media are done with little budget and resources. In fact, when you try and fail, it helps others to see you are authentic and trying to connect. Use what you learn from each post and communication to get better, but do not spend too much time polishing and too little time posting.

When to Disconnect

Technology provides new, unique opportunities and new issues we have not had to address before. As the internet made its way into our homes, parents and youth ministries spent time and energy to ensure young people knew how to be safe online. We warned of predators and encouraged parents to know the digital activity of the teens. While we do need to encourage online safety, most teens have internalized these lessons. The issues in front of us now may be a bit harder to address.

Fear of Missing Out, often shortened to FOMO, has begun to infect both teens and adults with serious ramifications for their mental health and social lives. Seventy-eight percent of teens check their devices at least hourly and 69 percent of parents do as well. Thirty-six percent of parents say they argue with their child daily about device use.[4] We live in a world where constant communication means plans change by the moment. With home phones and slower communication media, appointments and plans were set weeks and months in advance. Now, time with friends and family, practices, and group project work are planned minutes ahead, rather than days. Consequently, teens may be hesitant to commit to events because they can't be sure something else won't come along. We become tethered to our devices. Separation from technology could mean we are missing something important.

Challenging teens and their parents to set sacred time for worship, Bible study, and other faith practices means taking FOMO straight on. Help teens consider their priorities and how their phones and devices may keep them from focusing on the gifts of God. Give teens an excuse to disconnect and encourage them to be present wherever they are. The flip of this challenge is that youth leaders can be more spontaneous with their plans, and still find youth interested in engaging. Take advantage of openings in your schedule to feed into the lives of young people, rather than waiting for the first and third Sunday of the month to come around.

---

4   Kelly Wallace, "Half of Teens Think They're Addicted to Their Smartphones," CNN, July 29, 2016, http://www.cnn.com/2016/05/03/health/teens-cell-phone-addiction-parents/index.html.

Another issue of social media is online bullying. Social media may be public, but it often gives people the ability to hide from the ramifications of their words. It is much harder to insult someone to his face than it is to say it to his profile. This perceived separation between the person and his digital presence has given rise to online bullying. Online bullying can take many forms, from spreading negative rumors to sharing embarrassing material. Even worse, the person being bullied cannot escape by walking away. Online bullying can take place day or night, following the victim around. Staying offline is no longer an option. Rather, youth ministries need to be aware and teach teens how to promote healthy positive digital behavior.

We can no longer afford to turn a blind eye when a teen shows unhealthy, unsafe, or unkind behavior online. As difficult as it might be, adults should be willing to speak with teens one-on-one when they see them posting inappropriate or hurtful material online. Call out bullying when you see it. Often, it's adults who can be the most vicious online attackers, and teens are watching us. This means youth ministry volunteers or staff members must hold themselves to a higher standard online. Take time to address not only how teens should speak and act in their school and home, but in their digital lives as well.

Social media also presents another issue—it encourages us to cultivate our appearance to others and put our best selfie forward. We find the best light, best camera angle, and best filter for the picture on Instagram. We spend fifteen minutes composing the wittiest tweet. As we scan our feeds over and over again, it is easy to forget that everyone is cultivating their character online. Teens begin to compare their broken, hot-mess selves to what they see on everyone else's feed. This comparison almost always leaves them feeling as though they are not enough. In fact, the rise in teen suicide rates from 2010–2015 has been tied to the rise in social media usage in our society.[5]

The comparison of your real life to cultivated characters on social media puts the focus on your identity in the hands of others. Teens value and limit their identity to the number of likes and comments. God desires more for them. Youth ministries should reinforce for teens that their true identity is in Christ. They are baptized children of God, and that's more important than any post they could possibly make.

What's Next?

The inherent problem with talking about technology and social media is that it becomes obsolete so quickly. Social media evolves new platforms every day, and as new technology is adopted changes are coming we haven't even yet seen. Ministries cannot master one or two types of social media and then continue using those without ever considering anything new. Social media is a moving target, ever growing and changing. While it is vital to understand how to best use social media right now, it is important to continue to look ahead to what is next.

Churches have not traditionally been early adopters of new technology, in part because

---

5   Associated Press, "Rise in Teen Suicide Connected to Social Media Popularity: Study," *New York Post*, November 14, 2017, https://nypost.com/2017/11/14/rise-in-teen-suicide-connected-to-social-media-popularity-study/ .

of the cost. However, as new sites and technology change, nonprofits must stay open to trying new things. Keep on top of new developments, because the people who use a media first tend to be the people who do it best over time. Consider it an investment. Keep working, and it will have outstanding results.

Social media presence is critical to helping people learn about your church and creating the potential for action. I hope I have provided you with the tools to navigate any social media and allow it to amplify your message to reach people for Christ. Remember, in order to create a successful campaign toward a specific goal, start by calling on your community to help and participate in the process. Keep in mind that while there are very few strict rules for social media, there are specific pitfalls to avoid, as outlined above. Finally, always look at what is next. The reality of our ever-changing technology is that there will always be a new platform. A new way to connect people to our church, where we receive God's gifts.

RESOURCES

Associated Press, "Rise in Teen Suicide Connected to Social Media Popularity: Study." *New York Post*. November 14, 2017. https://nypost.com/2017/11/14/rise-in-teen-suicide-connected-to-social-media-popularity-study/.

Lenhart, Amanda, "Teens, Social Media & Technology Overview 2015." Pew Research Center, Internet & Technology. April 9, 2015. http://www.pewinternet.org/2015/04/09/teens-social-media-technology-2015/.

Patel, Neil. "How Frequently You Should Post on Social Media according to the Pros." Forbes. September 16, 2016. https://www.forbes.com/sites/neilpatel/2016/09/12/how-frequently-you-should-post-on-social-media-according-to-the-pros/#75dc3f3f240f.

Ross, Paula Schlueter. "LYF Youth Poll Results Reflect Headlines, Scriptural Stance." *Reporter*. January 24, 2017. Updated February 1, 2017. https://blogs.lcms.org/2017/lyf-youth-poll-results.

Wallace, Kelly. "Half of Teens Think They're Addicted to Their Smartphones." CNN. July 29, 2016. http://www.cnn.com/2016/05/03/health/teens-cell-phone-addiction-parents/index.html.

TERMINOLOGY

CONNECTED TO YOUNG PEOPLE

adolescence: A phase or stage in life for young people.

student(s): A vocation of someone learning in a systematic way in the church or school setting.

teens/teenagers/adolescents: Young people in the teenage years (13–19).

youth/young people: General term used to describe young people 18 or under, not graduated from high school. This may mean middle school youth or high school youth.

Note: We try to avoid "kid" or "child" (as a generic term to discuss middle or high school youth), or adolescents (except when talking about this stage in life).

CONNECTED TO ADULTS WHO WORK WITH YOUNG PEOPLE

director: Regardless of training or role, the person who "directs" or is responsible for a ministry or program for a congregation or organization.

layperson: Member of a Christian community who is neither ordained nor commissioned to do ministry. They play a vital role in supporting young people.

mentor: A person, regardless of role, who spends considerable time supporting young people.

pastor: Ordained minister.

professional (church worker): People who have been trained to perform ministry to young people. In the LCMS, this would usually mean ordained pastors and commissioned ministers.

volunteer (worker): A person who gives of his or her time to work with young people and receives little or no financial benefit and often is not responsible to the local church for specific outcomes of youth ministry.

youth pastor/minister: Ordained minister who specifically works with youth.

youth worker: General term for professionals or volunteers who work with young people.

LEADERSHIP/CHURCH TERMINOLOGY

congregation/church: A people called by God to receive the gifts of Christ together in one place.

youth (ministry) leadership team: A core group of leaders (professional or lay) who are key leaders of youth ministries or programs in a congregation or organization. This might be a youth board, youth steering committee, or other terms.

youth (ministry) staff: Professional/paid people who work with young people in a church or organization.

youth (ministry) team: General term for all people (professional, lay, parents, volunteers) who serve young people and connect them to Jesus.

OTHER

catechesis: Teaching of the doctrine of the Christian Church.

Christian Education: The teaching of God's truth found in the Holy Scriptures. Christian Education can take on many forms, modes, and settings.

confirmation: Formal process of teaching the one Christian faith, especially in the context of a local church. The process ends with a confirmation of one's faith in Jesus and His teaching in His Word and Church. In the LCMS, this is done after educating adults or youth. For youth, confirmation generally culminates in the eighth grade.

disciple: General term of listeners/learners of Jesus Christ, of all ages.

faith formation/faith journey/faith development/faith walk: Terms to describe the work of the Holy Spirit in calling people to repentance and faith in Jesus Christ.

practices of the faith/faith practices: Actions performed by those of the Christian faith to find Christ where He is promised (e.g., worship, Holy Communion, God's Word), converse with their heavenly Father (prayer), and serve others.